UNRAVELLING THE EVOLUTION OF LANGUAGE

"This book is a sound and sober, yet sympathetic, extensive comment on the widely publicised current debate on the evolution of language. While fully acknowledging the great interest of the question, Botha shows that the biologists, paleontologists, linguists, psychologists, philosophers and other participants in this unique interdisciplinary debate, are in dire need of clarification and explicitation of the assumptions, presuppositions, established forms of argument and theoretical premises current in the sister disciplines involved. Besides taking part in the actual process of unravelling the evolution of language, Botha also unravels the debate itself, and he does so with the typical combination of acumen, merciless systematicity and empathy that we know from his previous writings. Like his other works, this new book makes for great reading."

Pieter A. M. Seuren, Max Planck Institute for Psycholinguistics, The Netherlands

"The evolutionary emergence of language is an exciting new field, generating a rapidly expanding scientific literature. But is it really science? This razor-sharp, relentlessly critical book – the first systematic overview of recent thinking in this area – shows that the problems run deep. Competing hypotheses recall ships passing in the night, their concepts and terminologies wholly incommensurable. Scholars on all sides feel misunderstood, lacking even the rudiments of a conceptual framework which might allow them to settle their differences. What, for example, is 'language'? Not even on this fundamental point is agreement in sight. No currently available paradigm offers hope of unifying the field. The irony of the situation is therefore painful. Lacking a scientific language of their own, Botha reveals 'evolutionary linguists' to be in disarray. It is precisely these scholars who illustrate – perhaps more poignantly than any other known population – the complications of life in the absence of language."

Chris Knight, University of East London, UK

LANGUAGE & COMMUNICATION LIBRARY
Series Editor: Roy Harris

Related Elsevier books

HARRIS & WOLF (eds.)
Integrational Linguistics: A First Reader

JENKINS (ed.)
Variation and Universals in Biolinguistics
(Forthcoming)

Related Book Series:

LANGUAGE & COMMUNICATION LIBRARY

STUDIES IN PRAGMATICS (Forthcoming)

Related Elsevier journals:

LANGUAGE AND COMMUNICATION
Editors: Roy Harris and Talbot J. Taylor

LANGUAGE SCIENCES
Editor: Nigel Love

LINGUA
Editors: Johan Rooryck, Neil Smith and Diane Blakemore

JOURNAL OF PRAGMATICS
Editor: Jacob Mey

For free sample chapters, abstracts, tables of contents, sample journal issues and our online catalogue visit: www.socscinet.com/linguistics

Language & Communication Library

This series features books and edited collections of papers which focus attention on key theoretical issues concerning language and other forms of communication. The history of these issues and their cultural implications also fall within its scope, as do radical proposals for new approaches in linguistics and communication studies. The series has already published important contributions to critical debate both by younger writers and by established scholars, and welcomes more. Inquiries from potential contributors should be addressed to the Series Editor, Roy Harris.

UNRAVELLING THE EVOLUTION OF LANGUAGE

Rudolf P. Botha
Stellenbosch University, South Africa

2003

ELSEVIER

Amsterdam – Boston – Heidelberg – London – New York – Oxford
Paris – San Diego – San Francisco – Singapore – Sydney – Tokyo

ELSEVIER Ltd.
The Boulevard, Langford Lane
Kidlington, Oxford OX5 1GB, UK

© 2003 Elsevier Ltd. All rights reserved.

This work is protected under copyright by Elsevier, and the following terms and conditions apply to its use:

Photocopying
Single photocopies of single chapters may be made for personal use as allowed by national copyright laws. Permission of the Publisher and payment of a fee is required for all other photocopying, including multiple or systematic copying, copying for advertising or promotional purposes, resale, and all forms of document delivery. Special rates are available for educational institutions that wish to make photocopies for non-profit educational classroom use.

Permissions may be sought directly from Elsevier via their homepage (http://www.elsevier.com) by selecting 'Customer support' and then 'Permissions'. Alternatively you can send an e-mail to: permissions@elsevier.com, or fax to: (+44) 1865 853333.

In the USA, users may clear permissions and make payments through the Copyright Clearance Center, Inc., 222 Rosewood Drive, Danvers, MA 01923, USA; phone: (+1) (978) 7508400, fax: (+1) (978) 7504744, and in the UK through the Copyright Licensing Agency Rapid Clearance Service (CLARCS), 90 Tottenham Court Road, London W1P 0LP, UK; phone: (+44) 207 631 5555; fax: (+44) 207 631 5500. Other countries may have a local reprographic rights agency for payments.

Derivative Works
Tables of contents may be reproduced for internal circulation, but permission of Elsevier is required for external resale or distribution of such material.
Permission of the Publisher is required for all other derivative works, including compilations and translations.

Electronic Storage or Usage
Permission of the Publisher is required to store or use electronically any material contained in this work, including any chapter or part of a chapter.

Except as outlined above, no part of this work may be reproduced, stored in a retrieval system or transmitted in any form or by any means, electronic, mechanical, photocopying, recording or otherwise, without prior written permission of the Publisher.
Address permissions requests to: Elsevier Science Global Rights Department, at the fax and e-mail addresses noted above.

Notice
No responsibility is assumed by the Publisher for any injury and/or damage to persons or property as a matter of products liability, negligence or otherwise, or from any use or operation of any methods, products, instructions or ideas contained in the material herein. Because of rapid advances in the medical sciences, in particular, independent verification of diagnoses and drug dosages should be made.

First edition 2003

Library of Congress Cataloging-in-Publication Data
A catalog record from the Library of Congress has been applied for.

British Library Cataloguing in Publication Data
A catalogue record from the British Library has been applied for.

ISBN: 0-08-044318-4

∞ The paper used in this publication meets the requirements of ANSI/NISO Z39.48-1992 (Permanence of Paper).
Printed in The Netherlands.

For my Family

Contents

Acknowledgements		ix
Chapter 1	**Preamble**	
1.1	Central concerns	1
	1.1.1 "Mere windy talk"	2
	1.1.2 "Reopening the question"	3
	1.1.3 "Academics gotta write"	4
1.2	Scope	5
1.3	Focus	6
1.4	Core finding	7

Part I Linguistic Entities Involved in Evolution

Chapter 2	**Language and the Language Faculty**	
2.1	Terminological profusion	13
2.2	"Language" vs. "the language faculty"	15
2.3	A Chomskyan non-distinction	18
2.4	"Language" as "shared language"	20
2.5	"The language faculty" vs. "parts of the language faculty"	21
2.6	General perspective	23
Chapter 3	**The Formal Grammatical System**	
3.1	A reappropriationist scenario	27
3.2	Disconnected discussion	28
3.3	Reasonable response	30
Chapter 4	**Language in Multiple (Dis)guises**	
4.1	A "new approach"	33
4.2	Some of the (dis)guises	34
4.3	The (dis)continuity of language evolution	36
4.4	The (non)gradualness of language evolution	39
Chapter 5	**A Theory of Linguistic Entities**	
5.1	Ontological opacity and arbitrariness	43
5.2	A cure	44
5.3	A non-remedy	45

Part II Processes of Language Evolution

Chapter 6 Co-optation in Language Evolution
6.1	Snails' brooding chamber and the discrete infinity of language	49
6.2	A theory of by-producthood	51
6.3	Identifying evolutionary by-products	52
6.4	Chomsky's by-product "speculations"	55
	6.4.1 The language faculty	55
	6.4.2 The number faculty	57
6.5	Gould's "translation" of Chomsky's "speculations"	59
6.6	Wayward criticisms	62

Chapter 7 Preadaptation in Language Evolution
7.1	Birds' feathers and sentence structures	67
7.2	Lieberman's preadaptive model	68
	7.2.1 The model	68
	7.2.2 "Preadaptive links"	69
	7.2.3 "Syntax"	72
7.3	Wilkins and Wakefield's' reappropriationist scenario	73
	7.3.1 The scenario	73
	7.3.2 Conditions on reappropriation	74
7.4	Calvin and Bickerton's exaptationist theory	76
	7.4.1 The theory	76
	7.4.2 Appraising the exaptationist claims	78
7.5	Carstairs-McCarthy's co-optationist scenario	81
	7.5.1 The scenario	81
	7.5.2 Structural parallels	84
	7.5.3 Neural contiguity	86
	7.5.4 Neurological correspondences	89

Chapter 8 Natural Selection in Language Evolution
8.1	The vertebrate eye and Universal Grammar	93
8.2	The "crux" of the selectionist account	94
8.3	Evolutionarily significant function	96
	8.3.1 Dysfunctionality	97
	8.3.2 Non-uniqueness	99
	8.3.3 Functionlessness	101
	8.3.4 Arbitrariness	103
8.4	Complex adaptive design	104

	8.4.1 Design	104
	8.4.2 Adaptive complexity	106
8.5	General problems	111

Chapter 9 Theories of Evolutionary Processes

Part III Evidence and Argumentation

Chapter 10 Testability: a Litmus Test?

10.1 The role of testability	121
10.2 Claims expressed by selectionist accounts	123
10.3 Claims about function	124
10.3.1 Inherent trade-offs	126
10.3.2 Built-in arbitrariness	129
10.4 Claims about design	132
10.5 Claims about complexity	135
10.6 Testability tested	136

Chapter 11 Indirect Evidence

11.1 New sources of data	141
11.2 Indirect historical evidence	142
11.2.1 Doubting the data	144
11.2.2 The relevance condition	145
11.2.3 Inferential jumps	146
11.2.4 Bridge theories	147
11.3 Indirect nonhistorical evidence	150
11.3.1 "Postulates" about the evolution of language	151
11.3.2 Evidence for genetic variation	152
11.4 Building bridges	155

Chapter 12 Non-empirical Argumentation

12.1 Some consequences of evidential paucity	157
12.2 Arguments from analogy	158
12.3 Arguments from necessity and probability	159
12.3.1 The "onliness" of natural selection	159
12.3.2 "God's-eye" estimate of probability	161
12.3.3 "Ultra-Darwinism"	162
12.3.3.1 Professing pluralism	163
12.3.3.2 Improbable complexity	164

12.4	Arguments from ignorance		165
12.5	Rhetoric		168
12.6	Argument clusters		170

Chapter 13 Plausible Evolutionary Stories

13.1	Introduction		173
13.2	*Just-so* stories		173
13.3	Pinker and Bloom's selectionist "story"		175
	13.3.1	Some charges	175
	13.3.2	An assessment	177
13.4	Chomsky's "fable" of instantaneous language evolution		178
	13.4.1	An unlikely story-teller	178
	13.4.2	On the perfection of language	179
	13.4.3	Specifications for the design of language	180
	13.4.4	The fables	180
	13.4.5	The analogy	183
		13.4.5.1 Basic problem	183
		13.4.5.2 Poverty of the evidence	183
		13.4.5.3 States of a faculty	184
		13.4.5.4 Factors abstracted away from	184
		13.4.5.5 Function and epistemological status	187
	13.4.6	Appraisal	189

Chapter 14 Theories of the Substance of Science

Chapter 15 Capstone

15.1	Closing the argument	195
15.2	"Steps" in the evolution of language	195
15.3	Some language "fossils"	197
15.4	A theory of "degraded" language	198
15.5	A bridge theory	199
15.6	A theory of language "fossils"	200
15.7	Conclusion	201

Notes	203
Bibliography	223
Index	239

ACKNOWLEDGEMENTS

Work on the evolution of language, it is widely recognized, includes addressing questions of a foundational sort. A number of these, I have discussed in a series of articles published in the interdisciplinary journal *Language & Communication*. The present book seeks to extend this discussion in both scope and depth. It presents an analysis of what I believe to be major obstacles to progress in unravelling the evolution of language. It puts forward, too, an argument for adopting restrictive theory as a means to overcome some of these obstacles.

I would not have been able to complete this book without the generous support of various people and institutions and would like to express to them here my sincere gratitude. First of all, there is the Netherlands Institute for Advanced Study (NIAS), which hosted me as a Fellow-in-Residence for the duration of the academic year 2001–2002, thereby affording me a rare opportunity for uninterrupted reading, thinking and writing. The management and other staff of NIAS created an academic, social and physical environment that was uniquely supportive. Special mention has to be made of the ways in which Henk Wesseling, Wouter Hugenholtz, Jos Hooghuis, Rita Buis, Ruud Nolte, Jaklien Gillis, Yves de Roo and Erwin Nolet contributed to making my stay at NIAS so rewarding an experience.

Stellenbosch University generously granted me an extended period of study leave, and my departmental colleagues – Johan Oosthuizen and Christine Smit, in particular – went out of their way to free me from the daily chores of university life.

Various Dutch universities offered me the opportunity to lay my views before fellow linguists and advanced students for critical scrutiny. Thus lectures at the University of Amsterdam, Utrecht University, the University of Groningen and the Catholic University of Brabant elicited questions and comments that have led me to rethink certain ideas and reformulate others.

Walter Winckler went through the entire manuscript, reading many sections more than once. With characteristic acuity, he put his finger on a range of problems of conceptualisation and formulation and suggested solutions that I was unable to think of myself. Without his continuous probing and prodding, this book would have retained many of its first-draft features.

Acknowledgements

As far as word-processing is concerned, I received valuable assistance from Elize Lizamore. Christine Smit gave freely of her time and expertise in taking care of the final formatting of the text, weeding out in the process formal errors to which I was blind.

My family – Hanna, Philip, Liesbet and Gabriël – were wonderful in so many ways: together, they made up the secure home base which time after time I could return to for encouragement and emotional replenishment.

R.P.B.
Stellenbosch
October 2002

1

PREAMBLE

1.1 CENTRAL CONCERNS

Attempting any work on the evolution of language was long considered disreputable. Or, at best, futile – an exercise in trying to unravel something that we all know will be shrouded in mystery forever. Scholarly judgements seem to have been softening, though. That is, if there is any real significance to the rapid growth in the volume of work done on this topic in the past decade or two. Or to up-beat assessments of advances in investigating the evolution of language. But how well are such positive assessments justified, soberly speaking? That is, how much has modern work really added to our understanding of when, where, how and why human language emerged and/or developed in a distant past? What are the main obstacles to discovering things of substance about the evolution of language? And what, if anything, could we do to get these obstacles out of the way?

These questions point to the central concerns of this book. It will pursue them by way of a critical analysis of a varied set of assumptions that have been foundational to modern work on language evolution. Those assumptions – it will turn out – are in essence about three things: about what language is, about what evolution involves, and about what good science is about.

But what would be the point of taking a close look at assumptions of a foundational sort? To answer this question in a concrete way, let us consider how a specific foundational assumption has featured in the history of work on the evolution of language. It takes the form of a requirement that says roughly the following:

(1) In order to be of scientific value, accounts of the evolution of language should be supported by evidence of a factual sort.

We will turn in a moment to three clusters of episodes in the history of work in the evolution of language in which requirement (1) has featured in one or another form. First, though, we have to be clear about our use of the phrase "the evolution of language". It will, for convenience, do duty as an umbrella term at this early stage of the discussion. As such, it will stand for what has been referred to loosely in the literature as "language/linguistic evolution", "the genesis of language", "the origin of language", "the (first) appearance or emergence of language (in the human species)", "the origin of the first language", "the (phylogenetic) development of language", "linguistic phylogeny" and so on. It will later become quite clear that, when they form part of the phrase "the evolution of language", it is essential to use the terms "evolution" and "language" in a more highly constrained way.

1.1.1 *"Mere windy talk".* In the first and historically earliest of the clusters of episodes referred to above, accounts of the evolution of language were disparaged as products of subjective speculation. Thus, in 1873, the eminent American philologist William Whitney depreciatingly characterized as—

... mere windy talk, the assertion of subjective views which commend themselves to no mind save the one that produces them, and which are apt to be offered with a confidence, and defended with a tenacity, that are in inverse ratio to their acceptableness. This has given the whole question a bad repute among sober-minded philologists. (Whitney, 1873, p. 279)

And, in the same year, Alexander Ellis, the then president of the Philological Society of London, declared:

We [philologists – R.P.B.] shall do more by tracing the historical growth of one single work-a-day tongue, than by filling wastepaper baskets with reams of paper covered with speculations on the origin of all tongues. (Kendon, 1991, p. 199, Stam, 1976, p. 256)

Earlier still, in 1866, the Société de Linguistique de Paris had gone so far as to adopt a bylaw, Article II, which placed a ban on "communications" about the origin of language:

The Society will accept no communication dealing with either the origin of language or the creation of a universal language. (Kendon, 1991, p. 199, Stam, 1976, p.254)

The kind of speculation scorned by Whitney and Ellis and banned by the Société de Linguistique de Paris is illustrated by Christoph Voigtmann's contention that all the beauties and subtleties of language began in the throats of singing fowl; Jean-Jacques Rousseau's belief that language originated in primitive song, the first language having been a love song; Lorenz Oken's thesis that linguistic beginnings derive from the fact that all natural things have vibrating resonance; Archibald Sace's "Jellyfish Theory", on which speech evolved out of the unformed and undeveloped primitive sentence in the same way that the animal creation evolved in Darwinian terms out of the gelatinous matter of infinite potentialities; Éttiene Bonnot de Condillac's view that language had its origin in instinctive cries of pain, joy and other ancestral emotions; Ludwig Noiré's idea that language began in the involuntary grunts made by primitive humans doing communal labour; Johann Gottlieb Herder's view that language originated by ancestral humans imitating animals.[1] For centuries, all sorts of scholars routinely engaged in "creative" speculation about the origin of language.

The problem which Whitney and others had with these speculations was that they were not supported by evidence of a factual sort: the scholars who propagated them were either ignorant of or indifferent to the requirement that claims about what happened in a distant past have to be supported by factual evidence. This requirement is a clear example of a foundational assumption about what it is that would make an account of language evolution scientific.[2]

1.1.2 *"Reopening the question"*. Which brings us to the second, more recent, cluster of episodes in which scholars from diverse fields have expressed the view that it has become possible to do respectable work on the evolution of language. Some have even gone so far as to claim that significant progress has been made recently in attempts to unravel the nature and properties of this process. In 1990, for example, the (psycho)linguist Steven Pinker and the psychologist Paul Bloom published in the interdisciplinary journal *Behavioral and Brain Sciences* a Neo-Darwinian account of linguistic evolution in terms of which language evolved by natural selection like the vertebrate eye. They have found it possible to propose this account because they believe that—

> ... there is a wealth of respectable new scientific information relevant to the evolution of language that has never been properly synthesized ... [making them – R.P.B.] optimistic that there are insights to be gained, if only the problems are properly posed. (Pinker and Bloom, 1990, p. 727)

By offering their selectionist account, Pinker and Bloom (1990, p. 727) hope to have done something to counter the "skepticism about the possibility of saying anything of scientific value about language evolution".

On the judgement of a well-known philosopher, Pinker and Bloom have indeed succeeded in this and, moreover, are not the only ones to have done so. Thus, Daniel Dennett has expressed the belief that —

[m]any linguists and biologists have tackled the problem of the evolution of language, using the same methods that have worked well on other evolutionary puzzles, and getting results, or at least what seems to be results. (Dennett, 1995a, p. 389)

Significantly, the eminent evolutionary biologist John Maynard Smith agrees that the question of the origin of language can be reopened and investigated in a respectable way. Thus he asserts in tandem with Eörs Szathmáry that—

[the origin of human language – R.P.B.] is a topic that has a bad reputation among linguists ... but the time has come to reopen the question. (Maynard Smith and Szathmáry, 1995b, p. 71)

Scholars such as Pinker and Bloom, Dennett, and Maynard Smith obviously accept one or another version of the foundational requirement that accounts of language evolution should be supported by evidence of a factual sort. And they believe that it can be met.

1.1.3 *"Academics gotta write"*. In a third and equally recent cluster of episodes, however, various scholars have voiced grave misgivings about the success with which the problem of the paucity of the factual evidence about language evolution has been solved in modern work, including that of Pinker and Bloom. It has even been maintained that, in the case of some questions about language evolution, this problem is insoluble. Massimo Piattelli-Palmarini, for example, has charged that it is impossible to "refute" or even "substantially weaken" Pinker and Bloom's selectionist account since—

[r]esting their case on data that their own approach would have made impossible to collect ... they proceed to construct an a posteriori, ad hoc, irrefutable explanation. (Piattelli-Palmarini, 1990, p. 754)

This is to state, in contemporary terms, the view that certain claims in Pinker and Bloom's account of language evolution are what Whitney might have called "mere windy talk". Similar sentiments are expressed by the renowned palaeontologist Richard Lewontin when he concludes his critique of Pinker and Bloom's account of language evolution with the following sceptical, if not cynical, remarks:

And finally, to repeat my first problem, how much change in the brain really had to take place to make linguistic competence [in the human species – R.P.B.] and how many independent neurodevelopmental changes were needed? Does anyone know? The fact that they do not and often cannot know the basic facts on which theory rests does not seem to deter academics [such as Pinker and Bloom – R.P.B.] from presenting speculations as if they were well founded. Fish gotta swim, birds gotta fly, people gotta talk, and academics gotta write. (Lewontin, 1990a, p. 741)[3]

Noam Chomsky is another leading scholar who has held the view that there is just not enough factual information about what actually happened in the evolution of language for anyone to be able to tell anything other than speculative stories about the events in question:

> We can make up a lot of stories ... The story you choose is independent of the facts, pretty much. (Chomsky, 2000, p.24)

In keeping with this position, Chomsky has on the whole presented his own views on the emergence and evolution of language as "speculations", "Just-so stories" or "fables".[4] Finally, Jerry Fodor (1998, p. 176) is of the opinion that "... we'll just have to wait and see how, and whether our minds [including language – R.P.B.] evolved. As of this writing, *the data aren't in*".[5]

For nearly a century and a half, then, the possibility of doing respectable work on the evolution of language has been assessed with reference to the requirement of factual support stated as (1) above. But what does this requirement involve in terms of specifics? And is it possible to adopt this requirement in a strong form if it is true that there is virtually no factual evidence about what actually happened in the evolution of language? Moreover, is it true that there is virtually no such evidence? Who has it right on this score – the Pinkers and Blooms, Dennetts and Maynard Smiths or the Piattelli-Palmarinis, Lewontins, Chomskys and Fodors? Ultimately, just how valuable or respectable is modern work on the evolution of language? The only way to pursue these questions is to take a close look at how the foundational assumption embodied in requirement (1) has featured in this work.

1.2 SCOPE

The requirement of factual support represents but the tip of the proverbial iceberg: work on language evolution proceeds from a variety of other foundational assumptions as well, many of which are neither recognized for what they are nor discussed explicitly in the technical literature. Evidently, if flawed, such submerged assumptions would pose a serious threat to the value of this work.

Which brings us to the range of the foundational assumptions that will be subjected to critical scrutiny in this book. It includes—

(2) (a) Assumptions about the identity and nature of the linguistic entity or entities whose evolution is at issue – Part I;
    (b) Assumptions about the nature of (biological) evolution, including the processes through which it takes place – Part II;
    (c) Assumptions about the nature and properties of the structure of language, about the functions of language and about the neuroanatomical and neuropsychological bases of language – Parts I and II; and

(d) Assumptions about the "respectability", "value" or "substance" of accounts of language evolution, about the relevance and strength of the various types of evidence brought to bear on such accounts, and about the power of the non-empirical arguments that may be offered for or against them – Part III.

The aim of the analysis of the foundational assumptions is to pin down: (a) what it is that they involve in terms of content; (b) what it is that makes them problematic (if such they are); and (c) what, if anything, could be done to remove or reduce the problem(s). To identify the problem(s) with an assumption, one has to invoke appropriate criteria. I will make a point of not using any criteria of an esoteric sort. Instead, I will draw on values that are basic to good scholarship in general. Central to the values so used will be clarity of content, conceptual well-foundedness, and non-arbitrariness.

1.3 Focus

An analysis of foundational assumptions should of course meet certain minimal requirements in order to be sufficiently insightful. In particular, it has to deal with concrete instances of the use of specific assumptions and it has to subject these to fine-grained analysis. To meet this dual demand, this book focuses on foundational assumptions which underpin accounts that deal with a specific issue, namely that of the nature of the evolutionary processes taken to be central to the genesis of language. The rough comparisons below point to some of the main ideas expressed by modern accounts about the processes believed to be central to the evolution of language or features of it.

(3) (a) Language or certain fundamental features of it arose like the brooding chamber in certain snails.
 (b) Certain fundamental features of language originated like bird's feathers.
 (c) Language or some of its features evolved like the vertebrate eye.

In terms of comparison (3)(a), co-optation was a central process in language evolution – as has been claimed, for example, by Chomsky (1982a, 1988, 1991a), Gould (1991), Piattelli-Palmarini (1989, 1990) and Jenkins (2000). On comparison (3)(b), in turn, this status goes to exaptation in the sense of preadaptation or function shift – which is the claim of Lieberman (1984, 1990, 1991a), Wilkins and Wakefield (1995, 1996), Carstairs-McCarthy (1999), Calvin and Bickerton (2000) and others. Finally, in terms of comparison (3)(c), adaptation by natural selection is central to the evolution of language – a view that has been put forward by Pinker and Bloom (1990) amongst others. This book, then, offers a detailed analysis of concrete instances of foundational assumptions that are central to co-optationist, exaptationist, and selectionist accounts of language evolution, respectively. Some of these accounts – as will become clear – are held to be representative of the best modern work on language evolution.

Which leaves the question of what it is that makes work on language evolution "modern"? "Modern" is not to be taken in just a temporal sense – that of "having been produced in, say, the past decade or two". Rather, modern work has two more properties, both more central than this temporal one. Firstly, and above all, such work is informed by some understanding of contemporary evolutionary theory. Secondly, it is sensitive in at least some degree to insights that have been gained in diverse fields into phenomena that are believed to have a bearing on the evolution of language and speech. These fields include areas of linguistics, phonetics, psycholinguistics, neuroanatomy, palaeontology, archaeology, anthropology, evolutionary biology and genetics. There are good reasons – to be brought out in later chapters – why it is desirable for work on language evolution to proceed from a sound knowledge of linguistic theory in general and of theories of syntactic structure in particular. As will become clear, however, only a quite small body of work on language evolution would pass as "modern" if this property were adopted as criterial.

1.4 CORE FINDING

The analyses to be presented in subsequent chapters yield a wide range of quite specific findings about assumptions that have been taken as foundational in modern work on the evolution of language. Of course this first chapter, being merely introductory, is not the place for a preview of such specifics. It may be useful though to give a "core finding" here: a finding to which a large number of specific ones reduce and which, accordingly, serves to unify the analyses in regard to content and argument. Here it is:

(4) The main obstacle to gaining a better understanding of central aspects of the evolution of language is a poverty of restrictive theory.

What is interesting is that this "core finding" flies in the face of a view held by many (if not most): the view that the main obstacle to a better understanding of language evolution is the paucity of the factual evidence about that evolution. In order to gain such an understanding, the analyses offered in this book show, it is necessary to construct or adopt in a revised form various theories that will be new in the context of the investigation of language evolution. They will be theories that give restrictive characterizations of various sets of things: first, the (pre)linguistic entities that are believed to have undergone evolution; second, the processes by which these entities are believed to have evolved; third, the ways in which these (pre)linguistic entities link up with entities that are believed to be correlates of them; fourth, the sources of data that are believed to yield indirect evidence about the evolution of language; and, fifth, the factors that add to or subtract from the scientific substance of accounts of language evolution. The core finding of this book contradicts the widely held belief that, to be able to say things of scientific value about the evolution of language, we need more in the way of facts, rather than theory. The paucity of the factual evidence about the evolution of language, however, is found to be to a significant extent a consequence of the poverty of restrictive theory. As a whole, then, the book argues for an approach to the evolution of language that recognizes the priority of a specific kind of theoretical work in the areas identified above.

But what is it that makes a theory of something – an object, event, state, process, relation, class, system or the like – a restrictive theory of it? An example may be helpful in dealing with this question. Consider a theory – call it "T" – of what human language is. T will be restrictive to the extent that T's characterization of human language makes it possible to discriminate in a non-arbitrary way between human language and all things which, though they may be related to it, are in fact distinct from it. These "related-but-distinct" things could include, for example,—

(5) (a) forms of linguistic behaviour engaged in by people;
    (b) human linguistic capacities, abilities and skills;
    (c) non-linguistic cognitive systems including the language of thought; and
    (d) formal languages, artificial languages, animal languages, symbolic systems taught to chimps and so on.

In essence, then, a theory T of something, say S, will be restrictive to the extent that the characterization which T gives of S makes it possible to discriminate in a non-arbitrary way between S and things whose properties don't match those of S in the respects that matter. Should it turn out impossible to give a restrictive characterization of S, that in itself would be a good reason to suspect that S does not exist as something distinct. The characterization given by a restrictive theory of something can take the form of conditions on assigning a specified ontological status to the things in question. In the case of a theory of human language, needless to say, this status will be that of "human language-hood". On the basis of its characterization of human language, the theory will assign this status in a restrictive way, denying it to, for example, the things listed in (5)(a) – (d). As used in this book, "restrictive", in sum, means "(appropriately) discriminating".[6]

These are but the bare bones of the idea of "(a) restrictive theory". Coming chapters will flesh out these bones in the discussion of a considerable number of instances to which it is crucial.

PART I

LINGUISTIC ENTITIES INVOLVED IN EVOLUTION

Work on the evolution of language has to meet a condition that might seem to be too obvious to need explicit statement:

(1) The linguistic entity or entities whose evolution is at issue should be identified unequivocally and be characterized in a transparent, non-arbitrary way.

Unless such work does meet this condition of ontological transparency, it will leave it unclear what exactly the linguistic entity or entities are whose evolution is to be accounted for. The discussion of questions fundamental to language evolution may, as a result, be both inconclusive and internally disconnected. It may be inconclusive in the sense of failing to narrow down significantly the range of alternative answers to such fundamental questions. And it may be internally disconnected in at least two senses. One: scholars, though believing that they are discussing the same question, may in fact be talking about different matters. Two: scholars, though believing that they are responding (critically) to each other's views, may not really be addressing them.

Now, a sizable amount of work recently done on language evolution fails the condition of ontological transparency stated as (1) above. Scholars generally agree, on the face of it, that the entity whose evolution is at issue is language. But on closer inspection, this agreement turns out to be more apparent than real, since different scholars, often implicitly, proceed from different assumptions about what the entity is that they refer to as *language*. These scholars start out, in other words, from ontologically distinct conceptions of language. Some even hold more than one ontologically distinct conception of language, invoking in what seems to be a non-deliberate way now one and then another.

Even among the more sophisticated modern accounts of language evolution there are those that are marked by ontological opacity. And even among the more highly structured discussions of those same accounts there are those that are striking in their inconclusiveness and their internal disconnectedness. In Part 1 of this book, I will substantiate these points with reference to the ways in which "language" has been construed in four major discussions of language evolution:

(2) (a) the 1990 *BBS* discussion of Steven Pinker and Paul Bloom's selectionist account of language evolution;
(b) the 1995 *BBS* discussion of Wendy Wilkins and Jenny Wakefield's reappropriationist scenario of the emergence of neurolinguistic preconditions for language;
(c) the 1996 Edinburgh conference on the evolution of human language; and
(d) the 1999 Berlin colloquium on the origin of language.

In Chapters 2 – 4, these discussions will be shown to be problematic in virtue of certain foundational assumptions which are made in them about the nature of the linguistic entity or entities whose evolution is at issue. Then, in Chapter 5, I will identify the reason why those assumptions are problematic and indicate what a cure for the problem would have to involve.

2

LANGUAGE AND THE LANGUAGE FACULTY

2.1 TERMINOLOGICAL PROFUSION

Here are some of the remarks that Pinker and Bloom make in putting forward their selectionist account:

> It would be natural, then, to expect everyone to agree that human language is the product of Darwinian natural selection.
>
> We will argue that there is every reason to believe that language has been shaped by natural selection as it is understood within the orthodox "synthetic" or "neo-Darwinian" theory of evolution (...). In one sense our goal is incredibly boring. All we argue is that language is no different from other complex abilities such as echolocation or stereopsis, and that the only way to explain the origin of such abilities is through the theory of natural selection. (Pinker and Bloom, 1990, p. 708)

In these remarks, Pinker and Bloom use the terms "language" and "human language" to identify the entity for whose evolution they are proposing a selectionist account. They also, however, use several other terms and expressions for the same purpose. Here are some examples:

the/a (human) language faculty
Many people have argued that the evolution of the human language faculty cannot be explained by Darwinian natural selection. (Pinker and Bloom, 1990, p. 707)
But accounting for the evolution of a language faculty permitting restricted variation is only important on the most pessimistic of views. (Pinker and Bloom, 1990, pp. 715-716)

In the evolution of the language faculty, many 'arbitrary' constraints may have been selected simply because they defined parts of a standardized communicative code. (Pinker and Bloom, 1990, p. 718)

the language acquisition device
More generally, these *considerations* suggest that a preference for arbitrariness is built into the language acquisition device at two levels. (Pinker and Bloom, 1990, p. 718)

universal grammar
Does universal grammar in fact show signs of adaptive complexity? (Pinker and Bloom, 1990, p. 773)

grammar(s)
Evolutionary theory offers clear criteria for when a trait should be attributed to natural selection: complex design for some function, and the absence of alternative processes capable of explaining such complexity. Human language meets these criteria: Grammar is a complex mechanism tailored to the transmission of propositional structures through a serial interface. (Pinker and Bloom, 1990, p. 707)
A more serious challenge to the claim that grammars show evidence of good design may come from the diversity of human languages. (Pinker and Bloom, 1990, p. 715)
The nature of language makes arbitrariness of grammar itself part of the adaptive solution of communication *in principle*. (Pinker and Bloom, 1990, p. 718)

the cognitive mechanisms underlying language
Do the cognitive mechanisms underlying language show signs of design for some function in the same way that the anatomical structures of the eye show signs of design for the purpose of vision? (Pinker and Bloom, 1990, p. 712)

the ability to use a natural language
This list of facts ... suggests that the ability to use a natural language belongs more to the study of human biology than human culture. (Pinker and Bloom, 1990, p. 707)

Formulations such as these give rise to questions about the identity of the entity or entities for whose evolution Pinker and Bloom are offering a selectionist account. Are expressions such as "(human) language", "the (human) language faculty", "the language acquisition device", "universal grammar", "grammar(s)", "the cognitive mechanisms underlying language", "the computational mechanisms underlying the psychology of language" and "the ability to use natural language" intended to denote the same entity or different entities? What exactly is/are the entity/entities for whose evolution Pinker and Bloom are offering a selectionist account?

They do not address any such questions in explicit terms. Which is puzzling, since they do seem aware of the importance of setting up clear ontological distinctions and of reflecting these in unambiguous terminology. For instance, when they comment on the shortcomings of some of the evolutionary accounts that have been put forward in sociobiology, they remark as follows.

> The main flaw in many applications of sociobiology to human psychology is that their proponents do not focus on cognitive and emotional *mechanisms*, which are the proper subject for studies of adaptive complex design, but on particular *behaviors* (such as female infanticide) or on folk-psychological personality *traits* (such as "indoctrinability"), which are far too superficial and variable for such studies ... (Pinker and Bloom, 1990, p.766)

So why is it that scholars who are at pains to distinguish among (i) "cognitive and emotional **mechanisms**", (ii) "particular **behaviors**" and (iii) "folk-psychological personality **traits**" omit to make a clear distinction between "language" and "the (human) language faculty", between "language" and "the cognitive mechanisms underlying language" or between "language" and "the ability to use natural language"? What does this terminological or conceptual inexactitude do to the sharpness of the explanatory focus of their selectionist account? And to the coherence of the discussion of this account?

2.2   "LANGUAGE" VS. "THE LANGUAGE FACULTY"

> Consider the following remarks by Pinker and Bloom [emphases added – R.P.B.]:
> Many people have argued that the evolution of **the human language** *faculty* cannot be explained by Darwinian natural selection. Chomsky and Gould have suggested that **language** may have evolved as a by-product of selection for other abilities or as a consequence of as - yet unknown laws of growth and form. (Pinker and Bloom, 1990, p. 707)
>
> In the evolution of **the language faculty**, many "arbitrary" constraints may have been selected simply because they defined parts of a standardized communicative code in the brains of some critical mass of speakers. Piattelli-Palmarini may be right in claiming that there is nothing adaptive about forming yes-no questions by inverting the subject and auxiliary as opposed to reversing the order of words in the sentence. But given that **language** must do one or the other, it is highly adaptive for each member of a community of speakers to be forced to learn to do it the same way as all the other members. (Pinker and Bloom, 1990 p. 718)

Passages such as these seem to suggest that, in Pinker and Bloom's ontology, language and the (human) language faculty are one and the same entity. And yet, in responding to criticisms by Dan Sperber and by Anat Ninio of their selectionist account, they seem to say that language and the language faculty are in fact different objects.

Sperber criticizes Pinker and Bloom for extrapolating in their account tacitly and uncritically from "language" to "language faculty", as he puts it:

> Many of their [i.e., Pinker and Bloom's – R.P.B.] arguments consist in showing how aspects of language are advantageous. Arguments showing the advantageous (or non-advantageous) character of properties of language, however, don't automatically carry over to properties of the language faculty itself, and, of course it is the language faculty, rather than languages or grammars, that should be explained in terms of biological adaptation and selection. P&B tend to extrapolate tacitly and uncritically from language to language faculty, with some questionable results. (Sperber, 1990, pp. 756–757)

In support of his general point, Sperber (1990, p. 757) argues that some linguistic properties may well relate to language and to the language faculty in quite distinct ways. Thus, on the one hand, it may well be that linguistic diversity is a non-advantageous property of "language". On the other hand, it may well be that linguistic diversity not only is "compatible with" the underlying "language faculty" but is an effect of the "good design" of this faculty. What is more, Sperber (1990, p. 757) argues, Pinker and Bloom's extrapolation from "language" to "language faculty" leads them to underestimate the difficulty which arises when one gives the label of "adaptation" to a mutation *only if* it is advantageous in a population in which it is widely shared.

Ninio, likewise, contends that Pinker and Bloom in their target article subscribe to two "mutually exclusive conceptions of language":

> ... the most salient feature of this rich and complex target article is the evidence of a tension between two mutually exclusive conceptions of language. On the one hand, Pinker and Bloom (P&B) appear to subscribe to a view of language as a communicative code, inherently dependent on the existence of conventions shared among a group of people, an interpersonal rather than a private system of knowledge (sect. 3.1). On the other hand, they also see language as a genetically fixed, individually owned property of an organism (Ninio, 1990, p. 746).

This conceptual "tension", Ninio (1990, p. 746) argues, leads to "several ambiguities and inconsistencies in the evolutionary theory" presented by Pinker and Bloom. She charges, in fact, that their theory "actually consists of two mutually contradicting versions". In version A it is "language itself" that is claimed to have undergone evolution by natural selection. In this version "natural selection started to operate on the human language faculty from the initial grammarless moment, so that all development of language is itself simultaneously a development of the innate grammar". In version B, Ninio (1990, p. 746) claims, "what is evolving is the portion of all existing grammatical rules set genetically in individuals, when language itself is constant". In this version, on her reading, "natural selection started to operate on a full-blown language and has consisted only of the gradual genetic fixing of grammatical knowledge".

Lumping Sperber's and Ninio's criticisms together, Pinker and Bloom reject the "suggestions" of both of them, however:

> Contrary to the suggestions of **Ninio** and **Sperber**, there are no paradoxes, or confusions between language and the language faculty, in such an argument. (Pinker and Bloom, 1990, pp. 776-777)

In the "argument" that they refer to, the Baldwin effect is used to explain how innate grammatical mechanisms might have developed gradually from communication systems that were originally supported by general cognitive processes.[1] The reason why there are no such confusions or paradoxes, according to Pinker and Bloom, is that—

> [i]f some people are using a grammatical construction (either because of a special genetic property or general cognitive talents), there could be an advantage in others' evolving to be able to process it automatically, with dedicated hardware, as opposed to conscious inferential reasoning ... Moreover, a genetic change in the language faculty need not simply generate the ambient language verbatim, in which case ease of processing would be the only selection pressure, and further evolution would halt. It can generate a superset of the language (or a partially overlapping set), much the way contemporary children go beyond the information given in the development of creoles, sign languages, and their frequent creative inventions. If such creations increased expressive power and were comprehendable by others by any means, it could set the stage for the next iteration of the evolution process. (Pinker and Bloom, 1990, p. 776)

What is interesting about this response is that Pinker and Bloom do not argue that the distinction between "language" and "the language faculty" invoked by Sperber and by Ninio is purely terminological, or is obscure, or is flawed in some other way. Moreover, Pinker and Bloom seem to agree in principle that "language" and "language faculty" can be confused with each other as the target of a selectionist account in a way that would do harm to such an account. And they go on to introduce the notion of "the ambient language" into the discussion, without explicitly clarifying its ontological import *vis-à-vis* that of either of the concepts of "language" and "the language faculty". The argument between Pinker and Bloom on the one hand and Sperber and Ninio on the other hand is significant in at least three ways. First, it concerns the specificity and appropriateness of the focus of Pinker and Bloom's selectionist account. Second, it concerns the soundness of some of the inferences drawn by them. Third, and most important, it starts from a foundational assumption that is neither as obvious nor as clear as it might seem at first blush.

So let us explore the third point further. For ease of reference, we will state the foundational assumption at issue as (1):

(1) Language and the language faculty are distinct entities.

The question, of course, is this: What does the distinction between "language" and "language faculty" involve in a principled linguistic ontology? The distinction is not made in any explicit way by Pinker and Bloom, by Sperber or by Ninio. Pinker and Bloom, moreover, do not explicitly consider even just the possibility that the distinctions used by them, by Sperber and by Ninio may not be one and the same.

Could it be that "the" distinction between "language" and "the language faculty" is so evident, clear and unproblematic that there is no need for drawing it explicitly? Not really. To see this, let us consider how this distinction could, or could not, be drawn within the framework of one of the most clearly articulated linguistic ontologies yet proposed, namely Noam Chomsky's. Pinker and Bloom, after all, propose their account of language evolution within a broadly Chomskyan framework.

2.3 A CHOMSKYAN NON-DISTINCTION

As conceived of by Chomsky, the language faculty is a "mental organ" or "module of mind" and, as such, has two states that are of special significance.[2] One of these significant states of the language faculty is the initial state, taken by him to be "genetically determined".[3] That is to say, Chomsky sees the initial state of this faculty as incorporating the "genetic language program", or "(the set of) genetically encoded linguistic principles"; this, in turn, he sees as representing the child's innate linguistic endowment. The language faculty is in its initial state in a child that has not had any linguistic experience in the sense of having been exposed to utterances of or data about its language.[4] The other significant state of the language faculty is an attained, and stable, state.[5] This state develops or grows out of the initial state under the "triggering" and "shaping" influence of the child's linguistic experience.[6] It is this development or growth that has conventionally been called "language learning" or "language acquisition". And it is the attained, and stable, state of the language faculty that incorporates what Chomsky has characterized as "knowledge of a language".[7]

So, on Chomsky's linguistic ontology, to which the language faculty as characterized above is central, what would language or a language be? Chomsky has considered this question with reference to a language. On the one had, he identifies a language with a system of knowledge of language which, in turn, he takes to be a specific attained stable state of the language faculty. He comments, for example, that—

> [t]he language... constitutes one of the many systems of knowledge that the person has come to acquire, one of the person's cognitive systems.[8] (Chomsky, 1988, p. 36)

On the other hand, Chomsky draws a distinction between "knowledge of language" and "the object of knowledge":

> Taking knowledge of language to be a cognitive state, we might construe the "language" as an abstract object, the "object of knowledge", an abstract system of rules or principles (or whatever turns out to be correct) that is an image of the generative procedure, the I-language, represented in the mind and ultimately in the brain in now-unknown "more elementary" mechanisms.[9] (Chomsky, 1991a, p. 21)

Yet he sounds a warning about this further step of construing "language" as an abstract object:

> Since the language in this sense is completely determined by the I-language [i.e., by an attained state of the language faculty – R.P.B.], though abstracted from it, it is not entirely clear that this further step is motivated, but perhaps it is. (Chomsky, 1991a, p.21)

The question, then, is whether anything of substance can be claimed about "an abstract(ed) language" that cannot be claimed about the state of the language faculty from which it has been abstracted. Chomsky offers no examples of claims that apply to "an abstracted language" only.[10] In sum: it is doubtful that a Chomskyan linguistic ontology allows a distinction to be drawn between a language and a specific attained state of the language faculty.

So what does this imply for the ontological status of language, as distinct from a language? In other words: What could language be, given Chomsky's conception of the language faculty? An obvious possibility is to consider language to be an abstracted object too: specifically the entity abstracted from the initial state of the language faculty. But could language in such a sense be something that was not "completely determined" by the initial state of the language faculty? In other words, again: Could there be, distinct from a domain of "truths" about the initial state of the language faculty, an additional domain of facts about language as an abstracted object? Moreover, would such an object be a biological entity in a conventional sense: that is to say, an entity that could have evolved by a process such as natural selection? Is there a distinct domain of facts about the evolution of language which is not a domain of facts about the evolution of the initial state of the language faculty as well? These are examples of the questions that would have to be addressed by a Chomskyan ontology that drew a distinction of substance between language and the initial state of the language faculty. Similar questions would have to be raised and faced by Pinker and Bloom's ontology, should it differ in significant ways from Chomsky's. To my knowledge, they have not addressed questions such as these, which means that the following assumption would not be well-founded within their (broadly Chomskyan) linguistic ontology:

(2) Language could have evolved separately from the initial state of the language faculty.

2.4 "LANGUAGE" AS "SHARED LANGUAGE"

Would it not be possible to impute substance into Pinker and Bloom's distinction between "language" and "the language faculty" by taking "language" to mean "shared language"? In this connection, Jennifer Freyd has suggested in her *BBS* commentary that—

> Pinker and Bloom fail to distinguish adequately *language* – the public, shared system multiple humans create over time – from the human *language faculty* – the mental mechanisms that support the ability to acquire and use language. (Freyd, 1990, p. 732)

Freyd contends that "the language faculty" must have evolved through natural selection. But "language" as a "public shared system" – or "external language structure" – could not have done so. For, in Freyd's (1990, p. 733) view, "shared knowledge evolves at a much faster rate than our genetic code", and, consequently, cannot be "fully predicted from our genetic code". The evolution of "shared knowledge" cannot be "fully understood through an analogy "to physical evolution", moreover, since it does not "evolve through sexual reproduction".

On closer inspection, however, Freyd's ideas cannot be used for fleshing out Pinker and Bloom's distinction between "language" and "the language faculty". First, there are serious problems with the well-foundedness of notions of "shared language", as Chomsky (1989, pp. 10) has argued. In general, he sees no use for a notion of "shared language". As he puts it:

> For the inquiry into the nature of language, or language acquisition and change, or any of the topics of linguistic inquiry, the notion would appear to have no use ... [not] even for sociolinguistics, if we treat it seriously. (Chomsky, 1989, p. 9)

And, in regard to specifics, Chomsky has illustrated the flawed nature of the "logic" of Dummett's notion of "shared language" by inviting his readers to consider the fact that Jones understands Smith when the latter uses the word "tree" to refer to trees. Here is how Chomsky argues:

> Does it follow that Jones and Smith grasp the same meaning, an object of the common or abstract language? If so, then we should draw the analogous conclusion about pronunciation, given that Jones understands Smith to be saying "tree"; since Jones understands Smith, it must be that there is some object of the common

language, the real or common pronunciation of "tree", that Jones and Smith both grasp. No one is inclined to make the move. Rather, we say that Jones and Smith have managed a mutual accommodation that allows Jones, sometimes at least, to select an expression of his own language that, for the purposes at hand, matches well enough the one that Smith has produced. (Chomsky, 1989, p. 10)

Chomsky sees no need to draw the "absurd conclusion" that there is a common pronunciation shared by Smith and Jones. Clearly, one cannot operate, as Freyd does, with a notion of "shared language" without having shown that it is immune to Chomsky's objections. The same goes for Freyd's notion of "external language structure". To proceed in a nonarbitrary way, she has to show that this notion is free of the defects which Chomsky has diagnosed in well-known notions of "E(xternal)-language".[11] Freyd accordingly has not shown the following foundational assumption to be well-founded in the context of work on language evolution:

(3) Language should be conceived of as "shared language".

Second, Freyd invokes another distinction that is not made within a Chomskyan linguistic ontology: the distinction between "the human language faculty" and "the ability to acquire and use language". The former faculty, she asserts, is "the mental mechanisms that support" the latter ability. But she does not clarify this distinction, not even from her own evolutionary perspective. For example, does natural selection "operate" on the latter ability as it supposedly does on "the human language faculty"? Or does this ability, like "language", "evolve at a much faster rate" than the "human language faculty"?

Third, Freyd maintains that "shared knowledge" evolves much faster than our genetic code and that it does not evolve through sexual reproduction. Purely for the sake of argument, let us make two assumptions here. One: there does exist an entity such as "shared language". Two: "shared language" has the evolutionary properties attributed by Freyd to shared knowledge: those referred to above. Under this second assumption, however, "shared language" is something that could not evolve through natural selection. Which means that it cannot be the entity denoted by Pinker and Bloom's term "language".

2.5 "THE LANGUAGE FACULTY" VS. "PARTS OF THE LANGUAGE FACULTY"

What, then, is the entity that Pinker and Bloom mean to talk about when they make claims about the evolution of "language" or of "the language faculty"? Their selectionist approach requires this entity to be a biological one with a genetic base.

This means that, as used by them, the expressions "language" and the "language faculty" should be taken to refer to the initial state of a Chomskyan language faculty. And the specific claims made by Pinker and Bloom (1990, pp. 713-714) about the evolution of this entity are indeed claims about the evolution of U(universal) G(rammar) which in Chomsky's view is embodied in the initial state of the language faculty. But this is where it becomes unclear again what the entity/entities is/are for the evolution of which Pinker and Bloom have offered a selectionist account. For this is where a fundamental distinction drawn by Elliot Sober (1990) in his *BBS* commentary is fudged by Pinker and Bloom.

The distinction drawn by Sober is that between a compound entity or "complex phenotype" considered as a "unitary object" and the "specific features", "characteristics" or "parts" of such an entity.[12] This is an important distinction from the point of view of giving an account of the object's evolution, as Sober (1990, p. 764) explains with reference to the object known as the "human birth canal". In Sober's view:

> It is a waste of time to wonder whether "the human birth canal" is the product of natural selection. Rather, one wants to focus on specific features that the canal possesses. Some may be adaptive; others not. Presumably, we would want to tell quite different stories and to muster quite different kinds of evidence when we replace a single phenotype with a set of more finely individuated phenotypes. (Sober, 1990, p. 764)

Sober maintains that the distinction between a complex phenotype taken as a unitary object and the specific characteristics of such a phenotype is applicable to the language faculty as well. And he notes that Pinker and Bloom do recognize the need to distinguish some "features" of the language faculty from others. They (1990, p. 718) hold, for example, that "even if it could be shown that one part of language has no function, that would not mean that all parts of language had no function."

In their response to Sober's comments, however, Pinker and Bloom (1990, pp. 765–766), do not take up his point that, from an evolutionary perspective, a distinction needs to be drawn between (the) language (faculty) as a unitary object and specific "parts" or "features" of it.[13] Nor do they take up his point that a selectionist account should be given for specific features rather than for the whole. Instead, Pinker and Bloom switch back and forth, in what seems to be a non-deliberate way, between talking about the evolution of (the) language (faculty) as a unitary object and talking about the evolution of features of it. About the evolution of features, they make such general statements as the following:

In the evolution of the language faculty, many arbitrary constraints may have been selected simply because they defined parts of a standardized communicative code ... (Pinker and Bloom, 1990, p. 718)

And about the evolution of the unitary object, Pinker and Bloom say things in the vein of statements such as this one [emphases added – R.P.B.]:

The way to explain the evolution of **language** may not be to look for some climatic or ecological condition to which **it** was a direct selective response. (Pinker and Bloom, 1990, p. 773)

How does the evolution of the language faculty as a unitary object relate to the evolution of the specific parts of the language faculty? This broad question is not considered by Pinker and Bloom. It can be broken down, of course, into narrower questions such as the following two. First example: If one holds that basic parts of the language faculty did not evolve by natural selection, how can one hold at the same time that the faculty as a whole evolved by natural selection? Second example: Before one can properly take it as true that an individual part of the language faculty evolved by natural selection, what are the conditions which one will need to know to have obtained? We will go into these and related questions below, when we turn to some of the conceptual, epistemological and logical problems that are raised for selectionist accounts such as Pinker and Bloom's by the distinction between the language faculty as a unitary object and characteristics of the language faculty.[14] For now, it is enough to note that Pinker and Bloom do not make it clear which of the three assumptions below they are in fact adopting as foundational:

(4) (a) The entity whose evolution is to be accounted for is language taken as a unitary whole.
(b) The entities whose evolution is to be accounted for are individual parts of language.
(c) The entities whose evolution is to be accounted for include both language as a unitary whole and individual parts of language.

2.6 GENERAL PERSPECTIVE

Pinker and Bloom's selectionist account is instructive in the way it illustrates two of the fundamental ontological problems that have to be dealt with in all comprehensive accounts of language evolution.

The first of these two ontological problems involves the status of the entity conceived of as "language" – a matter that is left unclear by them. On Pinker and Bloom's account, language is portrayed both as an entity that is distinct from the initial state of the language faculty and as one that is identical to this state. Their portrayal of language as other than the initial state of the language faculty leaves two questions unanswered. Question one: On this portrayal, is language an entity (of a kind) that could have been subject to biological evolution? Question two: Are there facts about the evolution of this entity that are not facts about the evolution of the initial state of the language faculty as well?

Pinker and Bloom's account of language evolution is not unique in leaving it unclear how, on an essentially Chomskyan linguistic ontology, language could be distinct from the initial state of the language faculty. For example, at the Berlin Colloquium on language origin, Manfred Bierwisch (2001) presents his views on language origin in the framework of such an ontology, but leaves it unclear how language and its origin could be distinct from the language faculty or capacity – his term – and *its* origin. Thus, in some passages, he seems to use the expressions "(human) language" and "the language capacity" interchangeably [all emphases added – R.P.B.]:

> Did **language** emerge gradually from phylogenetic forerunners? To answer this question it is sometimes revealing to compare human languages with animal communication systems, including those – like birdsong – that are phylogenetically unrelated to **human language.** It is by now generally agreed that **the language capacity** is not a phylogenetic continuation of animal communication such as the gestural systems of nonhuman primates ... (Bierwisch, 2001, p. 70)

In other passages, however, Bierwisch uses the expression "(human) language" to refer to an entity that is distinct from the one he refers to as "the language capacity" [all emphases added – R.P.B.].

> The origin of the language capacity is either taken for granted or confused with the origin of (the first) **language.** The combinatorial properties of **human language** have largely been ignored. (Bierwisch, 2001, p. 70)
>
> In Bickerton's (1995) view, (18) and (19) represent two stages in the development of both the language capacity and of **language.**[15] (Bierwisch, 2001, p. 71)

How, on a Chomskyan linguistic ontology, language could be distinct from a state of the language faculty Bierwisch, like Pinker and Bloom, does not explain. Equally unclear is how, on such an ontology, it is possible for "the first language" or " a primordial language" to have originated – as Bierwisch (2001, p. 71) holds – separately from the language faculty. As he (2001, p. 71) sees it, "... the origin of a first language ... eventually activated the language capacity".[16]

The second of the two fundamental ontological problems that need to be dealt with in all comprehensive accounts of language evolution ties in with the distinction between language as a whole, or language as a unitary object, and the features or parts of language. An account of the evolution of an entity construed as a unitary whole does not relate in a simple way to accounts of the evolution of the features or parts.

Accounts of these two sorts differ, firstly, in the conceptual means needed for their construction; secondly, they differ in not only the criteria of adequacy but also the argument forms that are needed for their appraisal. These points will be taken up again in sections that are to follow.

3

THE FORMAL GRAMMATICAL SYSTEM

3.1　A REAPPROPRIATIONIST SCENARIO

Taking "language" to be a "formal grammatical system" embodied in a "human capacity", Wendy Wilkins and Jenny Wakefield (1995) in a target article in *Behavioral and Brain Sciences* present "a scenario for the emergence of the neural preconditions for language in the hominid lineage" (p. 161). At the core of this scenario is the claim that—

> [t]he neuroanatomical structures that underlie linguistic ability ... arose in human taxa as a direct result of evolutionary reappropriation. (Wilkins and Wakefield, 1995, p. 162)

The term "reappropriation" is used by Wilkins and Wakefield (1995, p. 162) in the sense of "the means by which a structure or function in the repertoire of a species reaches an evolutionary state that is compatible with, and facilitates, a new function". They note that the phenomenon they call "reappropriation" is referred to by Darwin as "preadaptation". Since the latter term has developed an "unintended connotation of premeditation", Wilkins and Wakefield (1995, p. 162) prefer not to use it.[1]

In outline, Wilkins and Wakefield (1995, pp. 161–172) maintain that certain adaptive changes produced in pleistocene primate lineages a paired expansion of the frontal and parietal cortex associated with manual throwing behaviours. This expansion resulted in the appearance, simultaneously with the emergence of *Homo habilis*, of two interconnected cortical areas: Broca's area and the POT. The latter area is a configurationally unique junction of the parietal, occipital and temporal lobes of the brain indicative of Wernicke's area. In their expanded form Broca's area and the POT had a motor function only.

The neuroanatomical structures associated with Broca's area and the POT were, on Wilkins and Wakefield's scenario, reappropriated for a new function: that of processing sensory input into conceptual structures that are both amodal and hierarchically ordered. More specifically, conceptual structure, according to Wilkins and Wakefield (1995, p. 175), is a cognitive construct that is produced by the POT through its interaction with Broca's area. By virtue of the POT, human sensory input is processed in a way that causes it to lose its modality-specific character. And by virtue of Broca's area, these amodal representations get structured in a hierarchical way. Structured modality-neutral representation is according to Wilkins and Wakefield's the essence of conceptual structure. In Wilkins and Wakefield's view, conceptual structure is but "a prerequisite to language"; having conceptual structure is **not** the same as having language, yet it does offer the hierarchical ordering necessary for modern syntax and morphology.[2]

3.2 DISCONNECTED DISCUSSION

Pinker and Bloom's account of language evolution is an example of an account which is inherently opaque in its identification of the entity/entities whose evolution is at issue. Wilkins and Wakefield's scenario for the emergence of the neural preconditions of language, by contrast, is not opaque in this regard. The entities whose evolution is at issue are clearly identified by them (1995, p. 161) as neural preconditions for language or, equivalently, as the neuroanatomical substrate of language.

And Wilkins and Wakefield (1995, p. 162) set out from an explicitly stated foundational assumption about what language is:

(1) Language is a formal grammatical system (as portrayed by theories of UG).

The *BBS* discussion of Wilkins and Wakefield's scenario, however, is internally strikingly disconnected: various commentators criticize Wilkins and Wakefield as if they offered an evolutionary scenario not of a formal grammatical system but of some other entity called "language". The resulting criticisms, accordingly, are misdirected and Wilkins and Wakefield (1995, pp. 206–208) have been able to counter them with relative ease. Though these misdirected criticisms have added little of substance to our understanding of linguistic evolution, they are instructive from a foundational perspective. So let us consider a number of them.

A first category of misdirected criticisms is based on conceptions of language that are **wider** than Wilkins and Wakefield's. These include—

(2) (a) Hauser and Wolfe's (1995, p. 190) conception in terms of which "language" is construed so broadly that even the categorical perception in chinchillas, macaques and quail is relevant to the appraisal of Wilkins and Wakefield's reappropriationist scenario;

    (b) Jacobs and Horner's (1995, pp. 194–195) non-homocentric conception in terms of which language is a multimodal enhancement system, which allows them to find evidence of "language" in non-human species;

    (c) Donald's (1995, p. 188) conception in terms of which aprosodias and difficulties in discourse comprehension are included in the category of language disorders, whereby it becomes necessary to assume a neurolinguistic model that is more inclusive than Wilkins and Wakefield's; and

    (d) Liska's (1995, pp. 198–199) conception on which language is so broadly construed that it involves sign use in general.

Underlying these conceptions of language is the foundational assumption statable as follows:

(3) Language is **more than** a formal grammatical system.[3]

On this foundational assumption, it becomes possible to criticize Wilkins and Wakefield's ideas about the neurolinguistic preconditions for language as incorrect and so on. An example is the criticism that the preconditions proposed by Wilkins and Wakefield do not account for the emergence of whatever it is that underlies categorical perception in chinchillas, macaques and quail. Criticisms such as these are offered on the basis of data about phenomena that fall outside the scope of the conception of language as a formal grammatical system; as a result, they miss their target.

Which brings us to a second category of misdirected criticisms of Wilkins and Wakefield's scenario for the emergence of neural preconditions for language. These criticisms are based on the foundational assumption that:

(4) Language is an entity that is **distinct from** the entity referred to as a "formal grammatical system".

This assumption underlies, for example,—

(5) (a) conceptions that equate language with communication – for example, that held by Walker (1995, p. 203); and

(b) conceptions that make no clear distinction between language and speech or speech perception – for example, those subscribed to by Catania (1995, p. 203), by Dingwall (1995, p. 187), and by Fitch and Tallal (1995, p. 189).

Assumption (4) makes it formally possible to criticize Wilkins and Wakefield for not providing an account of (the neural preconditions for) the emergence of communication, speech or speech perception. But this is not the purpose of their scenario: they (1995, p. 162) emphasize the point that language, as they define it, should not be equated with communication, speech, speech perception or conceptual structure.

3.3 Reasonable Response

To proceed from assumption (3) or (4) in critically appraising Wilkins and Wakefield's reappropriationist scenario is not to act in a reasonable way. In principle, there are various more coherent lines of response of which a first would involve arguing that there is no such thing as a formal grammatical system as portrayed by theories of UG. This would mean that Wilkins and Wakefield have proposed an account of the emergence (of the neural preconditions for) a non-existing entity. In view of the substantial amount of work that has been done over the years on the nature and specifics of UG, it would take not a little ingenuity to develop this argument. But from a formal point of view it would at least have some bearing on Wilkins and Wakefield's reappropriationist scenario.

A second line of response would involve: (i) granting the point that the formal grammatical system called "language" by Wilkins and Wakefield does exist; (ii) denying, however, that this system should be equated with "language"; (iii) proceeding, nevertheless, with appraising Wilkins and Wakefield's scenario for the emergence of (neurolinguistic preconditions for) this system on the basis of evidence or general considerations that do bear on it. In terms of (iii), Wilkins and Wakefield's scenario would still be appraised as a scenario of the emergence of (neural preconditions for) the formal grammatical system in question, in spite of their referring to it as "language".

This second line of response is a reasonable one in that it does not allow terminological disagreement about the use of the expression "language" to prevent critical appraisal of specific substantive claims about the emergence of neural preconditions for the formal grammatical system postulated by theories of UG. In Chapter 5, I will consider some of the reasons why Wilkins and Wakefield's critics have not been able to adopt such a more reasonable line of response.

The general approach underlying the second line of response can be adopted to enhance the cohesiveness of many discussions of language evolution that are in jeopardy by virtue of the fact that language is identified with different entities by different participants. It could, for example, have been used in the case of the Berlin Colloquium on language evolution for getting around the disagreement between Philip Lieberman and Eörs Szathmáry about the identity of the entity referred to as "language".

Lieberman proceeds from the foundational assumption that:

(6) Speech is the central "unique" aspect of language.

Thus, he maintains that:
> In the past forty years, linguists adhering to Noam Chomsky's theories have equated language with syntax, hypothetically specified by an innate, cortical organ, the "Universal Grammar". I shall attempt to shift the focus. I shall show that speech is perhaps the central "unique" aspect of human linguistic ability which also includes lexical and syntactic components ... (Lieberman, 2001, p. 21)

Using further the expression "(human) language" in the sense of "speech", Lieberman argues that its neural basis is a distributed network that crucially involves subcortical structures, the basal ganglia. The evolution of these structures can be traced back in time to animals similar to present-day frogs. This, to Lieberman, means that "the evolution of human language ... can be traced back hundreds of millions of years."

On the face of it, this view of Lieberman's clashes with Wilkins and Wakefield's scenario on which the neuroanatomical substrate of language emerged no more than two to two and half million years ago. And it would be unacceptable to Szathmáry as well who professes to subscribe to a Chomskyan position that involves the following as core assumption:

(7) Language is syntax.

In Szathmáry's view there is a "language amoeba" in the brain:
> The language amoeba is the neural activity pattern that essentially contributes to processing linguistic information, especially syntax. It is a sort of dynamic manifestation of Chomsky's language organ. (Szathmáry, 2001, p. 42)

Clearly, Lieberman and Szathmáry have different views of how "language" originated; clearly, too, this difference is at heart the difference between incompatible assumptions – namely (6) vs. (7) – about what "language" is. For reasons to be given in Chapter 5, it is highly doubtful that Lieberman and Szathmáry share a conceptual framework that might enable them to settle their disagreement about speech or syntax being central to language. Yet this lack of common ground need not of and by itself keep them from responding to each other's account of language evolution in a reasonable way: Szathmáry, by dealing with Lieberman's as an account of the evolution of speech; and Lieberman, by dealing with Szathmáry's as an account of the evolution of syntax.

4

LANGUAGE IN MULTIPLE (DIS)GUISES

4.1 A "NEW APPROACH"

In introducing the volume that resulted from the 1996 Edinburgh conference on language evolution, the editors distinguish two approaches to the topic: indirect (the old approach) and direct (the new one).[1] As this distinction is stated by Michael Studdert-Kennedy, Chris Knight and James Hurford (1998, p. 1), the old, indirect, approach is based on inferences from supposed correlates of language, including tools and artifacts as well as lateral biases in human brain morphology and handedness. The new approach, by contrast, "confronts language directly" by taking on questions such as these: "What was the nature of the hominid social matrix within which language arose, and what was the function of language in that matrix? How did its biologically unique hierarchical structure of phonology and syntax evolve?" These were in fact the general questions to be discussed at the Edinburgh conference.

The conference papers published in the resulting volume, according to Studdert-Kennedy, Knight and Hurford (1998, p. 4), address such more specific questions as the following: "How did a domain of collective rules emerge from, and come to constrain, the epigenetic course of individual development? How did the dual hierarchy of phonology and syntax emerge from perceptual, motoric, cognitive and social capabilities? How should we conceive the interactive evolutionary spiral through which both individual language capacity and a communal system of symbolic communication must have more or less simultaneously emerged?"

The general questions that set the agenda for the Edinburgh conference and the more specific ones dealt with in the resulting volume are all put in what seem to be carefully considered terms. Yet if the published papers are anything to judge by, the discussion that was meant to address these questions has turned out to be a strikingly disconnected whole. And one of the reasons for this – it will be shown below – is that:

(1) Different participants depict language as different (kinds of) entities.

Indeed, even one and the same participant seems to be able to think of language as being various distinct (kinds of) entities. The Edinburgh discussion, in short, treats language as a linguistic menagerie – ontologically speaking.

4.2 SOME OF THE (DIS)GUISES

Here is a sample of the ways in which participants in the Edinburgh conference use the term "language" [all emphases added – R.P.B.]:

Aitchison
Language, like many other aspects of **human behaviour**, is a case of "mosaic evolution"... (Aitchison, 1998, p. 19)
Language, like an orchid, ... [a]t its simplest ... involves three constituents: **auditory mechanisms**, **articulatory mechanisms**, and **a brain** which coordinates these. (Aitchison, 1998, p. 19)

Donald
... language is too broad a **process** ... (Donald, (1998, p. 46)
... language is really a gigantic **meta-task** ... (Donald, 1998, p. 56)
The acquisition of any special **human skill**, including language ... (Donald, 1998, p. 58)

Dunbar
... the function of language (as an **activity**) is to ... (Dunbar, 1998, p. 107)

Studdert-Kennedy, Knight, Hurford
However, historical changes within, and divergences among, languages are largely cultural matters, biologically constrained, no doubt, but quite distinct from the evolution of language as a **species-specific capacity**. (Studdert-Kennedy *et al.*, 1998, p. 2)
What we need therefore is an account of language evolution, sensitive both to language as **'a sort of contract signed by members of a community'** and to language as **hard-wired (individual) competence** generated under standard processes of Darwinian natural selection. (Studdert-Kennedy *et al.*, 1998, p. 2)
We need to place language among those many **group behaviours** of social animals – from the reproductive processes of social insects to the hunting routines of a wolf pack – that can only emerge through interactions among individuals. (Studdert-Kennedy *et al.*, 1998, p. 2)

Worden

Social intelligence and a theory of mind are vital pre-requisites for language. I propose that language is not just a new mental faculty. (Worden, 1998, p. 149)

Steels

Language is emergent in two ways. First of all, it [i.e., language – R.P.B.] is **a mass phenomenon actualized by different agents interacting with each other** ... Second, language is emergent in the sense that **it spontaneously forms itself** once the appropriate physiological, psychological and social conditions are satisfied ... (Steels, 1998, p. 384)

Language is not a mere **complex system of labels for concepts and conceptual structures** which already exist prior to language, but, rather the complexification of language contributes to the ability to form richer conceptualizations which in turn cause language itself to become more complex. (Steels, 1998, p. 385)

Ulbaek

Language is a task- and species-specific module of the human mind, a "language organ". [as Chomsky has maintained – R.P.B.] (Ulbaek, 1998, p. 30)[2]

These are not the only ways in which language is characterized in the Edinburgh discussion. For instance, when he introduces the contributions by Steels (1998) and Batali (1998), Hurford (1998, p. 303) asserts that "This genre of work assumes that language is *essentially* coordinated communicative behaviour, rather than an individual factual knowledge of rules of grammar". The contribution by Kirby (1998, pp. 360, 369, 379), moreover, provides for linguistic entities that he calls "language itself" and "languages themselves". These entities are supposed to be distinct from the entity/entities that he calls "human language learning mechanisms" or "the LAD". Kirby holds that "languages themselves" and the "LAD" came about by evolutionary processes of different kinds. But he does not clarify either the ontological status or the nature of "language itself", of "language themselves" or of the non-biological evolutionary process, what he calls "the linguistic process of selection", by which "languages themselves" are to have evolved.

By allowing language to be characterized in the ways exemplified above, the Edinburgh discussion gives rise to various questions. For example: What is/are the entity/entities whose evolution is meant to be at issue? How could language be at one and the same time an "aspect of human behaviour", a "process", a "meta-task", a "special human skill", an "activity", an "application of social intelligence and a theory of mind", a "species-specific capacity", "a sort of contract signed by members of a community", "hard-wired (individual) competence", a "group behaviour" and an entity "spontaneously [formed by] itself"? Are these expressions, ontologically non-identical as they are, being used to refer to one and the same entity rather than to various distinct entities? If there is more than one distinct entity, could they have all been subject to evolution in a non-outlandish sense? For instance, is it possible for a "giant meta-task" or a (social) "contract" to have evolved in the same sense as a "species-specific capacity" or a "hard-wired (individual) competence"? If scholars in using one and the same term "language" are **not** all referring to one and the same entity, then surely in effect they doom their treatments of the evolution of "language" to being **unlikely** to connect up with one another? The brute fact is that the Edinburgh discussion of new approaches to the evolution of language goes its way in the absence of a well-articulated and shared conception of the linguistic entity/entities whose evolution is at issue. As a line of conduct, this would seem to reflect an approach to the study of language evolution that takes the following for granted as a foundational assumption:

(2) Language can be various distinct entities at one and the same time.

The Edinburgh discussion does not in itself give any grounds, however, for thinking of assumption (2) as heuristically fruitful. Nor has the discussion advanced the search for an answer to the organizers' question: "How, perhaps most problematic of all, should we conceive the interactive evolutionary spiral through which both individual language capacity and a communal system of symbolic communication must have more of less simultaneously emerged?" (Studdert-Kennedy *et al.*, 1998, p. 4)

4.3   THE (DIS)CONTINUITY OF LANGUAGE EVOLUTION

The lack of a well-articulated and shared conception of the linguistic entity/entities whose evolution is at issue has been largely to blame, at the same time, for the internal disconnectedness and the inconclusiveness of the discussions on specific questions of language evolution. A good example is to be seen in the ways in which some of the papers in the Edinburgh discussion deal with the question of the (dis)continuity of language evolution. On its construal by Jean Aitchison, this question can be stated as in (3):

(3) Did language develop out of animal communication systems in a continuous line of development, or was there a break?[3] (Aitchison, 1998, p. 19)

On affirmative responses to this question, language as a communication system is not something completely novel; negative responses to it portray language as a novel, uniquely human, entity. Aitchison argues that, because it is based on a dichotomy that

has become untenable, question (3) has served its purpose. She prefers the view that—
> [l]anguage, like many other aspects of human behaviour, is a case of "mosaic evolution" ... in which some aspects of language have strong continuity, others moderate, others little. (Aitchison, 1998, p. 19)

In justification of this view, Aitchison (1998, pp. 120) distinguishes among three "constituents" of language whose development has been characterized by different degrees of continuity. In the case of the first "constituent", namely auditory mechanisms, the continuity is strong; in the case of the second "constituent", referred to by her as "a brain", the continuity is weak; the third "constituent", namely articulatory mechanisms, shows "the greatest discontinuity". After discussing some cases of what she calls "ambiguous continuity", here is how Aitchison sums up her view of the continuity – discontinuity dichotomy:
> In short, the continuity – discontinuity dichotomy has provided us with a useful staging-post in discussions of language origin. We now know enough, however, to realize that the divide is oversimple, and that it is time to move on. (Aitchison, 1998, p. 22)

At least one participant in the Edinburgh discussion, though, does not share Aitchison's view of the usefulness of the continuity – discontinuity dichotomy. This is Ib Ulbaek. He (1998) offers a serious defence of a variant of the position that the development of language was characterized by continuity. The core of his position is as follows:
> The correct theory of evolution of language is this: *language evolved from animal cognition not from animal communication.* Here lies the continuity. Language grew out of cognitive systems already in existence and working: it formed a communicative bridge between already-cognitive animals. (Ulbaek, 1998, p. 33)

In defending this position, Ulbaek (1998, p. 32) explicitly distances himself from Chomsky's "rejection of continuity" and sides with Bickerton (1990) and Pinker (1994), whose views on continuity he reads as similar to his own. Unlike Aitchison, then, Ulbaek treats the question of the (dis)continuity of language evolution not only as fundamental but also as based on a dichotomy that is not "oversimple".

Which gives rise to the question: How is it possible for Ulbaek and Aitchison to be seriously expounding and advocating these opposite positions in one and the same discussion? The short answer is that, when they use the expression *the evolution of language*, they do not refer to the evolution of the same entity. Take first the nature of the entity called "language" by Aitchison.

Language, like an orchid, has been "jury-rigged from a limited set of available components" (Gould 1980, p. 20). At its simplest, it involves three main constituents:

auditory mechanisms, articulatory mechanisms, and a brain which co-ordinates these. (Aitchison, 1998, p. 19)

Language, then, for Aitchison, is a tripartite entity. But there is more: she also conceptualizes it as an aspect of human behaviour:

> Language, like many other aspects of human behaviour, is a case of "mosaic evolution" ... (Aitchison, 1998, p. 19)

Conspicuously absent from Aitchison's list of "main constituents" of language is a mental faculty such as that referred to by generativists as "the genetically determined initial state of the language faculty" or "universal grammar". But it is this same mental faculty that is referred to as "language" by Ulbaek. Here, as evidence, is what Ulbaek has to say on the matter:

> What Chomsky *has* claimed is that without a strong innate component, language cannot be learned. To my mind his arguments are convincing ... So, in conclusion, I follow Chomsky in claiming a strong innate component in human language. (Ulbaek, 1998, p. 32)

Further evidence that Ulbaek takes language to be a Chomskyan mental entity is the fact that he aligns his position on the continuity of language evolution with Pinker's (1994), a position which is distinctly mentalist.

At the heart of the disagreement between Aitchison and Ulbaek lie two different foundational assumptions about what language is:

(4) *Aitchison:* Language is a composite entity; even at its simplest, it is made up of auditory mechanisms, articulatory mechanisms and a brain.

(5) *Ulbaek:* Language is a Chomskyan mental faculty, namely Universal Grammar.

This foundational disparity has a pair of effects, closely related one to the other, that are worth noting here. One: When Aitchison and Ulbaek address "the question" of the (dis)continuity of language evolution, they are not in fact talking about the same question. Two: They are not going to be able to have a properly connected exchange of ideas about the (dis)continuity of language evolution, unless they settle their ontological differences first.

Aitchison's adoption of (4) makes for a striking illustration of the extent to which foundational assumptions shape substantive claims about language evolution. If language is being taken to be a composite entity (of a poorly demarcated kind) and if its constituents are being taken to be ontologically disparate, then it is unsurprising to find that language has been subject to mosaic evolution. Applied to the evolution of language, the idea of mosaic evolution would be interesting if it were put in the form of an empirical hypothesis about a linguistic entity whose constituents all belonged to the same ontological category. The initial state of a Chomskyan language faculty – that is, Universal Grammar – is an example of such a linguistic entity. Essentially, what Aitchison has done in forming her notion of language is to put together an entity – "language" – out of quite unlike kinds of components without (a) showing that this is proper from an ontological point of view or (b) showing that this is heuristically fruitful from an evolutionary point of view. To be of sufficient substance, answers to these questions would have to do more than invoke Gould's orchid metaphor.

4.4 THE (NON)GRADUALNESS OF LANGUAGE EVOLUTION

The coherence of the Edinburgh discussion of language evolution has also been affected by assumptions in a more specific vein about language, notably assumptions about syntactic design. An interesting instance of this presents itself where the discussion shifts to the question of whether language evolved in a gradual or non-gradual way. This question, which is related to the question whether language evolved in a (dis)continuous way, can be stated as (6):

(6) Did language evolve over a long period in an incremental way via intermediate steps or did it emerge without any step-by-step accumulation of its components or traits? In other words, did language evolve **gradually** or **abruptly**?

Opting for a generativist linguistic ontology, Berwick (1998) argues that language, and in particular its combinatorial component, emerged abruptly. The core of his position is that—

> ... while it is surely true that natural language, like the vertebrate eye, is in some sense an "organ of extreme complexity and perfection", in Darwin's terms, we shall argue that one does not need to advance incremental, adaptationist arguments with intermediate steps to explain much of language's specific syntactic design. (Berwick, 1998, p. 322)

Berwick accordingly rejects the "pan-selectionist stance", the core of which, on his construal, is that—

> ... all the special properties of language have been specifically selected for as directly adaptive, with gradual changes leading from non-language-using ancestors to speaking/gesturing hominoids ...[4] (Berwick, 1998, p. 321)

In the Edinburgh discussion, Frederick Newmeyer, by contrast, defends a gradualist view of language evolution as part of his critique of Chomsky's non-adaptationist view (of language evolution).[5] Thus, Newmeyer (1998, p. 317) expresses the belief that "the origins of the vast amount of grammatical properties that are still arguably provided for by an innate UG" required a gradualist, adaptationist account. Interestingly, the opposed views taken by Newmeyer and Berwick on the gradualness of language evolution do not rest on two different conceptions of what language is: both of these scholars adopt a broadly generativist linguistic ontology. They do hold different theories of syntax, though, and it is this difference that ties in with the difference between their positions on the gradualness of language evolution.

As for Berwick (1998, p. 324ff.), he subscribes to Chomsky's views on syntax that make up the "Minimalist Program". Central to this programme, as Berwick understands it, are the two assumptions about syntactic structure given in (7):

(7) (a) There is only one combinatorial operation in the derivation of sentences, namely the operation called "Merge", which combines words hierarchically into superwords, and superwords, in turn, into larger syntactic constituents.[6]

(b) Many (apparently) fundamental syntactic relations and constraints can be derived from Merge, including basic skeletal tree structure, movement rules, grammatical relations like object-of, locality constraints and so on.[7]

According to Berwick (1998, p. 337), these syntactic relations and constraints "fall into place once the fundamental operation of Merge is up and running." And, what is crucial from a genetic perspective, the operation called "Merge" originated in a single step, according to Berwick. He makes this plain when he asserts that—

... there is no possibility of 'intermediate' *syntax* between a non-combinatorial one and full natural language – one either has Merge in all its generative glory, or one has no combinatorial syntax at all. (Berwick, 1998, pp. 338–339)

Since other fundamental syntactic "details" are derivative from Merge, they too emerged abruptly in one step along with Merge. This implies, as Berwick (1998, p. 337) sees the matter, that "nothing here has to be specifically 'selected for' in the gradualist, pan-selectionist sense". Berwick's adoption of a non-gradualist position on language evolution, thus, clearly coheres with his adoption of a particular, minimalist, theory of syntactic structure. In Berwick's thinking, if syntactic design is minimalist, it had to emerge abruptly rather than gradually.

This brings us to Newmeyer who, on the one hand, adopts a gradualist position on the evolution of language and, on the other hand, rejects Chomsky's minimalist syntax. Newmeyer (1998, p. 311) continues to hold to the older Government-Binding model of syntactic structure, central to which are the assumptions given in (8):

(8) (a) Syntax is made up of various subsystems, each of which is governed by a distinct set of principles.[8]

(b) The principles of the various syntactic subsystems cannot be derived from a more fundamental principle or property.

Assumptions (8)(a) and (b) are difficult to reconcile with the view that the computational core of language emerged in just one step ("abruptly"). Rather, these assumptions are compatible with the position that the various syntactic principles evolved in an incremental way ("gradually").

Note that adoption of specifically the Minimalist Program – in terms of which Merge is the only combinatorial syntactic operation – is not a precondition for holding a nongradualist view of language evolution. What is required, rather, is the adoption of **some** syntactic theory in terms of which the details of syntactic structure could have emerged abruptly as consequences of **some** more fundamental property, Merge being just one instance of such a property. In the Edinburgh discussion, for example, Bickerton (1998) argues that language emerged in a "rapid" or "catastrophic" way, yet he does so without subscribing to the Minimalist Program. He holds a pre-minimalist theory of syntax, one that allows him to claim that the structure of syntax emerged abruptly as a collection of consequences of the more fundamental "mechanism of theta analysis". Thus, he asserts that—

> ... the linkage of theta analysis with other elements involved in protolanguage would not merely have put in place the basic structure of syntax, but would also have led directly to a cascade of consequences that would, in one rapid and continuous sequence, have transformed protolanguage into language substantially as we know it today.[9] (Bickerton, 1998, p. 353)

To return, however, to the differences that set Berwick and Newmeyer apart. How can they debate in a properly connected way whether language evolved gradually or emerged abruptly? For their discussion of this issue to become properly connected, it would first have to focus on the merits of the different syntactic theories they hold. As long as Berwick and Newmeyer disagree on fundamental notions about syntactic structure – those stated as assumptions (7) and (8) – there can be no real prospect of their resolving their differences on the (non)-gradualness of language evolution.

5

A Theory of Linguistic Entities

5.1   Ontological Opacity and Arbitrariness

Let us pick up again from the condition stated as (1) in the introductory paragraph of Part 1. What it says is that the linguistic entity or entities whose evolution is at issue should be identified unambiguously and characterized clearly in non-arbitrary terms. Next, in Chapters 2, 3 and 4, two sets of failures in terms of this condition have been shown. One: some of the most sophisticated modern accounts of language evolution fail to meet this condition at all or meet it to a limited extent only. Two: the same goes for discussions of such accounts. That is, we have seen that such accounts or discussions have one or more of the four shortcomings listed below:

(1) (a) It is unclear what the entity is or entities are for whose evolution an account is being offered.
(b) It is not evident that the entity or entities whose evolution is at issue exist or could exist.
(c) It is not shown that the entity for the evolution of which an account is being offered is of a kind that could have undergone (biological) evolution.
(d) It is not obvious why one entity rather than another is being equated with the "thing" whose evolution has to be accounted for.

Accounts of language evolution which have one or more of shortcomings (1)(a) – (d) are insufficiently transparent or well-founded in regard to ontological import. And, as we have seen, discussions of language evolution which exhibit one or more of shortcomings (1)(a) – (d) are on the whole internally disconnected and inconclusive.

So the question is: What could be done to eliminate shortcomings (1)(a) – (d) from those modern accounts and discussions of language evolution that exhibit them?

5.2   A CURE

In Chapters 2 to 4, we also pinned down the source of the ontological opacity or arbitrariness of which (1)(a) – (d) are symptoms; its source is the questionable assumptions which are made about the entities in the linguistic domain of reality. To cure such opacity or arbitrariness, and to prevent thereby the disconnectedness of discussion that it inevitably gives rise to, work on language evolution should set out from a linguistic ontology which is well founded. A well-founded linguistic ontology is a theory which unambiguously identifies and restrictively characterizes—

(2) (a) the basic linguistic entities – objects, states, events, processes and so on – that occur in linguistic reality,
   (b) the distinctive properties of those entities, and
   (c) the ways in which those entities are interrelated.

On the basis of this characterization, such an ontology discriminates in a non-arbitrary way among entities such as language, a language, knowledge of language, the language faculty, language behaviour, the capacities underlying language behaviour and so on.[1] In this way, it rules out whole classes of options. First example: it makes it impossible to distinguish between entities that do not have different properties. Thus, it makes it impossible to distinguish in an arbitrary way between an entity called "the (initial state of the) language faculty" and one referred to as "language". Second example: it makes it impossible to arbitrarily take two distinct entities, such as "language" and "speech", to be one and the same thing.

A well-founded linguistic ontology has as a core component a theory of language such as that referred to in Section 1.4 above. That theory, on the basis of its restrictive characterization of language, denies certain (kinds of) linguistic entities the ontological status of "language" or "a language" – and it does so not by means of some arbitrary stipulation. Recall that earlier chapters have pointed out many assumptions about language that are the products of just such stipulations. It is the lack of a well-founded linguistic ontology – with a restrictive theory of language at its core – that has caused accounts of language evolution to be misdirected or insufficiently well-focused. The lack of a well-articulated linguistic ontology and theory of language, moreover, has been a major cause of the disconnected state of the discussions of language evolution examined in earlier chapters. Disagreements about the identity or nature of the linguistic entities whose evolution is at issue cannot be discussed in a coherent way outside the framework of general theories of linguistic entities and specific theories of language.

5.3 A Non-Remedy

But is it really necessary for work on language evolution to set out from a sophisticated theory of what the fundamental linguistic entities are? Wouldn't it be possible to "get by on" less complex conceptual constructs such as those represented by the formula "language as (a/an) X"? These questions are to the point, since – as we have seen in earlier chapters – the entity whose evolution is believed to be at issue is often identified with the aid of phrases such as the following:

(3) (a) "language as hard-wired individual competence",
   (b) "language as speech",
   (c) "language as an activity",
   (d) "language as a sort of contract signed by members of a community", and
   (e) "language as syntax".

Surely the linguistic entity whose evolution is at issue is being indicated in an unambiguous way by expressions such as (3)(a) – (e)? So what would be wrong in using the "simple", "commonsensical" formula "language as (a/an) X" rather than a "technical" linguistic ontology of the sort discussed above?

There is indeed a sense in which "language as (a/an) X" formulations are harmless – the sense in which "language as (a/an) X" has the meaning "the linguistic phenomenon or entity called 'X'". In this sense, the phrase "language as hard-wired individual competence" would mean "the linguistic phenomenon or entity called 'hard-wired individual competence'", the phrase "language as syntax" would mean "the linguistic phenomenon or entity called 'syntax'" and so on. In this sense, clearly, hard-wired individual competence or syntax or whatever is not being equated with language.

At a deeper level, however, the formula "language as (a/an) X" is problematic in more than one way. First, it may give rise to incoherence or tautology: if language is **not** the same thing as what "X" may stand for – e.g., syntax – then language cannot coherently be construed as being identical to this thing. If language is the same thing as what "X" may stand for, the formula "language as (a/an) X" is a useless means for expressing tautologies.

Second, the formula "language as (a/an) X" may be used as a licence for arbitrariness. One scholar, for instance, may wish to substitute "speech" for "X":

another, "syntax"; yet another, "a sort of contract signed by members of a community"; and so on. To avoid such arbitrary stipulation, the value of "X" would have to be constrained in a principled way. For this, however, a well-founded linguistic ontology would be required.

Third, the use of the formula "language as (a/an) X" may give rise to disconnected, non-constructive discussion. This is what happens when a phrase such as "language as syntax" is understood as doing two things: identifying the entity – namely syntax – whose evolution is at issue, on the one hand, and covertly equating language with syntax, on the other hand. Scholars who reject the latter equation may dismiss the proposed account of the evolution of syntax without giving it serious consideration, when in fact this account does merit serious consideration. In outline, the argument behind such a dismissal runs as follows (where "S" is short for "the scholar in question"):

(4) S equates language with syntax.
    Language, however, does not equal syntax.
    Therefore, S's account of the evolution of language cannot be correct.

For various reasons, then, the formula "language as (a/an) X" should not be used for identifying the entity or entities whose evolution requires explanation.

To sum up. Work on language evolution needs to start out from a discriminating characterization of the entities that could have been subject to evolution. For this, one has to have a linguistic ontology that is clearly articulated and that has at its core a restrictive conception of language. Such an ontology needs to be complemented, however, by an equally restrictive theory of evolution – a point that will be taken up in Part II below.

PART II

PROCESSES OF LANGUAGE EVOLUTION

How did language evolve? This is one of the central questions that have guided modern work on language evolution. As such, it has typically been construed as a question about the nature and properties of the process(es) by which language evolved. In response to it, answers such as the following have been given:

(1) (a) Language or certain fundamental features of it arose – like the brooding chamber in snails – by a process of (spandrel) co-optation.

(b) Certain fundamental features of language originated – like bird's feathers – by a process of preadaptation or function shift.

(c) Language or some of its features evolved – like the vertebrate eye – through natural selection.

Claims such as (1)(a)–(c) presuppose, clearly, a principled theory of evolution that makes use of two sorts of general assumptions. One: the theory makes use of assumptions about the nature and properties of the evolutionary processes in question. Two: it makes use of assumptions about the conditions under which an entity may be claimed to have evolved by a specific evolutionary process and, therefore, may be assigned a matching evolutionary status. In the absence of assumptions of the first sort, claims such as (1)(a)–(c) would be unclear in terms of their content. And in the absence of assumptions of the second sort, it would not be possible to appraise such claims by bringing appropriate factual evidence or non-empirical considerations to bear on them. The evolutionary status assigned to an entity is generally taken to reflect (some aspect of) its evolutionary history. That is why it has become conventional to require that the evidence put forward in support of such status assignments should have some historical import.

Part II of this book examines some of the more highly rated modern accounts of language evolution from the perspective of the assumptions which they make about the processes believed to have been central to the evolution of language or features of it. It does this by going into questions such as the following: How clear are these assumptions? Are they non-ad hoc in being embedded in a general theory of evolution? Is this theory sufficiently restrictive? In Chapter 6 these questions are considered as they apply to exaptationist accounts of language evolution which express claim (1)(a) in one or another form. Chapter 7 pursues these questions with reference to preadaptationist accounts central to which is some version of claim (1)(b). And in Chapter 8 they are discussed with reference to a comprehensive selectionist account central to which is claim (1)(c). Chapter 9 brings Part II to a close by discussing a general shortcoming of the various accounts – exaptationist, preadaptationist and selectionist – that was focused on in the preceding chapters: the fact of their not being underpinned by evolutionary theories of a sufficiently restrictive sort.

6

CO-OPTATION IN LANGUAGE EVOLUTION

6.1 SNAILS' BROODING CHAMBER AND THE DISCRETE INFINITY OF LANGUAGE

Certain species of snails protect their eggs by using what Stephen Jay Gould (1997a, p. 10753) calls an "umbilical brooding chamber".[1] This chamber is a cylindrical space inside a coiled tube; the tube is laid down in a coil as the snail body grows. The chamber and the coil have the same geometric axis. Evolutionarily speaking, this central space did not arise as part of a design selected for the advantages of egg protection – indeed, no such design ever existed. Rather, the space arose nonadaptively, as a by-product of a biological process of the winding of a tube around an axis.

Various scholars, including Noam Chomsky (1982a, 1988, 1991b), Stephen Gould (1991), Massimo Piattelli-Palmarini (1989, 1990), Lyle Jenkins (2000) and Manfred Bierwisch (2001), have speculated that language or some fundamental feature(s) of language arose non-adaptively like the brooding chamber in snails. On such a conception, language or some of its features – it should perhaps be stressed – emerged initially as a consequence or by-product of something else. Chomsky's (1982a) speculations on the matter instantiates this point clearly. Taking it that humans' capacity to deal with discrete infinities is fundamental to the computational component of language, he has speculated that:

> ... it could, for example, be a consequence of the increase in brain size and complexity. (Chomsky, 1982a, p. 22)

Such conceptions of the origin of either language or some of its features will be referred to below as "by-product conceptions of language origin" or, more briefly, "by-product conceptions".[2]

The by-product conception of language origin held by Chomsky and Gould has been dismissively criticized as being characterized by "vacuity" (Pinker and Bloom, 1990, p. 711), as being "utterly implausible" (Newmeyer, 1998, p. 313), as being "more an *ex cathedra* proclamation than a theory" (Donald, 1999, p. 138) and so on. The proponents of this conception have shown no sign of abandoning it, however, at least not in public. This, of course, gives rise to questions such as:

(1) (a) How good is Chomsky's by-product conception of language origin really?
 (b) How forceful are the criticisms of this conception actually?

A first step in pursuing these questions is to note that claims to the effect that a particular biological entity or feature of such an entity arose nonadaptively as a consequence or by-product of something else presuppose a general theory of evolutionary by-producthood. And this applies to criticisms of such claims as well. A theory of by-producthood has to state the conditions under which an entity or feature may be properly assigned or denied the evolutionary status of "by-product". These conditions, moreover, will determine the kinds of evidence and forms of argument that can be properly used in justifying or criticizing claims which attribute by-product-status to entities or features of entities. In the absence of an adequate theory of by-producthood, claims to the effect that specific entities or features did or did not arise as by-products would be arbitrary and ad hoc.

Which brings us to two further questions that arise in connection with Chomsky's by-product conception of language origin:

(2) (a) Within what theory of by-producthood has Chomsky accorded language or fundamental features of language the status of "evolutionary by-product"?
 (b) Within what theory or theories of by-producthood have Chomsky's critics questioned or rejected this step of his?

These, of course, are questions about a particular category of foundational assumptions – assumptions about the nature of biological evolution – that have underpinned modern work on the evolution of language.

So let us pursue questions (2)(a) and (b) by considering Gould and Vrba's (1982) theory of evolutionary by-producthood, one of the better known theories of its sort. This theory – though controversial in various ways – gives us an idea of the kinds of grounds on which a particular biological entity or some feature of it could be assigned or denied the evolutionary status of by-product.[3] And it offers us a conceptual background against which the merit of Chomsky's by-product conception of language origin and the force of the main criticisms of this conception may be assessed.

6.2 A THEORY OF BY-PRODUCTHOOD

Gould and Vrba's theory of by-producthood forms part of their more general theory of exaptation. In their attempt to account for large-scale evolutionary change, Gould and Vrba (1982, pp. 4–6) draw a distinction between two categories of characters that enhance fitness.[4] The first category is the adaptations: characters shaped (or built) for their present use (or function) by natural selection. As instances of "true adaptation", Gould (1991, p. 47) cites the elaborate plumages and behavioural displays of male birds of paradise; the function of these characters is to help ensure the males' success in mating. Like the character shaped, the evolutionary process that shaped it is called "adaptation". The second category of fitness-enhancing characters is the exaptations: characters that enhance fitness in their present role but that, according to Gould (1991, p. 46), were not built for this role (or effect) by natural selection. The evolutionary process by which an exaptation arose is called "exaptation" or "co-optation".

Exaptations belong on Gould and Vrba's (1982, pp. 5–6) theory to one of two subcategories. The first comprises the characters previously shaped as adaptations by natural selection for a particular function but co-opted later for a new use (or effect). An example given by Gould and Vrba (1982, p. 7) is that of feathers which evolved initially as an adaptation for thermoregulation and were later co-opted for flight. The process of exaptation by which exaptations of this subcategory originate is referred to as "preadaptation" by some and "function shift" by others.[5]

To the second subcategory of exaptations, Gould and Vrba (1982, pp. 5–6) assign characters that did not originate by the direct action of natural selection and that were later co-opted for a current use (utility, role or effect). The umbilical brooding chamber of snails referred to in Section 6.1 above instantiates the second subcategory of exaptations. Characters belonging to this subcategory have been called "spandrels"; "spandrel" is a term borrowed by Gould and Lewontin (1979) from architecture, where it designates forms and spaces that arise as necessary by-products of another decision in design, and not as adaptations for direct utility in themselves. On Gould's (1997a, p. 10751) judgement, "spandrel" is "optimally suited" as a general term in evolutionary biology for "the concept of a nonadaptive architectural by-product of definite and necessary form – a structure of predictable size and shape that then becomes available for later and secondary utility".[6]

Within their general theory of exaptation, Gould and Vrba (1982, p. 11) provide for two other useful concepts: "primary exaptations" and "secondary adaptations". In their basic design, feathers are primary exaptations for flight, having evolved by adaptation for insulation. Once this new fitness-enhancing role in flying was added to the function of thermoregulation, feathers underwent what Gould and Vrba call "a suite of secondary adaptations" or "post-adaptations", which enhanced their utility in flight. In the view of Gould and Vrba (1982, pp. 11–12), the evolutionary history of any complex feature is likely to include a "sequential mixture of adaptations, primary exaptations and secondary adaptations". The reason why such secondary adaptations happen is that any exapted or co-opted structure "will probably not arise perfect for the new role".

6.3 IDENTIFYING EVOLUTIONARY BY-PRODUCTS

Determining whether a given structure or feature is to be assigned or denied the evolutionary status of "by-product" or "spandrel" is a complex matter for Gould:

> ... if we now have available only the modern structure with its mix of primary adaptations and secondarily exapted spandrels – the usual situation in biology when we do not have a fossil record of actual historical stages leading to a present structure – then how can we identify and allocate the proper statuses? (Gould, 1997a, p. 10752)

After all, both types of features may now be exquisitely well "crafted" for a current utility – for the exapted spandrel may work just as well, and may be just as crucial to current function of the whole, as the primary adaptation.

To make the matter more complex still, there is the possibility that by-products or spandrels may have been subject to a suite of the secondary adaptations. So what are the grounds – general considerations and kinds of evidence – that can be properly invoked in assigning or denying a "modern structure" the evolutionary status of "by-product" or "spandrel"? In addressing this question, Gould (1997a) uses the term "spandrel" rather than "by-product", a terminological practice without any deeper significance.

First there are some considerations which in Gould's view cannot be used as grounds for assigning or denying a structure S the status of "(biological) spandrel". These include:

(3) (a) the extent to which S is well-crafted for a current utility;
    (b) the nature of the current utility (role or effect) of S;
    (c) the evolutionary meaning or importance of S;
    (d) the (physical) size of S.

As for (3)(a), Gould believes, we have seen, that a structure which originated as a spandrel through primary exaptation may have been further "crafted" for its current utility by a "suite of secondary adaptations". Consequently, it may end up being "exquisitely crafted for its current utility" and may work just as well as an adaptation. How well-crafted S is or how well S works, accordingly, cannot be used as a ground for assigning or denying S the status of a structure that originated as a spandrel.

Turning to (3)(b), Gould (1991, p. 45) has insisted that "the clear separation of historical origin and current utility" is an important "conceptual tool" of the evolutionary biologist.[7] In his view, the inference of origin from current utility constitutes a "false conceptual passage".[8] The nature of the current utility of S accordingly does not provide a basis for assigning or denying spandrel status to S.

As regards (3)(c) – a ground related to (3)(b) – Gould (1991, pp. 54–55, 1997a, p. 10754) rejects what is referred to as the "sequelae argument". In terms of this argument, spandrels always occur later than and secondarily to primary adaptations, as "correlated consequences" of them, and never as "active phenomena themselves" or as "important components of a structural design". Gould (1997a, p. 10745) rejects these views because "manner of origin has no necessary relationship to the extent or vitality of a later co-opted role". And he (1991, p. 55) emphasizes that "[t]he important issue is not status at origin, but later evolutionary meaning; the last shall be first, and the correlated consequence may emerge as the directing feature". A notable implication here is that the status of "spandrel" cannot be withheld from S on account of its being an important component in the structural design of a more complex entity.

Concerning (3)(d), Gould (1991, p. 55, 1997a, pp. 10753–10754) rejects the "Nooks and Crannies Argument" as well. In terms of this argument, spandrels are "just funny little spaces" left over after the major features of form and behaviour have been shaped by adaptation. By analogy with the (architectural) spandrels of the San Marco Cathedral, Gould (1991, p. 55) offers two observations in rebuttal of this argument about (biological) spandrels. First, spandrels can be "spatially extensive" whatever their "temporal status".[9] Second, the "design" and "secondary utilization" of spandrels may "feed back" into the evolution process and thereby "determine major features of the entire structure".[10]

Which brings us to two grounds that Gould (1997a, pp. 10752–10753) does accept for the purpose of assigning or denying a structure S the status of "spandrel". These are:

(4) (a) historical order; and
    (b) comparative anatomy.

54 Unravelling the Evolution of Language

As for (4)(a), it involves the use of historical evidence to determine for two features, F_1 and F_2, which one arose first as a primary adaptation and which one subsequently as a co-opted by-product. If available, evidence of this kind would, for example, provide an answer to the question "Did the umbilical brooding chamber of snails arise as a nonadaptive geometric by-product of winding a tube around an axis or did it evolve as part of an actively selected design centered upon the direct advantages of protecting eggs in a cigar-shaped central space?" Since there is no historical evidence bearing on this question, we do not know according to Gould (1997a, p. 10753) whether the first coiled snails brooded their eggs in an umbilical chamber. In the case of a large number of structures or features, the use of what Gould (1997a, p. 10753) calls the "method of actual historical sequence" is ruled out by the lack of historical evidence.

As regards (4)(b), in the absence of historical evidence about what actually happened in the evolution of a particular structure or feature, biologists draw inferences about its evolution from evidence about comparative anatomy. Such evidence is obtained by tabulating the comparative anatomy of current examples of the structure or feature in question in a cladistic context and by subsequently trying to determine a historical order from the distribution yielded by such tabulation.[11] The use of what Gould (1997a, p. 10753) calls the "method of comparative anatomy" yields evidence that bears on the question of the evolutionary status of the brooding chamber in snails. Specifically, the use of this method reveals that, whereas thousands of species of snails have umbilical spaces, only a few use this space for brooding. In addition, the "umbilical brooders" occupy only a few tips on distinct late-arising twigs of the evolutionary tree in question and not a central position near its root. From these two observations, it may properly be inferred according to Gould (1997a, p. 10753) that the umbilical space under consideration had arisen as a spandrel and then became co-opted for later utility in only a few lines of brooders.

Gould considers the method of actual historical sequence as "evidently superior" to the method of comparative anatomy since the former relies on "raw observations rather than inferences". The use of the latter method, moreover, is limited in a fundamental way: it can only be used in the case of structures or features where cladistic comparison is possible. This means that this method cannot provide evidence bearing on the evolution of structures or features which are (believed to be) specific to a particular species. The comparison has to involve homologous structures or features, of course, rather than analogous ones.[12]

Notice that neither of the grounds on which a structure or feature can be assigned spandrelhood according to Gould applies to human language. As regards (4)(a), since

Co-optation in Language Evolution 55

there is no direct historical evidence about the events through which language originated, the method of actual historical sequence cannot be used to determine whether language did or did not arise as a spandrel or by-product. As for (4)(b), scholars who believe that language is specific to the human species cannot use the method of comparative anatomy, even in a suitably adapted form, in the case of language since the belief that language is species-specific rules out the cladistic comparison required by this method.

Gould's theory of spandrelhood can, in conclusion, play an indirect but nevertheless important role in determining the process(es) by which language initially arose. This role is indirect in the sense that Gould's theory does not articulate grounds that can be invoked in assigning or denying language the status of spandrel. The theory's role, however, is important in that it serves as an example of the kind of theory which is required for assigning or denying evolutionary by-product status to human language or some of its features in a principled and properly argued way.

6.4 CHOMSKY'S BY-PRODUCT "SPECULATIONS"

Over the years, Chomsky has speculated more than once about the possibility that a fundamental feature of the language faculty originated as a by-product.[13] And, in equally speculative terms, he has expressed the view that the human number faculty or capacity arose as a by-product likewise. Below, we will consider these two sets of speculations in turn.

6.4.1 The language faculty. Language is believed by Chomsky (1988, p. 169) to have a property that is "extremely unusual, possibly unique" in the biological world, the property of discrete infinity. This property is essentially involved in the fact that each sentence of a natural language has a fixed number of words, yet there is no limit to how many words a sentence may have. Referring to this property as a "capacity", Chomsky (1988, p. 170) stresses the evolutionary significance of its emergence by observing that "[w]ithout this capacity it might have been possible to think thoughts of a certain restricted character, but with the capacity in place, the same conceptual apparatus would be freed for the construction of new thoughts and operations such as inference involving them, and it would be possible to express and interchange these thoughts".

On the origin of the property of discrete infinity, Chomsky offers what he calls "some speculations, nothing more", including the following:

> It may be that at some remote period a mutation took place that gave rise to the property of discrete infinity, perhaps for reasons that have to do with the biology of

cells, to be explained in terms of physical mechanisms, now unknown. (Chomsky, 1988, p. 170)

Here is a first question that arises about these speculations: What is discrete infinity a by-product of? Chomsky has responded to this question in the most general of terms only. Thus, referring to the property of discrete infinity alternatively as "a system of discrete infinity" and a "computational capacity to deal with discrete infinities", he has speculatively pointed to increased size and complexity of the evolving brain as possibly the feature of humans that yielded discrete infinity as a "consequence" or "concomitant":

> It [i.e., the capacity to deal with discrete infinities – R.P.B.] could, for example, be a consequence of the increase in brain size and complexity. (Chomsky, 1982a, p. 22)
>
> It could be that when the brain gets so complex, it simply has to encompass systems of discrete infinity. (Chomsky, 1982a, p. 23)
>
> In this regard [i.e., that of the origin of an infinite digital system – R.P.B.], speculations about natural selection are not more plausible than many others; perhaps these are simply emergent physical properties of a brain that reaches a certain level of complexity under the specific conditions of human evolution. (Chomsky, 1991b, p. 50)

These speculations clearly have nothing specific to say about the way(s) in which human brains became so big and/or complex that discrete infinity resulted as a by-product. Where Chomsky does appear to furnish some specifics with the aid of such expressions as "more cortical surface" and "hemispheric specialization for analytic processing", he qualifies his further speculations to such an extent that it is unclear what they actually assert and how they could be tested. Consider in this regard the following example (all emphases added):

> These skills [e.g., learning a grammar and recognizing faces – R.P.B.] **may** well have arisen as a concomitant of structural properties of the brain that developed for others reasons. **Suppose** that there was selection for bigger brains, more cortical surface, hemispheric specialization for analytic processing or many properties that **can be imagined**. The brain that evolved **might** well have all sorts of special properties that are not individually selected; there would be no miracle in this, but only the normal workings of evolution. (Chomsky, 1982b, p. 321)

A second question that arises concerns the factors that were responsible for the brain's attaining the size and complexity of which discrete infinity is a consequence. Chomsky is equally nonspecific about these factors. He mentions factors involving the biology of cells (Chomsky, 1988, pp. 168–169), unknown physical laws relating to neuron packing or regulatory mechanisms (Chomsky, 1980a, p. 100, 1988, p. 169), and constraints on growth and form related to the ones proposed by D'Arcy Thompson (Chomsky 1982a, p. 23). But he makes no detailed claims about how these factors were either individually or collectively involved in the evolutionary events of which discrete infinity is a by-product.

A third question concerns the nature of Chomsky's justification of his by-product conception of language origin. What he has said in this regard does not ground the speculations under consideration in a principled theory of by-producthood. For instance, Chomsky (1982a, p. 22, 1988, p. 168) has observed that discrete infinity is "extremely unusual" and "possibly unique", an observation which may be taken to indicate that Chomsky proceeds from the following foundational assumption:

(5) The fact that an entity is "extremely unusual" or "possibly unique" indicate that evolutionarily it is a by-product.

Chomsky, however, has not attempted to show that these properties are diagnostically significant within the framework of some theory of by-producthood. It is therefore doubtful whether this observation yields evidence that supports the attribution of by-product status to discrete infinity.[14] Curiously, Chomsky has done more towards justifying his speculation that the human number faculty is an evolutionary by-product. What Chomsky has had to say on the origin of the number faculty actually highlights the absence of specifics that is so marked in his by-product conception of the origin of the language faculty.

6.4.2 The number faculty. In Chomsky's (1988, pp. 168–169) view, humans are the only species which has what he alternatively refers to as a "number faculty", a "number capacity" and a "number system" whose most elementary property is that of discrete infinity: "the series of numbers goes on indefinitely; you can always add one more". As regards the origin of the number faculty, Chomsky (1988, p. 168) finds it "impossible to believe that it was specifically selected for". The reason why he cannot believe this is that "cultures still exist today that have not made use of this faculty". The fact that this faculty was latent and unused for almost all of human history means, in Chomsky's opinion, that it did not bestow any selectional advantage on humans.[15]

On how the number faculty did "develop", one "can only speculate" at this point, according to Chomsky (1988, p. 169). And he has offered two main speculations about this development. In the first, the number faculty is assigned the evolutionary status of "by-product":

... it is possible that the number faculty developed as a by-product of the language faculty. (Chomsky, 1988, p. 169)

In the second speculation, however, Chomsky assigns the number faculty the status of an "abstraction":

> ... we might think of the human number faculty as essentially an "abstraction" from human language, preserving the mechanism of discrete infinity and eliminating the special features of language. (Chomsky, 1988, p. 169)

Chomsky offers two grounds for this second speculation. First, if the number faculty were an abstraction of the language faculty, that would explain on his (1988, p. 169) view "the fact that the number faculty is available though unused in the course of human evolution". Second, it would also explain why humans have two faculties which are both "quite unusual and perhaps even unique in the biological world".

Which brings us to the question whether (6)(a) and (6)(b) express one and the same claim about the origin of the number faculty:

(6) (a) The number faculty developed as a by-product of the language faculty.

(b) The number faculty is an abstraction from human language.

At issue is whether a by-product and an abstraction are the same kind of thing from an evolutionary perspective. On Gould's theory of by-producthood, a structure S can be a by-product of something else E without being an abstraction of E in Chomsky's (1988, p. 168) sense of a version "preserving the mechanism of E and eliminating the special features of E". And, indeed, not a single one of the examples of spandrels discussed by Gould, Vrba and Lewontin is an abstraction in Chomsky's sense from the entity from which it was exapted.

The root of the problem is that Chomsky makes the claims (6)(a) and (6)(b) without offering a theory which explicitly states conditions on evolutionary by-producthood or abstraction status. This is why these claims are ad hoc and obscure in regard to content. It is moreover the absence of such a theory that makes it difficult to judge whether the considerations adduced by Chomsky for (6)(a) and (6)(b) are appropriate and sufficiently strong. If these considerations were of the right sort, one would expect Chomsky to take them into account, in a suitably adapted form, when expounding the idea that the language faculty is a by-product. He has not, however, done so.

The following consideration – embodying a foundational assumption – is invoked, then, by Chomsky to argue against the idea that the number faculty evolved by natural selection:

(7) If a faculty is available but unused in the course of human evolution, it could not have evolved through natural selection.[16]

Chomsky, as we noted above, takes it to be a fact that the number faculty was latent and unused for almost all of human history and that even today there are cultures that have not made use of it. And, as we noted, these facts can be "explained" by assigning the number faculty by-product or abstraction status. If Chomsky set about the question of assigning faculties a particular evolutionary status in a principled way, one could have expected him to extend the use of consideration (7) from the number faculty to the language faculty. If he did this, two routes would be open to him. On the first route, he would have to address questions such as the following: Was the language faculty available but unused in the course of human evolution? Does the language faculty bestow a (significant) selectional advantage on humans? Are there even today cultures that have not made use of the language faculty? Taking the other route, Chomsky could have given reasons why consideration (7) and the questions associated with it do not apply to the language faculty. But he has not proceeded along either of these two routes.

Consider, finally, the way in which Chomsky has used the concept of "abstraction" in parallel to that of "by-product" to characterize the evolutionary status of the number faculty. The question arises as to why Chomsky has not also used the "abstraction" concept in characterizing the evolutionary status of the language faculty. And why he has refrained from considering questions such as: What entity could the language faculty be an abstraction from? What is the mechanism that was preserved in abstracting the language faculty from this entity? What are the special features that were eliminated in abstracting the language faculty from this entity? Alternatively, Chomsky could have made a principled case for not using his "abstraction" concept for capturing the evolutionary status of the language faculty. This line of thinking about the origin of the language faculty presupposes a theory of evolution that distinguishes in a non-ad hoc way between by-products and abstractions. The foundational assumptions (embodied in) (5) and (7), however, fall far short from constituting such a theory. It is the absence of such a theory which makes Chomsky's by-product conception of language origin ad hoc and minimal in what it speculatively claims. And it is the absence of such a theory which makes Chomsky's mode of approach to the origin of the language faculty hard to reconcile with his mode of approach to the origin of the number faculty.[17]

6.5 GOULD'S "TRANSLATION" OF CHOMSKY'S "SPECULATIONS"

As part of his argument for considering the concept of "exaptation" a "crucial tool" for evolutionary psychology, Gould (1991, p. 61) shows how it can be used for giving an account of "fundamental attributes" of humans, including human language. Fundamental attributes, in his view, are attributes which are unique to the human species. Gould rejects the "adaptationist and Darwinian tradition" of constructing scenarios in terms of which language grew in a gradual and continuous way out of gestural and calling systems of other species. Instead, he opts for Chomsky's conception of the origin of language; this, on Gould's (1991, p. 61) "translation", claims that "language is an exaptation of brain structure". This conception of the origin of language ties in with Gould's (1991, p. 57) view that "for something so complex and so replete with latent capacity as the human brain, spandrels must vastly outnumber original reasons, and exaptations of the brain must greatly exceed adaptations by orders of magnitude".

On the matter of the faithfulness of his "translation" of Chomsky's conception of the origin of language, Gould observes that:

> Chomsky, who has rarely written anything about evolution, has not so framed his theory, but he does accept my argument as a proper translation of his views into the language of my field – Chomsky, personal communications. (Gould, 1991, p. 61)[18]

Gould, moreover, offers some justification of the "translated" Chomskyan view that language is an exaptation of brain structure rather than an "adaptationist continuation" of an attribute of some other species. This justification is interesting both for what it does and does not include.

The justification mixes fact-like considerations with ones of a rhetorical sort. A first fact-like consideration involves "the spectacular collapse of the chimp experiments" which Gould (1991, p. 61) takes to weaken the adaptationist position that cross-species continuity exists in the case of language origins. Gould agrees that cross-species continuity must exist in the case of the growth of conceptual powers and rhetorically asks:

> ... but why should our idiosyncratic capacity for embodying much of this richness in the unique and highly peculiar mental structure called language be seen as an expression of this continuity? (Gould, 1991, p. 62)

For later reference, the properties of language involved in the first fact-like consideration adduced by Gould in support of the claim that language is an exaptation of brain structure can be stated as (8)(a) and (8)(b):

(8) (a) idiosyncratic, peculiar nature, and
(b) uniqueness in the species or species-specifity.[19]

As a second fact-like consideration supporting the claim in question, Gould (1991, p. 162) asserts that the "traits" attributed by Chomsky (1986) to language "fit far more easily with an exaptive, rather than an adaptive explanation". These "traits", in Gould's (1991, p. 62) phraseology, are:

(9) (a) "universality of generative grammar";
(b) "lack of ontogeny (for language 'grows' more like a programmed organ than like memorizing the kings of England)";
(c) "highly peculiar and decidedly non-optimal structure";
(d) "formal analogy to other attributes, including our unique numerical faculty with its concept of discrete infinity".

Having listed these "traits" of language, Gould observes once more that, in becoming large for whatever reason, the brain acquired a "plethora of co-optable features". And he appends two rhetorical questions to this observation:

Why shouldn't the capacity for language be among them [i.e., the plethora of co-optable features – R.P.B.]? Why not seize this possibility as something discrete at some later point in evolution, grafting upon it a range of conceptual capacities that achieve different expression in other species (and in our ancestry)? (Gould, 1991, p. 62)

These rhetorical questions conclude the justification offered by Gould (1991) for the claim that language is an exaptation of brain structure.

The question that now arises about this justification is: Just how good is it, given Gould's own theory of what exaptations in the sense of spandrels are and given his own methodology for determining whether a specific structure or feature should or should not be assigned the status of "spandrel"? An essential weakness of this justification lies in what is omitted from it: Gould fails to make any reference in it to the former theory or the latter methodology. On the one hand, he considers neither the question whether the grounds (4)(a) and (4)(b) should or could be invoked in attributing spandrelhood to language nor the question of what the most appropriate method would be for determining whether language is or is not a spandrel. On the other hand, he does not go into the question of why the properties (8)(a)–(b) and (9)(a)–(d) should be taken as distinctive of, criterial for or, more weakly, indicative of spandrelhood. This is curious since none of these properties is explicitly accorded such a status in Gould's theory of spandrelhood. His use of these properties is, in short, ad hoc and arbitrary in terms of his own theory of spandrelhood.

Superficially, one of the latter properties, namely that of species-specificity, seems to be related to a property that is pertinent to the use of the method of comparative anatomy. Within the framework of this method, we have seen in Section 6.3 above, the fact that a structure or feature is used by just a few of the species to which it is available is taken to be evidence of the spandrel status of this structure or property. It could now be contended that the fact that a structure or feature such as language occurs in one species only represents the strongest manifestation of the phenomenon of restricted use or spread and thereby constitutes a ground for assigning spandrel status to it. This line of argument, however, would be flawed in that it fails to take into account the distinction between the intraspecies and the interspecies distribution or occurrence of a structure or property. The fact that a particular structure or property is species - specific seems to be of methodological significance only: the evolutionary status of such a structure or property cannot be determined with the aid of the method of comparative anatomy.[20]

In conclusion: Gould's attribution of spandrel status to human language will remain ad hoc and arbitrary until such time as the properties (8)(a)–(b) and (9)(a)–(d) are accorded the status of "distinctive" or "indicative of spandrelhood" on principled grounds in terms of his own theory of exaptation.[21]

6.6 WAYWARD CRITICISMS

Chomsky's by-product conception of language origin has been criticized in the literature for what are obviously considered to be serious shortcomings. Pinker and Bloom (1990), for example, hold that this conception exhibits the following flaws:

(10) (a) As for Chomsky's idea that language emerged as a consequence of the application of physical laws, there isn't "any reason to believe that there are as yet undiscovered theorems of physics that can account for the intricate design of natural language". (Pinker and Bloom, 1990, p. 720)

(b) Concerning Chomsky's idea that language emerged as a consequence of constraints on its possible neural basis and epigenetic growth:

  (i) "[t]he space of physically possible neural systems can't be all *that* small as far as computational abilities are concerned". (Pinker and Bloom, 1990, pp. 720–721); and

  (ii) "... it is most unlikely that laws acting at the level of substrate adhesion molecules and synaptic competition, when their effects are projected upward through many levels of scale and hierarchical organization, would automatically result in systems that accomplish interesting engineering tasks in a world of medium-sized objects." (Pinker and Bloom, 1990, p. 721)

(c) As regards Chomsky's idea that language emerged as a consequence of the large size attained by human brains:

  (i) there are studies showing that "mere largeness of brain is neither a necessary nor a sufficient condition for language ...". (Pinker and Bloom, 1990, p. 721); and

Co-optation in Language Evolution 63

(ii) "... there may be direct evidence against the speculation that language is a necessary physical consequence of how human brains can grow." (Pinker and Bloom, 1990, p. 721)

Frederick Newmeyer (1998), in turn, has criticized Chomsky's by-product conception of language origin for such failings as the following:

(11) (a) I find a Thompsonian/spandrel explanation for the design features of any significant aspect of the language faculty to be utterly implausible. The hexagonal cell aggregate, the equiangular spirals, and so on found repeatedly in nature, and determined by the same laws of physics that suggest optimal design for a bridge or the arrangement of packing crates, have no counterpart in the language faculty. Indeed, perhaps the most salient (and at times, frustrating) aspect of UG is its lack of symmetry, the irregularity and idiosyncrasy that it tolerates, the widely different principles of organization of its various subcomponents and consequent wide variety of linking rules relating them. (Newmeyer, 1998, p. 315)

(b) [Chomsky has defended the autonomy thesis according to which – R.P.B.] underlying linguistic behavior there is a separate component of our knowledge, which is not reducible to other forms of knowledge. But we have a contradiction here. UG cannot be derivative and autonomous at the same time. What are the chances of UG emerging as an automatic consequence of *any* set of external principles, but having an internal algebra totally independent of those principles. Absolutely none, I would venture to say. (Newmeyer, 1998, p. 314)

(c) [Chomsky] wants, language, at one and the same time, to be an epiphenomenon and an 'organ', the latter by definition a product of a dedicated genetic blueprint. But it cannot be an 'organ', even in a metaphorical sense, if it is simply an inevitable consequence of a big brain. (Newmeyer, 1998, p. 316)

Finally, consider as a third set of sample criticisms of Chomsky's by-product conception of language origin the following ones as (re)phrased by Jean Aitchison (1994):

(12) (a) ... this by-product view is highly unlikely, as language is too complex. Exaptation – a re-use of an existing structure – is undoubtedly a powerful force in evolution. But in all documented cases, complex structures are used for simple purposes, and not vice versa. (Aitchison, 1994, p. 75)

(b) The complexity of language, and the interwoven adaptations of the mouth, larynx and brain make it unlikely that language could have developed as an accidental by-product. (Aitchison, 1994, p. 75)

The criticisms (10)(a)–(c), (11)(a)–(b) and (12)(a)–(b) of Chomsky's by-product conception of language origin are intended, clearly, to be criticisms of substance. But how pertinent are they really? On closer inspection, these criticisms turn out to be less than well aimed, since they fail to observe a number of fundamental distinctions.

First – as we have seen in Section 2.5 above – in accounts of the evolution of a biological entity (or structure), a distinction is standardly drawn between an entity as a unitary whole and specific features or components of it. This distinction applies to language in the sense of the language faculty too, as has been observed in the literature.[22] Though Chomsky's conception of the origin of language is in various ways insufficiently clear and specific – as has been shown in Section 6.4 above – his speculations on the origin of the language faculty are on the whole underpinned by this distinction. In particular what Chomsky has offered is a conception of a specific feature of the language faculty, namely discrete infinity. He has *not* offered this as a conception or theory of the evolution of the language faculty or Universal Grammar as a whole – as a whole that:

(13) (a) is characterized by "intricate design" [cf. (10)(a)];
 (b) "accomplish[es] interesting engineering tasks" [cf. (10)(b)(i)];
 (c) displays "design features" [cf. (11)(a)];
 (d) is characterized by a "lack of symmetry", by "irregularity" and "idiosyncrasies" [cf. (11)(a)];
 (e) is characterized by "widely different principles of organization" [cf. (11)(a)];
 (f) has an "internal algebra" [cf. (11)(b)];
 (g) is too "complex" a structure to be used for "simple purposes" [cf. (12)(b)]; and
 (h) is characterized by "complexity" that is "interwoven" with "adaptations of the mouth, larynx and brain" [cf. (12)(b)].

Chomsky's conception of language origin, in sum, cannot be properly criticized for failing to give an account of the evolution of the language faculty or Universal Grammar in its modern form. This conception should rather be criticized, if at all, for what it claims about the origin of discrete infinity as a fundamental feature of the language faculty.

Second, a distinction is standardly drawn between various phases in the evolution of a biological entity (or structure) or features of such an entity. These phases include those referred to in the literature by such expressions as "origin", "emergence", "appearance in the initial form", "elaboration and complexification leading to the current form", "initial spread (in a population)", "maintenance (in a population)", "atrophy", "loss" and so on.[23] On the whole, Chomsky has phrased his conception of the origin of discrete infinity in terms referring to the very first evolutionary phase, namely that of "origin", "(first) emergence" or "initial appearance". The following remarks by him are typical in this regard:

> [An innate language faculty] poses a problem for the biologist, since, if true, it is an example of the "emergence" – the appearance of a qualitatively different phenomenon at a specific stage of complexity of organization. (Chomsky, 1972a, p. 70)
>
> It may be that at some period a mutation took place that gave rise to the property of discrete infinity ... (Chomsky, 1988, p. 70)

Chomsky does provide for further phases in the evolution of the language faculty in which the process of natural selection played a role:

> In some cases it seems that organs develop to serve one purpose and, when they have reached a certain form in the evolutionary process, became available for different purposes, at which point the process of natural selection may refine them for further purposes ... Possibly human mental capacities have in some cases evolved in a similar way. (Chomsky, 1988, p. 167)[24]

But Chomsky has not offered his conception of language origin as a theory of how the language faculty evolved through any noninitial phases into its modern form.[25] Criticisms such as (9)(a)–(c), (10)(a)–(c) and (11)(a) and (11)(b) are wrong, therefore, to construe this conception as a theory of the latter sort. To be pertinent, these criticisms have to pinpoint flaws in Chomsky's by-product speculations on how discrete infinity originated or appeared in the (first) emergence of the language faculty. Interestingly, the critics in question do not seem to have the conceptual means that are required for criticizing Chomsky's attribution of by-product status to discrete infinity. Specifically, they seem to lack a restrictive theory of evolutionary by-producthood in terms of which they can question, in a non-ad hoc and sufficiently well-argued way, Chomsky's speculations on the by-product status of discrete infinity as a feature of the language faculty. In Gould's (1997a, p. 10752) terminology, this means that these critics themselves are not able to "identify and allocate the proper statuses" in the conceivable event that the language faculty, as a "modern structure", is a "mix of primary adaptations and secondary exapted spandrels."[26] The fact that critics of Chomsky's by-product conception of language origin fail to ground their criticisms of it in a restrictive theory of evolutionary by-producthood, obviously, does nothing at all to remedy the shortcomings identified in Section 6.4 above. And questioning the pertinence of these criticisms is in no way a defence of this conception of Chomsky's. The point, simply, is that the flaws of a conception of language origin cannot be laid bare by appraising it as if it were a theory of the evolution of the complexified modern language faculty as a whole. And such flaws cannot be laid bare without invoking a theory that gives a restrictive characterization of the evolutionary process(es) at issue.

7

PREADAPTATION IN LANGUAGE EVOLUTION

7.1 BIRDS' FEATHERS AND SENTENCE STRUCTURES

Skeletal features of the earliest known bird, *Archaeopteryx*, indicate that it was a "weak, flapping flyer", as John Ostrom (1979, p. 55) puts it. This prehistoric bird was thoroughly feathered, however, which suggests to scholars that feathers did not develop initially for the function of flight. Rather, on what is called by Stephen Jay Gould and Elisabeth Vrba (1982, pp. 7–8) a "common scenario from the evolution of birds",

> ... the basic design of feathers is an adaptation for thermoregulation and, later, an exaptation for catching insects. The development of large contour feathers and their arrangement on the arm arises as adaptations for insect catching and become exaptations for flight. (Gould and Vrba, 1982, p. 8)[1]

Recall that on Gould and Vrba's (1982, p. 5) theory of large-scale evolutionary change outlined in Section 6.2 above, adaptations are fitness-enhancing characters shaped (or built) for their present use (or function) by natural selection. Exaptations, by contrast, are taken by Gould and Vrba (1982, pp. 6–7) to be characters that enhance fitness in their present role (or effect) but that were not built by natural selection for this role.[2]

In terms of the scenario just mentioned, exaptation featured twice in the evolution of birds. First, having developed as adaptations for insulation, feathers were co-opted (or exapted) for prey-catching. Second, having been further adapted by natural selection for prey-catching, feathers were co-opted for flight.[3] The kind of exaptation involved in the evolution of feathers has also been referred to in the literature as "preadaption" or "function shift".[4] As we have seen in Section 6.2 above, Gould and Vrba (1982, pp. 5–6) provide for a second kind of exaptation as well: the co-option for a current use (utility, role or effect) of characters that do not originate by the direct action of natural selection.

On some modern accounts of language evolution, certain fundamental features of language arose, like bird feathers, through exaptation. Thus:

(1) (a) Philip Lieberman (1991a, p.4) postulates a "preadaptive link" from manual motor control to speech production and, again, from speech production to syntax.

(b) Wendy Wilkins and Jenny Wakefield (1995, p. 175) argue that the neuroanatomical structures associated with the purely motor function of Broca's area and the POT (i.e., the junction of the brain's parietal, occipital and temporal lobes) were "reappropriated" for the task of turning sensory input into conceptual structures.

(c) William Calvin and Derek Bickerton (2000, p. 126) propose that the social calculus categories of AGENT, THEME and GOAL were "exapted" to produce the basis for sentence structures.

(d) Andrew Carstairs-McCarthy (1999, p. 148) asserts that the neural organization underlying syllable structure was "co-opted" to provide a syntax for strings of words.

Central to an appraisal of these accounts of language evolution is the question:

(2) To what extent are these accounts of language evolution embedded in a restrictive theory of exaptation?

Ultimately, it is the latter theory which will determine whether the former accounts do or do not assign the (pre-) linguistic entities in question the evolutionary status of exaptation in a non-ad hoc and non-arbitrary way. So let us consider (2) in some depth.

7.2 LIEBERMAN'S PREADAPTIVE MODEL

7.2.1 The model. Lieberman (1984, p. 67) has proposed a "preadaptive model" of language evolution to which the following claims are central:

The brain mechanisms that control speech production probably derived from ones that facilitated precise one-handed manual tasks. Through a series of perhaps chance events they eventually evolved to allow us to learn and use the complex rules that govern the syntax of human language. (Lieberman, 1991a, p. 4)[5]

Preadaptation in Language Evolution 69

As regards the first claim, Lieberman (1995, p. 197) follows Kimura (1979) in accepting "a preadaptive link between manual motor control and speech", even though it is unclear to Lieberman "when vocal communication and 'phonology' came into being". In regard to the second claim, Lieberman (1990, p. 742) proposes that motor control for speech is "the preadaptive basis for the brain mechanisms underlying human syntactic ability".[6] More specifically, he believes that:

> Brain mechanisms adapted to handle the complex sequential operations necessary for speech production would have no difficulty in handling the comparatively simple problems of syntax. (Lieberman, 1991a, pp. 107–108)

On the "evolutionary model" proposed by Lieberman (1991a, p. 109), "speech motor control is the preadaptive basis, that is, the starting point [for syntax – R.P.B.]". Natural selection played a role at a later stage, once the selective advantages conferred by syntax became manifest. It enhanced the abilities characterized by Lieberman (1991a, p. 109) as those involved in increasing the speed of communication through encoding and through circumventing short-term memory limitations. And over the past 150,000 to 200,000 years natural selection, according to Lieberman (1991a, p. 109), "could have produced neural structures dedicated to syntax". Schematically, Lieberman's model of linguistic evolution may be outlined as follows:

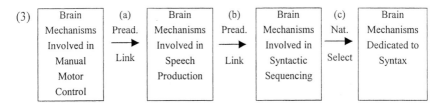

(Lieberman seems to use the expressions "brain mechanisms" and "neural structures" as synonyms; in (3), "Pread." is an abbreviation of "Preadaptive"; "Nat. Select." is an abbreviation of "Natural Selection".)

7.2.2 "Preadaptive links". At issue here are the "preadaptive links" (3)(a) and (3)(b) postulated by Lieberman in his model of linguistic evolution. More specifically:

(4) (a) What does preadaption involve in Lieberman's view?
    (b) How does preadaption differ from adaptation by natural selection?
    (c) What are the grounds on which it can be claimed that two (or more) entities are "linked" or related by preadaption?

Lieberman's response to the first question, (4)(a), is brief in the extreme. He (1990, p. 742) takes preadaption to be a "Darwinian mechanism" and characterizes it with the aid of a quotation from Darwin (1859, p. 190) as a mechanism whereby an "organ

70 *Unravelling the Evolution of Language*

originally constructed for one purpose ... may be converted into one for a wholly different purpose ...". On the nature of such conversion, Lieberman (1990, p. 742) observes that "Charles Darwin was not a fool and he realized that abrupt transitions occur in the course of evolution". Lieberman, however, does not ground his adoption of the Darwinian view of preadaptation in modern literature, refraining, for example, from relating it to the Gouldian theory of exaptation.[7]

As regards the second question, (4)(b), Lieberman (1975, p.3) equates preadaptation with a kind of natural selection:

We will ... make use of the principle of "preadaptation", that is, natural selection channelling development in a new direction because of previous modifications for some other role. This principle is extremely important, for it demonstrates how natural selection operating in small steps can effect radical changes in behavior. Darwin's comments on the evolution of the lung from the swim bladder make the principle clear: "The illustration of the swim bladder in fish is a good one, because it shows us clearly the highly important fact that an organ originally constructed for one purpose, namely floatation, may be converted into one of a wholly different purpose, namely respiration (1859, p. 190)." (Lieberman, 1975, p. 3)

Suppose now that one had to judge on the basis of the beliefs expressed in this quotation whether an arbitrary evolutionary development was effected by preadaptation by natural selection or by adaptation by natural selection. To be able to do so, one would need a clear and principled conception of what it is that makes the "direction" in which "development" takes place a "new direction". In addition, one would need a similarly well-founded conception of what it is that makes one purpose "wholly different" from another one. In the absence of these conceptions, assigning the development in question the evolutionary status of a preadaptation by natural selection rather than that of an adaptation by natural selection would boil down to a matter of arbitrary stipulation of a terminological sort. In short: without access to these conceptions it would be impossible to draw a distinction between preadaptation and adaptation.

Let us consider an example that illustrates the problem under consideration. The brain mechanisms involved in manual control are used for a purpose that can be characterized as "sequencing"; the brain mechanisms involved in speech production are used for a purpose that can, likewise, be depicted as "sequencing"; and the brain mechanisms involved in syntax are used for a purpose that can be portrayed as "sequencing" as well, on Lieberman's model. The brain mechanisms in question, thus, are used for fundamentally the same purpose, namely that of "sequencing". What differs is the nature of the entities subjected to "sequencing". But on what principled notion of a "wholly different purpose" can it be claimed non-arbitrarily that the mechanisms under consideration are used for three "wholly different purposes"? And what makes the use of the mechanisms involved in motor control for speech production a "development in a new direction" and the use of these mechanisms for syntax as development in yet another "new direction"? What are the conditions that a "direction" has to meet to qualify as a "new direction"? Lieberman does not address these questions and, moreover, does not seem to have the kind of principled theory of preadaption on the basis of which they could be answered in a non-ad hoc way. This means that he is not in a position to non-arbitrarily assign the brain mechanisms involved in speech production and those involved in syntax the evolutionary status of being preadaptive in origin, a point to which we will return in Chapter 9 below.

There is a second way in which Lieberman's distinction between preadaptation and adaptation is problematic. This involves his use of the notion of "generalization" in attempting to clarify the nature of the "preadaptive links" postulated by his model. Thus, with reference to the "preadaptive link" between the neural mechanisms involved in precise central motor control and those associated with the sequencing rules of syntax, he remarks that [emphases added – R.P.B.]:

> Broca's area, in my view, is a multifunction organ adapted to the regulation of sequential activity in several different domains that reflect its evolutionary history. It appears to function as Kimura (1979) proposed, in precise sequential hand manoeuvres. The lateralized brain mechanisms that were initially adopted for precise sequential manual control **generalized** to control the nearby orofacial motor control areas of the primate brain. A later change involved using these brain mechanisms (which accessed complex motor control "rules") for the sequential rules of syntax. (Lieberman, 1991b, p. 567)
>
> My proposal (Lieberman 1984, p. 67) was that "the rules of syntax derive from a **generalization** of neural mechanisms that gradually evolved in the motor cortex to facilitate the automatization of motor activity". This preadaptive model was elaborated in Lieberman (1985) and discussed in some detail in Lieberman (1991) [= Lieberman (1991a) – R.P.B.]. Unlike Wilkins and Wakefield (W&W), I do not believe that the neural bases of human syntactic ability can be completely dissociated from "communication" or other aspects of cognition. This position is based on neurophysiological and comparative data that show links between speech production, syntactic ability, and certain aspects of cognition. Unlike W&W I also posit a gradual increase in these aspects of human behavior. (Lieberman, 1995, p.197)

Lieberman leaves unclear how the kind of process, i.e., "generalization", posited by him could be construed as the channelling of development in a "new direction" or how it could be viewed as converting an organ originally constructed for one purpose into one for a "wholly different" purpose. Similarly unclear, is how the apparently gradual nature of the generalization in question should be reconciled with the abruptness of the evolutionary transitions that Darwin attempted to account for with the aid of the notion of "preadaptation". And, ultimately, it is unclear why the gradual way in which speech production and syntax evolved in response to selective pressures by means of a process of generalization is construed by Lieberman as preadaptation rather than "ordinary" adaptation by natural selection. Some of the core problems with Lieberman's "preadaptive model" of language evolution, thus, arise from the following foundational assumption of his:

(5) Preadaptation is a kind of natural selection.

To overcome these problems, Lieberman would have to embed his "preadaptive model" in a general theory of evolution that discriminates in a non–arbitrary way between preadaptation and adaptation.

7.2.3 "Syntax". Appraised from the perspective of theoretical embeddedness, Lieberman's preadaptive model of the origin of syntax has an additional shortcoming. Thus, as has been noted by Bickerton (1998, pp. 342ff.), Lieberman adopts a syntactic theory which is quite simplistic in its placing of sequencing rules at the core of syntax. On more sophisticated theories of syntax, by contrast, language uses a variety of syntactic mechanisms that are more complex than such sequencing rules are and that therefore could not have evolved by a process such as "generalization" from the sequencing mechanisms used by phonology.[8] Moreover, the rules or mechanisms that effect the sequencing of syntactic units are construed in some of these theories as epigenetic in the sense of being consequences of some other, more fundamental, feature(s) of language. Consider here just two, starkly contrasting, examples of such theories. On Berwick's (1998) construal of minimalist syntax – we have seen in Section 4.4 – sequencing rules are an automatic consequence of the fundamental hierarchical concatenation operator known as "Merge".[9] On the syntactic theory subscribed to by Calvin and Bickerton (2000, p. 139), however, sequencing – or "linearization" in their terminology – is "forced on us by our choice of a physical medium for language". In sum, a theory of linguistic evolution which is underpinned by foundational assumption (6) can at best be said to address the evolution of syntax in superficial terms:

(6) Sequencing rules form the core of syntax.

Over the years, Lieberman has consistently rejected Chomskyan Universal Grammar and along with it theories of syntax which are demonstrably superior to his own.[10] Thereby he has placed rather severe limitations on the explanatory power of his "preadaptive model" of linguistic evolution.

Preadaptation in Language Evolution 73

7.3 WILKINS AND WAKEFIELD'S REAPPROPRIATIONIST SCENARIO

7.3.1 The scenario. On a "scenario" developed by Wilkins and Wakefield (1995, p. 162) – we saw in Section 3.1 above – the neuroanatomical structures that underlie linguistic ability arose in human taxa as a direct result of evolutionary reappropriation. The term "reappropriation" is used by them (1995, p. 162) in the sense of "the means by which a structure or function in the repertoire of a species reaches an evolutionary state that is compatible with, and facilitates, a new function". They observe that the phenomenon they call "reappropriation" is referred to by Darwin as "preadaptation". Since the latter term has developed an "unintended connotation of premeditation", Wilkins and Wakefield (1995, p. 162) prefer not to use it. As used by them, "reappropriation" refers to the first kind of exaptation that has been distinguished by Gould and Vrba (1982, pp. 5–6): the co-optation of characters previously shaped as adaptations by natural selection for one function for a new "use" or "effect".

As observed by various scholars who offer critical commentary on it in *Brain and Behavioral Sciences* (1995), Wilkins and Wakefield's scenario is in more than one way unclear and less than sufficiently specific. This makes it difficult to give a full account of their views; below I will accordingly attempt no more than to outline the three main components of their re-appropriationist scenario, fleshing out in the process some of the points touched on in Section 3.1 above.

1. Certain adaptive changes produced in pleistocene primate lineages, a paired expansion of the frontal and the parietal cortex associated with manual manipulation and with throwing behaviours (Wilkins and Wakefield, 1995, pp. 161–172). This expansion resulted in the appearance, simultaneously with the emergence of *Homo habilis*, of two interconnected cortical areas: Broca's area and the POT, a configurationally unique junction of the parietal, occipital and temporal lobes of the brain indicative of Wernicke's area. In their expanded form, Broca's area and the POT had a motor function only.
2. The neuroanatomical structures associated with Broca's area and the POT were reappropriated for a new function: that of processing sensory input into conceptual structures – also referred to as "CS" – that are both amodal and hierarchically organized. More fully:

> CS is the cognitive construct that is produced by the POT through its interaction with Broca's area. By virtue of the POT, human sensory input is highly processed in association cortex and loses its modality-specific character; by virtue of the

74 *Unravelling the Evolution of Language*

influence of Broca's area on the POT, the amodal representations are subject to hierarchical structuring. Structured modality-neutral representation, we suggest, is the essence of CS. (Wilkins and Wakefield, 1995, p. 175)

As noted in Section 3.1 above, CS is on Wilkins and Wakefield's scenario "a prerequisite to language". Having CS is not the same as having language; it does however, offer the hierarchical ordering necessary for modern syntax and phonology.[11]

3. Though Wilkins and Wakefield's (1995, p. 218) target article "has focused solely on the reappropriation that made possible the first generation of language-capable hominids", they speculate under pressure of their peers that "the reappropriated structures were later modified through natural selection". Communicative interaction might, on their (1995, p. 218) view, be necessary for "the development of the complexity that characterizes all components of human language, including phonology, syntax and morphology".

Wilkins and Wakefield's claims about the origin of the preconditions for language and their speculations about the (further) evolution of language may be represented in outline as follows:

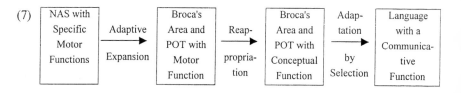

("NAS" is an abbreviation of "Neuroanatomical Structures")

Let us now turn to a fundamental question that arises in connection with Wilkins and Wakefield's reappropriationist scenario of the emergence of the neural preconditions for language:

(8) Under what conditions should a (neuroanatomical) structure be assigned the status of a reappropriated structure rather than that of a structure adapted by natural selection?

This question is in essence a question about the foundational assumptions about reappropriation that underpin Wilkins and Wakefield's evolutionary scenario.

7.3.2 Conditions on reappropriation. Wilkins and Wakefield do not address question (8) directly. The natural place for that would have been Section 2 of their article, the section bearing the title "Adaptation and evolutionary reappropriation". In this section, they do in essence three things that could be considered as having some bearing on question (8).

First, Wilkins and Wakefield offer an undocumented characterization of the process they refer to as "gradual adaptation shaped by forces of natural selection". On their characterization, it is—

> ... the process whereby individuals with certain (genetically transmissible) traits are better able to respond to environmental pressures, survive and reproduce in greater numbers. (Wilkins and Wakefield, 1995, p. 162)

Second, Wilkins and Wakefield offer a number of observations on the process called "preadaptation" by Darwin:

> But direct selection for an adaptive capacity is not the only evolutionary process conducive to the emergence of structural or behavioral innovation; a structure may arise through adaptively selective mechanisms and, by its conformation alone, be neutrally preadaptive (Darwin 1871) or exploitable for some function independent of the original function. It may produce a new capacity not already in the repertoire of the organism. This manner of exploitation converts the raw material provided by adaptation (or by the laws of growth and form) to a function that may itself prove beneficial to the organism or taxon. (Wilkins and Wakefield, 1995, p. 162).

Having offered the former observations on the process of adaptation and the latter ones on that of preadaption, the next thing for Wilkins and Wakefield to do, would be to derive from these two sets of observations some conditions on assigning an arbitrary (neuroanatomical) structure the status of "preadapted/reappropriated structure" rather than that of "adapted structure". Crucially, however, they omit to do so.

Third, Wilkins and Wakefield state what in their view is a requirement for the reappropriative component of their evolutionary scenario:

> To argue for our interpretation of the available data relevant to neurolinguistic capacity, we must specify which aspects of brain structure were available, compatible, and ultimately reappropriated. (Wilkins and Wakefield, 1995, p. 163)

In later sections of their article, Wilkins and Wakefield do in fact "specify" the aspects of brain structure which, on their view, were "available, compatible, and ultimately, reappropriated". To assign the evolutionary status of "reappropriated structure" to a given structure S, however, requires more than specifying the structure that was allegedly reappropriated. It requires evidence and/or general considerations – offered within the framework of a principled theory of reappropriation – which indicate that S arose by reappropriation rather than, say, adaptation. Specifying the ancestral structure from which S derives does not provide such evidence and/or considerations.

It might be contended that Wilkins and Wakefield should not be expected to explicitly address question (8). On this contention, one should rather inspect the specifics of their reappropriationist account with the aim of extracting from these what Wilkins and Wakefield implicitly assume about the conditions under which a structure may be assigned a reappropriationist rather than an adaptationist origin. Subjecting Wilkins and Wakefield's reappropriationist scenario to such inspection, however, is a less than rewarding exercise. It turns out that their article contains no more than a few remarks on the "moment" at which the brain structures in question were available for reappropriation:

> The appropriate brain structures evolved gradually, under pressure of natural selection, by the mechanisms typically subsumed under Darwinian theory. *Language* was made possible, however, only at the moment the brain achieved the appropriate internal configuration. The most convincing evidence points to a "moment" approximately 2 million years ago at which *Homo habilis* appeared in the fossil record.[3] (Wilkins and Wakefield, 1995, p. 162)
>
> This "moment" might have been even earlier with the appearance of *Australopithecus*. (Wilkins and Wakefield, 1995, p. 180, note 3)

From these remarks one could extract the following foundational assumption about or condition on reappropriation:

(9) A neuroanatomical structure S cannot be assigned the evolutionary status of reappropriated structure unless it emerged in a "moment".

This condition would tie in with the Darwinian view that preadaption involves an abrupt transition in the course of evolution. Condition (9), however, clearly cannot fulfil the function of the explicitly articulated and restrictive theory of reappropriation presupposed by Wilkins and Wakefield's reappropriationist scenario.[12]

7.4 CALVIN AND BICKERTON'S EXAPTATIONIST THEORY

7.4.1 The theory. Calvin and Bickerton (2000) have recently proposed a theory that provides for three stages in the evolution of human language.[13] In the first stage,

> ... language began in the form of a structureless protolanguage, something like an early stage pidgin without any formal structure – just handfuls of words or gestures strung together. (Calvin and Bickerton, 2000, p. 137)

In Calvin and Bickerton's (2000, p. 137) protolanguage, utterances would take the form of simple sequences such as "Ig take", "Ug meat", "hit Og" and so on. Since little is known about how protolanguage emerged, Calvin and Bickerton can only "speculate" in a relatively contentless way about its "spontaneous" appearance:

Somehow, somewhere, and at some time in the distant past – probably at least a million and a half years ago, maybe quite a bit longer – a language system similar to what can now be taught to apes and other brainy creatures must have emerged spontaneously. (Calvin and Bickerton, 2000, p. 103).

According to Calvin and Bickerton (2000, p. 199), our species "stumbled into protolanguage" whose first "major" use, they (2000, p. 149) believe, was "extractive foraging".[14]

The second and "exaptive" stage of language evolution is according to Calvin and Bickerton the one in which "syntax began":

What ... happened was that the social calculus set up the categories of AGENT, THEME, and GOAL, and that these categories (or *thematic roles*, which is what linguists call them) were exapted to produce a basis for sentence structures. (Calvin and Bickerton, 2000, p. 136)

In a species practising reciprocal altruism, according to Calvin and Bickerton (2000, p. 129), a social calculus is required by members in order to remember "who groomed whom and how often, who gave meat to whom and how often". In addition, members needed such a calculus "to keep track of how often partners stood by them in fights, how often they ran away and so on". A social calculus, accordingly, is needed by members of the species for detecting cheaters and for protecting their own interest. For these purposes, such a calculus should provide, amongst other things, for "tags" such as AGENT (the performer of the action) and THEME (whoever or whatever undergoes the action) to be attached to any individual whose role happens to fit on a particular occasion.[15] It is these thematic roles that are claimed by Calvin and Bickerton to have been exapted and mapped onto protolanguage utterances to form syntactically structured strings of words. What this means to them—

is simply that when they [i.e., "people" – R.P.B.] talked about anything that had happened, they would put in the obligatory arguments. Instead of saying things like "Ig take," they would have to say "Ig take meat," even if everyone knew it was meat they were talking about. Instead of saying "hit Og," they would have to say "Ig hit Og," even though everyone know it was Ig who had done it. (Calvin and Bickerton, 2000, p. 137)

Once the members of the species knew "what had to be there", they could form longer and longer sentences. Arguments could be combined not only with groups of words forming noun phrases, but just as easily with whole clauses which could be sentences in their own right.[16]

A third stage in language evolution was required, according to Calvin and Bickerton (2000, p. 146), since argument structure on its own cannot remove all ambiguities from syntax. In the third stage, devices evolved for making syntax more parsable, hence easier to understand automatically, thereby giving rise to what they call "true language". The process by which these devices evolved is depicted by Calvin and Bickerton (2000, p. 147) as one comprising a series of "Baldwin effects" or as one representing "organic selection". Through this process, what began as learned behaviour and acquired modification might become innately determined and part of the hereditary legacy of the species.[17]

The outlines of Calvin and Bickerton's exaptationist theory of language evolution may be represented schematically as follows:

(10)

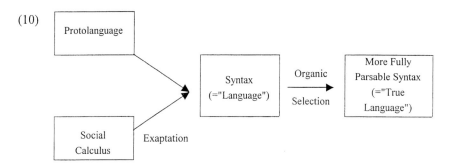

7.4.2 Appraising the exaptationist claims. To appraise the exaptationist claims expressed by Calvin and Bickerton's theory of language evolution, it is necessary to determine, on the one hand, the extent to which these claims are embedded in a general theory of exaptation and, on the other hand, the extent to which they are grounded in evidence of a factual sort. As for the former, Calvin and Bickerton do not present the claims in question within the framework of an explicitly articulated general theory of exaptation which constrains the way in which the status of "exaptation" is assigned to structures or characters. This means, for example, that their claim that the categories AGENT, THEME and GOAL were exapted to produce the basis for sentence structures is essentially an ad hoc one.

The lack of a general theory of exaptation, in addition, means that it is unclear what kinds of factual data or non-empirical considerations would provide evidence for or against Calvin and Bickerton's exaptationist claims. This point is illustrated rather well by the way in which these claims differ from the exaptationist claims expressed by Bickerton's (1998) earlier theory of language evolution referred to in Section 4.4 above. This difference, according to Bickerton, is that,

> ... what I formerly [i.e., in the 1998 theory - R.P.B.] conceived of as a single step from protolanguage to true language can be broken down into two stages, one of exaptation (the core phrase-and-clause producing argument structure machine) and

one of Baldwinian evolution (adding mechanisms useful for marking the new structures with grammatical morphemes and making them more readily processable). (Calvin and Bickerton, 2000, p. 148)

Bickerton's earlier theory, thus, expresses the claim that the emergence of syntax was not a gradual process comprising a series of several events but rather that it took the form of one catastrophic step. In support of this claim, Bickerton presents what he calls "five independent lines of argument". The gist of these lines of argument is that there is no evidence bearing out the expectations created by the "alternative claim", namely that the emergence of syntax was indeed a gradual process comprising a series of several events. These expectations, on Bickerton's construal, are the following:[18]

(11)(a) Cognition evolved (or "grew") gradually over the 2-million-plus years of hominid development (but had virtually no effect on behaviour or technology). (Bickerton, 1998, p. 354)

(b) There should be synchronic varieties of language intermediate between protolanguage and fully developed human language.[19] (Bickerton, 1998, p. 354).

(c) We should find a "stable level" of syntax between "true language" and protolanguage across the wide range of aphasic and dysphasic syndromes, cryptolects, stages of first and second language acquisition and other atypical manifestations of the human language faculty. (Bickerton, 1998, p. 355).

(d) It should not be "beyond human ingenuity" to hypothesize what the intermediate states between protolanguage, the initial stage, and (full) language, the final state would have been like (in the event that these latter stages might have permanently self-destructed and be irrecoverable today). (Bickerton, 1998, p. 355).

(e) The properties that distinguish language from protolanguage must be dissociable in the sense that the existence of one does not depend on the existence of another. (Bickerton, 1998, pp. 355–357)

Let us assume for the sake of argument that Bickerton is right in considering (11)(a)–(e) to be (test-)implications of the claim that syntax emerged gradually in a series of steps. Let us moreover assume, again for the sake of argument, that Bickerton is right in claiming that there is no evidence which bears positively on (11)(a)–(e). Interestingly, then, the lack of such evidence bears negatively also on Calvin and Bickerton's new theory on which syntax developed in two stages. For, given the way in which Bickerton (1998) reasons, this theory has test-implications – or gives rise to "expectations" – which are parallel to those of the theory that the emergence of syntax was a gradual process comprising a series of several events. Thus, on Calvin and Bickerton's theory:

(12)(a) There should be two stages in the evolution of cognition over the 2-million-plus years of hominid development: a first stage of abrupt appearance and a second stage of gradual step-wise evolution. (See (11)(a) above.)

(b) There should be synchronic varieties of language between protolanguage and fully developed human language: one of these varieties should correspond to poorly parsable syntax, the other should represent more parsable levels of syntax that came between poorly parsable syntax – or "language"– at the one extreme and fully parsable syntax – or "true language" – at the other extreme. (See (11)(b) above.)

(c) One should find one or more stable levels of syntax between protolanguage and "true language" across the wide range of aphasic and dysphasic syndromes, cryptolects, stages of first and second language acquisition and other atypical manifestations of the human language faculty. (See (11)(c) above.)

(d) It should not be "beyond human ingenuity" to hypothesize what the intermediate states between poorly parsable syntax – or "language" – and fully parsable syntax – or "true language" – were. (See (11)(d) above.)

(e) The properties that distinguish protolanguage from language – characterized by poorly parsable syntax – and those that distinguish language from "true language" – characterized by fully parsable syntax – must be dissociable. (See (11)(e) above.)

Bickerton, of course, has claimed that there is no evidence which bears out the expectations (11)(a)–(e). But this implies that there is no evidence bearing out the expectations (12)(a)–(e) either. And if there were evidence which bore out the latter expectations, this evidence would automatically bore out some of the expectations created by a theory on which the emergence of syntax was a gradual process comprising a series of several events as well. Calvin and Bickerton, regrettably, do not consider the question of why Bickerton's (1998) "five independent lines of argument" against a theory on which syntax emerged gradually in a series of several events are not "lines of argument" against their new theory as well. It would have been interesting to see how they reconciled the gradualist claims implicit to the role assigned to organic selection with the absence of the evidence in question. The existence of "language", characterized by poorly parsable syntax, should of course also be borne out by evidence of the kinds involved in Bickerton's five lines of argument.

The deeper question, however, is whether Bickerton's five lines of argument are indeed pertinent to the appraisal of the theory on which syntax evolved gradually in a series of steps as well as to that of Calvin and Bickerton's theory of the development of syntax. To be pertinent to the appraisal of these two theories, these lines of argument require as backing a number of theories, including the following:

(13)(a) a theory of exaptation which restricts in a non-ad hoc way the assignment of the evolutionary status of "exaptation" to biological structures or characters;

(b) one or more linguistic theories that warrant or license the use of data about the synchronic varieties of language referred to in (11)(b) and (12)(b) as evidence for or against claims to the effect that language or syntax developed gradually or nongradually in the species;

(c) one or more linguistic theories that warrant the use of data about such atypical synchronic manifestations of language as those referred to in (11)(c) and (12)(c) as evidence for or against claims to the effect that language or syntax developed gradually or nongradually in the species.[20]

In the absence of the theories referred to in (13)(b)–(c), it is simply not clear whether the evidence involved in Bickerton's five lines of argument has any bearing whatsoever on the theories of the evolution of syntax under consideration. Until the required inference licences have been furnished, both Calvin and Bickerton's (2000) theory and Bickerton's (1998) earlier theory will remain unappraisable. In Chapter 11 below, I will clarify the nature and function of linguistic theories from which such inference licences can be derived.

7.5 CARSTAIRS-MCCARTHY'S CO-OPTATIONIST SCENARIO

7.5.1 The scenario. In a recent book, Andrew Carstairs-McCarthy (1999) presents a "scenario for language evolution" by which he intends to account for the origin of three characteristics of "(modern) human language":

(14)(a) Large vocabulary size: languages typically have an enormous number of words with distinct meanings (pp. 8, 10–12);

(b) Duality of patterning: linguistic expressions are analysable at two levels – as composed of meaningless elements (sounds belonging to a finite inventory) and meaningful ones (words and phrases) (pp. 8, 13–15); and

(c) The distinction between sentences (Ss) and Noun Phrases (NPs) (pp. 9, 27–32).

In the scenario by Carstairs-McCarthy's (1999, p. 177), these three features of language, on the face of it unrelated, are turned into "joint consequences of the interaction of two factors: vocal tract changes and synonymy avoidance principles". The vocal tract changes in question were themselves, he claims, the results of a lowering of the larynx that had begun in the time of *Homo erectus*. All in all, the anatomical change brought with it a vast increase in our ancestors' potential for vocalization. Synonymy avoidance principles, according to Carstairs-McCarthy, dictated that in the call systems used by our ancestors, different calls should have different meanings. The great increase in our ancestors' capacity to form distinct sounds meant that there became available to them a vast number of forms that could all bear different meanings. In short, on Carstairs-McCarthy's scenario it was the availability of distinct forms that led to the creation of different meanings – he thus stands on its head the view conventionally taken in accounts of language evolution.

Carstairs-McCarthy's evolutionary scenario has a component that relates to the concerns of this Part II. To account for the origin of the distinction between sentences and Noun Phrases, he proposes that syntactic structure was modelled on phonetic and phonological organization – in particular, that the S/NP distinction was modelled on the structure of the syllable:

> ... since the syllable appeared as a unit of phonetic and phonological organization as soon as the lowered larynx and other vocal-tract changes made a more modern style of vocalization possible, it is reasonable to conclude that the neural organization underlying syllable structure was co-opted to provide a syntax for strings of "words" when the need became pressing. It was natural, therefore, that syntactic structure should possess features reminiscent of syllable structure. This resemblance was neither accidental nor analogical but rather homological in the evolutionary sense: that is, it came about because sentence structure had originally the same biological basis in neural organization as syllable structure had. (Carstairs-McCarthy, 1999, pp. 147–148)

In broad terms, for him (1999, pp. 134–139), the structure of phonological syllables is based on a hierarchy of sonority that can be characterized in acoustic terms.

Carstairs-McCarthy (1999, p. 139) takes the conventional view, in fact, that a syllable has a nucleus that corresponds to a sonority peak. On this view a syllable may, in addition, have an onset and/or a coda; this, if present, then constitutes the initial and/or final margin, respectively. He (1999, pp. 139–140) also adopts the "mainstream view" that the constituents of a syllable are linked by the hierarchical relations shown below.

(15)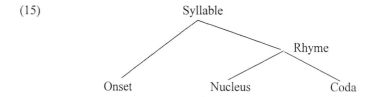

As for the ways in which syntactic structure is "reminiscent" of syllable structure, Carstairs-McCarthy (1999, p. 151) sees the following:

(16)(a) Every text is analysable into sentences such that each sentence obligatorily contains a nucleus-like position.
  (b) This nucleus-like position is filled by a class or classes of words that are substantially but not completely distinct from the classes of words that fill constituents occupying the margin-like positions.
  (c) Substantially the same classes of words are found in all constituents occupying margin-like positions.
  (d) Some non-nuclear constituent or constituents are privileged in onset-like fashion.
  (e) A sentence cannot occupy the nucleus-like position in a larger sentence.

Carstairs-McCarthy (1999, p. 151) points out, however, that if all of modern syntax derived from syllable structure, one would expect human language to exhibit the following syntactic property as well:

(17) A sentence cannot occupy a margin-like position in a larger sentence.

Since sentences can be embedded in other sentences, this syllable-based expectation is incorrect. To account for the origin of embedding, Carstairs-McCarthy (1999, p. 173) speculates that it arose later as a characteristic that "confer(red) an advantage on those humans experiencing it". He (1999, p. 191) accordingly provides for a further stage in the evolution of syntax, one that involved the "enrichment of syllable-based syntax" with properties that "would provide new ways in which people with bigger brains could enjoy selective advantage".

On Carstairs-McCarthy's scenario, in sum, the evolution of syntax had three broad stages:

84 *Unravelling the Evolution of Language*

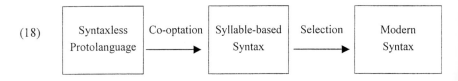

Protolanguage, as conceived of by Bickerton, is manifested in short structureless strings of words, as we saw in Section 7.4.1 above. Note too that, as it is used by Carstairs-McCarthy, the term "co-optation" does not bear the sense that came up in Section 6.4 in the discussion of Chomsky's conception of language origin. Under that conception, "co-optation" is used to refer to the later one of two evolutionary processes, if a structure or feature arose as a functionless by-product of the earlier process and is assigned a use or role by the later process only. Carstairs-McCarthy, by contrast, uses "co-optation" to refer to a process by which a structure or feature that (already) has a specific function acquires a new use or role. It is in fact for this reason that Carstairs-McCarthy's co-optationist scenario is not discussed along with Chomsky's views in Section 6.4.

Here, now, is the question: How principled is the co-optationist claim expressed by Carstairs-McCarthy's evolutionary scenario? That is to say: Is claim (19) constrained by a general theory of the conditions under which the evolutionary status of "(product of) co-optation" may be assigned in a restrictive way to a biological entity or a feature of one?

(19) The neural organization underlying syllable structure was co-opted to provide a syntax for strings of "words".

Carstairs-McCarthy does not present any theory of co-optation in an explicit way; he attempts, instead, to justify claim (19) by adducing various kinds of evidence for it. To be pertinent to claim (19), however, these kinds of evidence presuppose conditions of the kind mentioned above. So let us look into the conditions on co-optation which Carstairs-McCarthy has to appeal to implicitly in his attempt at justifying claim (18).

7.5.2 Structural parallels. The first kind of evidence put forward by Carstairs-McCarthy (1999) for claim (19) points, he believes, to there being "quite close parallels" (p. 147), "resemblance[s]" (p. 148) or "a close match" (p. 151) between syllable structure and syntactic structure. In fact, he (1999, pp. 151ff.) takes it that he has evidence for five distinct parallels, those set out in (16)(a)-(e) above. For such evidence to be pertinent to claim (19), though, Carstairs-McCarthy must implicitly assume that (20) – in one or another form – is a valid condition on assigning the evolutionary status of "co-optation" to an entity or a feature of one.

(20) An entity/feature X is properly assigned the evolutionary status of "co-optation", if two requirements are met: (i) there are close parallels (or, there is a close match) between the structure of X and the structure of an entity/feature Y; and (ii) the neural basis of Y is used for X as well.

Condition (20) – which represents a foundational assumption about (biological) evolution in general – gives rise to such questions as the following two:

(21)(a) Just how close do the parallels or match between (the structural characteristics) of X and Y have to be?
 (b) On what basis is it to be decided what the structural characteristics are in regard to which X and Y have or do not have to parallel each other?

The point of these questions comes out clearly in some of the criticisms that have been made of Carstairs-McCarthy's co-optationist evolutionary scenario.

As for question (21)(a): in his review of Carstairs-McCarthy's book, Frederick Newmeyer (2000, p. 389) argues that the structural parallels between syllable structure and syntactic structure identified by Carstairs-McCarthy are not sufficiently close. In phonological structure, for example, there is nothing that (closely) parallels the lexical categories, N, V, P and A that occur in syntactic structure. As a consequence, Carstairs-McCarthy's co-optationist scenario does not offer an account of the origin of these categories. Moreover, the parallels identified by Carstairs-McCarthy account for the internal structure of sentences only. Phrases also have an internal structure; yet, as Newmeyer (2000, p. 389) points out, PPs and APs do not exhibit characteristic (16)(c) since "their 'onsets' and 'codas' do not contain the same type of grammatical elements". With question (21)(a), then, here is how things stand. The observations by Newmeyer cast doubt on the grounds on which it might be maintained by Carstairs-McCarthy that the parallels between syllable structure and syntax were close enough to warrant co-optationist claim (19). Condition (20) does not furnish a basis for settling that doubt. Therefore, it is not clear that the structural evidence adduced by Carstairs-McCarthy in support of (19) has the required force.

Turning to question (21)(b): it differs from (21)(a) in an important way. The earlier one of the two questions bears on syntactic properties that should naturally fall within the domain of syllable-based syntax as construed by Carstairs-McCarthy. Question (21)(b), by contrast, is about features which, on modern syntactic theories, are so central to syntax that any scenario of the origin of syntax should be able to account for them in a non ad hoc way. In this connection, two reviewers of Carstairs-

McCarthy's book – Newmeyer (2000) and Uriagereka (2001) – have argued that recursion or embedding and displacement, along with the various principles that constrain them, are just such central or "robustly manifested structural characteristics" of syntax. Neither of these features, however, is a characteristic of that part of syntax which can be naturally construed as syllable-based. In terms of an expectation – (17) – which is set up by Carstairs-McCarthy's notion of syllable-based syntax, recursion/embedding ought actually not to be a property of human language at all. And yet, of course, it is: sentences can be embedded inside other sentences, a fact noted by Carstairs-McCarthy himself.

In order to retain the position stated – in a strong form – in (19), Carstairs-McCarthy would have to come up with some account of the way in which recursion/embedding could have arisen. As we have seen above, he provides for a second, evolutionarily later, phase in the development of syntax in which recursion could have evolved by natural selection. Unfortunately this step by Carstairs-McCarthy is a dubious one, though, as both Newmeyer (2000, p. 389) and Uriagereka (2001, p. 371) point out. Here is how Uriagereka puts it:

> The author [i.e., Carstairs-McCarthy – R.P.B.] seems to be taking the position that something like recursion will adaptively spread once it arises, for some more or less trivial reason. But aside from not spelling out that obvious reason, this brings the book to the familiar territory it rightfully seeks to avoid: the just so story. (Uriagereka, 2001, p. 371)[21]

Uriagereka observes, in addition, that he sees "absolutely no adaptiveness in any properties that characterize displacement". Which means that, in his view, it is not even possible to think up what would amount to a *Just-so* story for this "robustly manifested structural characteristic" of syntax.

To sum up: Foundational assumption (20) fails to warrant the use of evidence about structural parallels for the purpose of supporting the claim that the neural organization underlying syllable structure was co-opted to provide a syntax for strings of "words". That inability is due to (at least) two factors. One: (20) is not sufficiently specific about how close the required parallels between syllable structure and syntactic structure should be. Two: (20) is not sufficiently specific about what the features are that should be taken as the central or "robustly manifested syntactic characteristics" for the origin of which a non-ad hoc account is being required.

7.5.3 Neural contiguity. In addition to putting forward evidence about structural parallels for the co-optationist component of his evolutionary scenario, Carstairs-McCarthy (1999, p. 176ff.) argues that evidence from three other areas "is consistent" with this scenario. These areas are biological anthropology, brain neurophysiology and studies of the linguistic abilities of the great apes. In the case of the first two of these areas, Carstairs-McCarthy finds evidence for claim (19) – i.e., the claim that the neural organization underlying syllable structure was co-opted to provide a syntax of strings of words – by invoking in an implicit way certain conditions on assigning the status of "co-optation" to (linguistic) entities or features.

Central to the first of these conditions is the notion of "neural contiguity" or "closeness". This condition is invoked by Carstairs-McCarthy in his appraisal of proposals about the origin of syntax made by Patricia Greenfield (1991) and William Calvin (1993). There are two, related, suggestions to the proposal by Greenfield:

(22)(a) In early childhood, before neural specialization takes place, object manipulation and linguistic structure are controlled by the same neural mechanisms.

(b) In evolutionary terms, object manipulation and linguistic structure are homologous.

It is Greenfield's proposal, then, that it was the neural basis of object manipulation – not that of syllable structure – that served as the evolutionary source of syntactic structure.

In defending (19), Carstairs-McCarthy comments as follows on Greenfield's proposal:

> Greenfield is correct in drawing attention to the fact that the manual motor area of the cortex is next to the orofacial area, and the orofacial area in turn is next to Broca's area, which is widely seen as having a special role in the grammatical organization of speech. But the manual motor area is not directly next to Broca's area; and this lack of contiguity counts against the suggestion that the manual motor area (as opposed to the orofacial area) has something directly to do with how language is learned. (Carstairs-McCarthy, 1999, p. 187)

On Carstairs-McCarthy's interpretation, the evidence rather supports Thomas Wynn's view that in tool behaviour there is no equivalent to linguistic syntax. This view weakens the idea that prehistoric tools could shed light on the evolution of language. These comments by Carstairs-McCarthy point to a certain foundational assumption about when it is (not) permissible to infer that the neural basis of one entity or feature was co-opted for another one. Here, roughly stated, is that assumption:

(23) Unless the neural basis of an entity X and that of an entity Y are contiguous, it cannot be the case that the neural basis of X was co-opted for Y.

This condition on co-optation can also be stated in positive terms; nothing, however, in the present discussion hinges on this possibility.

Before we examine (23) more closely, let us first consider a case in which Carstairs-McCarthy implicitly appeals to a slightly different version of it. Calvin (1993) proposes what Carstairs-McCarthy (1999, p. 188) refers to as a "ballistic model of syntax". In terms of this model, syntax did not evolve from (the neural basis of) slow-speed object manipulation in tool use, as proposed by Greenfield. Instead, it evolved from the way in which high-speed neural impulses are organised for accurate throwing. Specifically, the neural sequencer for throwing and similar high-speed skills was co-opted for language. This proposal offers a basis for understanding the origin of syntactic category distinctions. In Calvin's own wording,—

> [o]ne can imagine a manual-brachial sequencer being adapted to simple kinds of language. A verb is usually a stand-in for a movement. And the targets of a ballistic movement are examples of nouns: "Throw at that rabbit!" or "Hit that nut". This seems just like the predicate of a sentence: the verb and its object. (Calvin, 1993, pp. 238–239)

To Carstairs-McCarthy's mind, Calvin's ballistic model does not "achieve" all that his own syllable model of the evolution of syntax does.[22] But he believes Calvin's ballistic model to "complement" his syllable model. In attempting to justify this belief, Carstairs-McCarthy implicitly invokes (a version) of assumption (23). Here is how his argument runs:

> Although the lowering of the larynx is the most prominent of the physiological changes that triggered syntactic development according to the syllabic model, it is not the only one. It would have had much less effect on the human vocalization repertoire if the tongue, lips, and soft palate had not acquired the agility that they exhibit in speech. And Calvin's ballistic model suggests a source for that agility. Of course the tongue, lips and soft palate are not used for throwing; but the area of cortex most closely implicated in controlling movement of the tongue and lips is next to that which controls the hand, and the idea that finer neural control of hand movement could have leaked across so as to yield finer control of the tongue and lips too seems compatible with what we know of how the cortex works. So more accurate throwing could indeed have contributed to the development of syntax, but by a more indirect rout than Calvin suggests. (Carstairs-McCarthy, 1999, pp. 188–189)

Relevant here is the reason why Carstairs-McCarthy seems to think that neural control of hand movement could have been the source of the refinement of the control of the tongue and lips: the area of the cortex that controls the hand is next to the one most closely implicated in controlling the movement of the tongue and lips. Without implicit appeal to a version of assumption (23) in terms of which contiguity includes closeness, Carstairs-McCarthy's argument lacks the required warrant.

Preadaptation in Language Evolution 89

As observed above, although Carstairs-McCarthy's arguments take for granted some version of assumption (23), he omits to state it explicitly and to embed it in a general theory of evolution which restrictively assigns co-optation status to biological entities or features of such entities. And he does not attempt to show why it should be considered a valid condition on co-optation. Had he attempted this, Carstairs-McCarthy would have had to argue for the two further claims shown below:

(24)(a) Assumption (23) has the required sort of generality.
 (b) The neurolinguistic theory presupposed by assumption (23) is not untenably localizationist.

To substantiate (24)(a), Carstairs-McCarthy would have had to address questions such as the following: Can condition (23) be applied outside the domain of language as well? Are there paradigmatic instances of co-optations outside this domain which indicate that (23) represents a valid condition on co-optation? Does the use of (23) in conjunction with other conditions on the assignment of co-optation status lead to converging judgements or does it lead to contradictions in the (non-)assignment of co-optation status to entities/features?

As regards (24)(b): condition (23) presupposes a neurolinguistic theory which is localizationist in associating specific components of language or aspects of linguistic function with specific areas of the brain. Strongly localizationist neurolinguistic theories have become untenable in view of the increasing amount of evidence showing that the ways in which components of language – or aspects of linguistic function – are associated with areas of the brain are highly complex and less than well understood. In justifying (23), Carstairs-McCarthy, accordingly, would have had to show that the neurolinguistic theory he subscribes to does not belong to the sort that has been discredited by the evidence in question. In Section 11.2.4 below it is shown why this would be all but simple.

7.5.4 Neurological correspondences. In discussing the sources of evidence for his syllabic model of the origin of syntax, Carstairs-McCarthy asserts that—

[t]here are three independent correspondences between the syllabic model for syntactic evolution and the neurological basis of language. These correspondences tend to confirm the syllabic model in the sense that, although the model does not predict them in detail, their absence would have required extraneous explanation of a kind that turns out to be unnecessary. (Carstairs-McCarthy, 1999, p. 195)

One of these correspondences is to do with what Carstairs-McCarthy's calls "the broad characteristics of Broca's and Wernicke's aphasia". The significant thing to him here is that slow and laboured articulation generally accompanies, not the lexical confusion of Wernicke's aphasia, but the agrammatism of Broca's aphasia.[23] In his view, what is more, the fact that these associations are as they are "fits" the syllable model. These observations by Carstairs-McCarthy can be construed as pointing indirectly to a condition on co-optation which is statable as follows:

(25) Two linguistic entities may be assumed to be related through the evolutionary process of co-optation if they are affected by the same specific pathology.

The foundational assumption stated in (25) is affected, however, by a pair of related problems.

First, what is at issue here is an evolutionary relationship, of a certain kind, that holds between the neurological basis of syntax and that of phonology. The "association" referred to by Carstairs-McCarthy (2000, p. 196) holds, however, between what he calls "disturbances in syntax" and "articulatory disturbances". Articulation and phonology, of course, are different phenomena. Consequently, for Carstairs-McCarthy to be able to appeal – be it implicitly – to condition (25), he has to make an additional assumption:

(26) Phonology and articulation have the same neurological basis.

He does not, however, justify this assumption in any way. Nor does he argue, in line with assumption (25), that the neurological basis of phonology and that of articulation are contiguous with some "leakage" between the two.

Second, a number of different factors may play a causal role in aphasia. This means that it is quite difficult, if not impossible, for any correct conclusion about features of components of language such as phonology and syntax to be straightforwardly drawn from data about aphasia. And such inferences become even more tenuous if a localizationist neurolinguistic theory is assumed on which the features or components in question are taken to be localized in such specific brain areas as Broca's area or Wernicke's area. The reason for this is put as follows by Elizabeth Whitcombe in her *BBS* commentary on Wilkins and Wakefield's reappropriationist scenario:

> All current maps of human cerebral function rely heavily on localization by lesion and are at bottom unsound, because the method is fallacious. Carpenter (1990, pp. 17–18) provides an ideally simple demonstration of the fundamental fallacy: a lesion may indeed cause loss of function by direct inference, but it may do so "equally" by interrupting pathways, obstructing blood-flow, or extinguishing excitatory input. Localization of lesion must therefore be inconclusive. (Whitcombe, 1995, p. 204)

On the basis of various studies – not referred to by Carstairs-McCarthy – Lieberman (2000, p. 101) concludes that subcortical damage that leaves Broca's area intact can result in Broca-like speech production deficits. To him (2000, p. 101), it is evident "that the neuroanatomical basis of Broca's aphasia is *not* simply a lesion localized to this region of the neocortex". And he cites work indicating that a similar situation holds in the case of Wernicke's aphasia. In general, then, discussions such as those by Whitcombe, Lieberman and others show that it is a highly complex matter to determine the neurological basis of the pathologies in question. This means, in turn, that inferences from data about pathologies to the neurolinguistic bases of such components of language as phonology and syntax are, of necessity, poorly warranted at best.

How good then, overall, is Carstairs-McCarthy's co-optationist scenario of the origin of syntax? In particular, is it embedded in a well-articulated general theory of exaptation? As shown above, some of the conditions on co-optation that Carstairs-McCarthy implicitly invokes do admit of reconstruction. And in this respect his co-optationist scenario is better than some of the exaptationist accounts that have been considered in earlier sections. But the conditions just referred to fall far short, in at least two ways, of the theory of exaptation which his scenario takes for granted. One: They have not been explicitly articulated. Two: They are essentially ad hoc. In Chapter 11 below, we will return to the general question of the relevance of the kinds of evidence adduced by Carstairs-McCarthy for his co-optationist scenario. And pursue it further from a more principled perspective.

8

NATURAL SELECTION IN LANGUAGE EVOLUTION

8.1 THE VERTEBRATE EYE AND UNIVERSAL GRAMMAR

The vertebrate eye is regularly cited as a classic example of an organ that evolved through natural selection. It is accorded this evolutionary status on the grounds that it exhibits complex design for an adaptive function – that of seeing. Charles Darwin (1859, p. 79) found the complexity or "perfection" of the eye manifested in "its inimitable contrivances for adjusting the focus of different distances, for admitting different amounts of light, and for the correction of spherical and chromatic aberration".[1] Having defined natural selection as the "preservation of favourable variations and rejection of injurious variations", Darwin gave three reasons for his belief that the eye evolved through natural selection (he stated these reasons in the form of conditions):

> Yet reason tells me that if numerous gradations from a perfect and complex eye to one very imperfect and simple, each grade being useful to its possessor, can be shown to exist; if, further, the eye does vary ever so slightly and the variations be inherited, which is certainly the case, and if any variation or modification in the organ be ever useful to an animal under changing conditions of life, then the difficulty of believing that a perfect and complex eye could be formed by natural selection, though insuperable by our imagination, can hardly be considered real. (Darwin, 1859, p. 79)

In support of each of these three reasons, Darwin adduced considerations which collectively convinced him that "a structure even as perfect as the eye of an eagle might be formed by natural selection".[2]

As we have seen in preceding sections, it has been contended that human language or some of its features evolved like the vertebrate eye through natural selection.[3] Thus Steven Pinker and Paul Bloom claim that:

> ... there is every reason to believe that language has been shaped by natural selection ... [and] that language is no different from other complex abilities such as echolocation or stereopsis, and that the only way to explain the origin of such abilities is through the theory of natural selection. (Pinker and Bloom, 1990, p. 708)

These claims are fleshed out by Pinker and Bloom in an account of language evolution which has sparked a robust debate about, amongst other things, the conditions on assigning to language or to features of it the evolutionary status of an adaptation that evolved by natural selection.[4] From the exchanges in this debate, it is clear that these conditions are problematic in being based on questionable assumptions many of which are not stated explicitly. Specifically, in regard to these conditions questions such as the following arise:

(1) (a) What are the conditions on assigning language or features of it the status of "adaptation by natural selection"?

(b) What are the assumptions underpinning these conditions?

(c) What is it that makes certain conditions and assumptions questionable?

This chapter pursues these questions by examining both Pinker and Bloom's selectionist account itself and the debate set off by it. This account deserves such scrutiny: it has been offered as a synthesis of some of the best work on the evolution of language done within a neo-Darwinian framework, and its relative sophistication has drawn favourable comments from supporters and critics alike.[5] No selectionist account of language evolution that compares in scope with Pinker and Bloom's has recently been published. The BBS debate of this account, in turn, has been relatively coherent: thanks to the structured format of the exchanges, it is one of the more highly focused modern debates on issues of language evolution.[6]

8.2 THE "CRUX" OF THE SELECTIONIST ACCOUNT

On Pinker and Bloom's own portrayal, their selectionist account of language evolution is quite simple in regard to what is argued:

> All we have argued is that human language, like other specialized biological systems, evolved by natural selection. Our conclusion is based on two facts that we would think would be entirely uncontroversial: Language shows signs of complex design for the communication of propositional structures, and the only explanation for the origin of organs with complex design is the process of natural selection. (Pinker and Bloom, 1990, p. 726)

The argument outlined in this quotation has recently been recast by Bloom in the following format:

(2) Natural selection is the only explanation for the origin of adaptive complexity. Human language shows complex design for the adaptive goal of communication.
Hence, language has evolved through natural selection. (Bloom, 1998, p. 209)

Before we proceed, a terminological matter requires some clarification: Pinker and Bloom use the expressions "complex design", "adaptive complexity", "complex adaptive design" and "complex design for an adaptive goal" interchangeably for denoting what they take to be one and the same property of entities such as human language or the vertebrate eye.

From the remarks by Pinker and Bloom quoted above and from their (1990, p. 766) assertion that "complex design is indeed the crux of our argument", it may be inferred that there are only two conditions on assigning language the evolutionary status of an adaptation by natural selection:

(3) Language can be accorded the evolutionary status of an adaptation by natural selection:
    (a) if it is a specialized biological system, and
    (b) if it exhibits complex adaptive design for some evolutionarily significant function.

The seeming simplicity of conditions (3)(a) and (b) is, however, deceptive. First, though it does not appear to be the case, (3)(b) is in fact a compound condition incorporating various more specific conditions each of which involves assumptions that are complex in themselves. Thus each of the constituent concepts of (3)(b) – "language", "complex adaptive design", "evolutionarily significant function" – has to be constrained in regard to content by one or more specific conditions. Second, (3)(b) has to be applied in conjunction with a number of other general assumptions, a fact not reflected in its formulation. Some of these assumptions derive from the theory of natural selection and others from more general considerations of the philosophy of biology. Having already considered Pinker and Bloom's concept of "language" in Chapter 2 above, we will focus in Sections 8.3 and 8.4 below on some of the more specific conditions that have to be placed on the concepts of "evolutionarily significant function" and "complex adaptive design" as constituents of (3)(b). A number of the more general assumptions to which I have just referred will be discussed in Section 8.5.

8.3 EVOLUTIONARILY SIGNIFICANT FUNCTION

Selectionist condition (3)(b) incorporates two requirements, the first of which is that language has to serve an evolutionarily significant function. The second, related, requirement is that language has to exhibit complex adaptive design (for this function). In the present section, the first of the two requirements, as it features in Pinker and Bloom's selectionist account, is considered from the perspective of some of the constraints that need to be placed on their concept of "function". The guiding question will be whether these constraints are sufficiently well articulated to distinguish in a non-arbitrary way among the various kinds of aberrant functionality of parts of language.

Pinker and Bloom assign to both language as a whole and specific parts or features of language a function which they claim to be significant from an evolutionary point of view. As for language as a whole, according to them (1990, pp. 712-720, 726, 763, 767), it shows signs of complex design for carrying out a function that is "reproductively significant". This function they (1990, p. 712) characterize as that of "communicating propositional structures over a serial channel". In less technical terms, Pinker and Bloom (1990, p. 766) alternatively describe it as the function of "mapping meanings onto pronounceable and recoverable sounds". On their (1990, p. 712) view, this function is reproductively significant in the sense that it allows humans to acquire and exchange information. Exchanging information makes it possible for humans to deal with causal contingencies of the environment as these change within a lifetime. This, Pinker and Bloom (1990, p. 712) claim, provides humans with a decisive advantage in competition with other species, which can only defend themselves against new threats in evolutionary time. The advantage of being able to acquire information about the world second-hand from the reservoir of knowledge accumulated by other individuals is that "one can avoid having to duplicate the possibly time-consuming and dangerous trial-and-error process that won that knowledge". Moreover, Pinker and Bloom (1990, p. 712) observe, the internal states of cooperating individuals within the same group are amongst "the most significant things in the world worth knowing about". The communication of knowledge and internal states useful for surviving and reproducing, thus, is on Pinker and Bloom's view the function central to the evolution of language that "shaped" language in human species.[7]

Turning to the functions of the parts of language, Pinker and Bloom (1990, p. 713) maintain that language fulfils its general communicative function in virtue of being "a complex system of many parts tailored to mapping a characteristic kind of semantic or pragmatic function onto a characteristic kind of symbol sequence". The parts in question are substantive (linguistic) universals, also called by them "the building blocks of grammar that all theories of universal grammar posit". Pinker and Bloom's (1990, pp. 713-714) list of substantive linguistic universals and their presumed functions includes, for example:

(4) (a) lexical categories – such as noun, verb, adjective and preposition – whose function is to distinguish basic ontological categories such as things, events and states, and qualities;
   (b) major phrasal categories – such as noun phrase, verb phrase and so on – whose function is to describe particular things, events, states, locations and properties;
   (c) verb affixes whose function is to signal the temporal distribution of the event that the verb refers to (aspect) and the time of the event (tense);
   (d) pronouns and other anaphoric elements whose function is to convey patterns of coreference among participants in complex relations without the necessity of repeating lengthy definite descriptions.

What Pinker and Bloom do is to divide or anatomize the function of language – or the "language function", as it is also called – into subfunctions and to associate specific subfunctions with individual substantive universals. These universals are functional to the extent that they play a role in the mapping of propositional structures on to a serial channel.[8]

Central to the concept of function as a component of selectionist condition (3)(b) is the following assumption:

(5) The individual parts of language have (sub)functions that match the function of language as a whole.

As argued by various BBS commentators, however, the fit between many parts – also referred to as "linguistic forms", "structures" or "features" – and functions deviates from what is to be expected on assumption (5). Below we consider various kinds of deviation or "misfit" and the way in which they bear on the adequacy of selectionist condition (3)(b).

8.3.1 Dysfunctionality. Dysfunctionality represents a first kind of form-function fit that is problematic within the context of condition (3)(b). A formal feature of language is considered dysfunctional if it has some function but does not fulfil this function particularly well. An instance of a dysfunctional feature, on Piattelli-Palmarini's (1990, p. 750) analysis, is the formal feature of tenses. It serves the function of expressing temporality, but does this less than well. For example, Piattelli-Palmarini (1990, p. 753) observes, the "resources of tenses" do not allow us to express the simultaneity of two events by syntactic means alone if that simultaneity occurs at a time that lies in the future with respect to the time of utterance. On his analysis, we *have* to use some "elaborate, strained, prolix periphrasis, supplemented with lexical pointers".[9]

Piattelli-Palmarini uses the dysfunctionality of tenses as the basis for stating a general "challenge" to Pinker and Bloom's selectionist account of the evolution of language:

> How *inadequate* (how dysfunctional) must a structure be before an adaptationist admits that it cannot have been shaped by the proposed function? How does adaptive *under*determination differ from the claim that the structure is only *compatible* with the function? (Piattelli-Palmarini, 1990, p. 753)

Pinker and Bloom's direct response to this challenge by Piattelli-Palmarini is to turn his question around:

> How adequate (how functional) must a structure be before an antiadaptationist admits it was shaped by the proposed function? (Pinker and Bloom, 1990, p. 773)

This response, though it might score points in a debate, does not address the substance of Piattelli-Palmarini's questions. It is therefore not surprising that Pinker and Bloom (1990, p. 773) offer a second, more substantial, response to Piattelli-Palmarini's challenge. They maintain that the criterion demanded by Piattelli-Palmarini is not whether there are some things that grammar cannot do (well), but whether there are things it can do "that cannot be done by a system designed at random". By "at random" they mean "unrelated to the task that the system is to be used for". They illustrate their point by posing two questions. Their first question is about a computational system that is either assembled at random or designed for some specific, but randomly selected, task:

> Would it [this computational system – R.P.B.] be capable, without modification, of encoding into strings of words the tense distinctions that human language can express? (Pinker and Bloom, 1990, p. 773)

Their second question is about random neural spandrels:[10]

> What does an arbitrary cell adhesion molecule know about computational systems that can encode tense distinctions (as opposed to building feathers) – unless it is nonarbitrary because it had been selected to build a system that can do so? (Pinker and Bloom, 1990, p. 773)

Central to this line of argument is the replacement of one criterion of functionality by another which, in the short run, shields Pinker and Bloom's selectionist account from criticisms based on the alleged dysfunctionality of elements of linguistic form. To show, however, that the threat posed by such dysfunctional elements is not a real one, it would have to be argued that Pinker and Bloom's substitution of one criterion of functionality for another is justified on principled grounds. The argument, if successful, would turn the substitution into more than merely an evasive stratagem. Pinker and Bloom, however, have not presented such an argument in any explicit way.

8.3.2 Non-uniqueness. The non-unique way in which specific linguistic forms are associated with specific functions represents a second kind of form-function fit that has been considered a problem for selectionist condition (3)(b). Thus, in the BBS debate, Piattelli-Palmarini (1990, p. 753) has observed that according to Pinker and Bloom one of the central communicative functions of language is to enable speakers to establish and manage social relations. Universal grammar, in Pinker and Bloom's view, has been significantly shaped by the need to promise, instruct, threaten, persuade, order and so on. Piattelli-Palmarini accordingly finds it a puzzle that:

> Although there are syntactic constructions especially suited to these situations (modals, hypotheticals, conditionals, and so forth), this "function" does not uniquely pick out any syntactic construction or module. (Piattelli-Palmarini, 1990, pp. 753-754)

He observes that there are "endless ways" to promise, threaten, induce and so on. Conditionalization and contract-making, likewise, "map onto a *desperately* mixed syntactic bunch". The phrasing of *bona fide* contracts, according to Piattelli-Palmarini, is exhausting and frustrating. Ordinary speakers, he contends, feel "that they can be fooled in a thousand ways, by the mere *wording* of contracts".

All this, then, in Piattelli-Palmarini's opinion, goes to show that UG is "a very bad device for cheater detection". And so he draws the general conclusion that:

> The function explains next to nothing of the structure that it has allegedly shaped through natural selection. (Piattelli-Palmarini, 1990, p. 754)

This conclusion is seen by Piattelli-Palmarini as "refuting" Pinker and Bloom's selectionist account, "or at least weakening [it] substantially". What seems "vastly more plausible" to Piattelli-Palmarini is that, possessing the languages we happen to possess, we human beings have "managed somehow to coax them into the uses we see fit, getting plenty of glitches ... as a result".

Pinker and Bloom's (1990, p. 773) response to Piattelli-Palmarini's criticism based on the non-uniqueness of the link between specific forms and specific functions is cryptic in the extreme:

Piattelli-Palmarini's demand that there be a unique pairing of syntactic constructions with social functions (e.g., a construction for cheater detection) is not reasonable; see our response to **Hornstein**. (Pinker and Bloom, 1990, p. 773)

To see what it is that makes Piattelli-Palmarini's demand "not reasonable" we will have to consider, first, Hornstein's critique of Pinker and Bloom's selectionist account and, then, their response to that critique.

One of Hornstein's (1990, pp. 735-736) criticisms of Pinker and Bloom's selectionist account is that it does not offer an evolutionary model for the selection of specific grammatical properties. Such a model, in Hornstein's view, should for example answer the question: "What evolutionary pressure selects for the case filter or structure-dependence or the binding theory or X' [= X-bar − R.P.B.] theory?" Hornstein (1990, p. 736) contends that a perfectly serviceable communication system that did not mark "abstract" case on NPs could be just as good a medium of communication as one that did. And he comes to the conclusion that:

> In fact, despite Pinker and Bloom's sensitivity to providing "just-so" stories ... that is indeed all they provide. They do not begin to offer even the outlines of an account of what *specific* environmental pressures *specific* grammatical properties are responses to, let alone evidence that these pressures were actually impinging on our ancestors. Nor do they suggest what sorts of tradeoffs might have led to natural selection choosing some specific principle of grammar. Until this is done, however, very little has been accomplished by way of evolutionarily explaining these properties. (Hornstein, 1990, p. 736)

If Pinker and Bloom wish to show that the complex properties of language are due to the "workings of natural selection", Hornstein stresses, nothing less will do than their spelling out the environmental pressures that would cause specific grammatical properties or principles to be selected. But, he points out, "Pinker and Bloom never provide a single detailed discussion of this type for a grammatical principle".

Pinker and Bloom respond to this criticism of Hornstein's by presenting an argument from analogy. First, they state that:

> Demanding to know what environmental pressure selected for X-bar theory is like demanding to know what environmental pressure selected for the third metacarpal or the right iris. (Pinker and Bloom, 1990, p. 772)

By implication, they are saying that this demand would be "not reasonable". But this line of argument requires that, as a component of language, X-bar theory should have approximately the same status as the third metacarpal has as a part of the anatomy of the hand or the right iris has as a part of the anatomy of the eye. It is not evident that this is the case, nor do Pinker and Bloom show that it is.

Second, Pinker and Bloom maintain that:

Natural selection is not a list of environmental forces each tugging at its own bit of anatomy. (Pinker and Bloom, 1990, p. 772)

Elaborating on this point, Pinker and Bloom observe that acute vision depends on several factors: a controllable iris, transparent vitreous humour, a focusing lens, a densely packed fovea all contribute to acute vision. Vision they portray, moreover, as a general function: vision is adaptive across a wide range of environments. It would be a mistake therefore, they claim, to assign each of these a different environmental pressure.

Third, to clinch the argument, Pinker and Bloom state that:

Likewise, the value of each component of universal grammar is its contribution to how the entire language faculty allows complex thoughts to be communicated, an ability that is useful across a huge range of environments. (Pinker and Bloom, 1990, p. 772)

The acceptability of Pinker and Bloom's second and third points depends on the tenability of what they assume about the way in which parts of a structure – as opposed to the structure as a whole – are or are not shaped by specific environmental pressures.

The question, ultimately, is whether the requirement of complex adaptive design expressed in selectionist condition (3)(b) should (be made to) apply to components of a structure as well. And, if so, in what non-arbitrary form? These questions, regrettably, are not explicitly addressed by Pinker and Bloom — a point to which we will return in Section 8.4.2 below.

8.3.3 Functionlessness. In the case of dysfunctionality, a given form can be assigned some (discernible) function. In the case of functionlessness, however, it is not possible to assign the form any function that could explain its existence in selectionist terms. Interestingly, now, several of Pinker and Bloom's critics have argued that certain features or formal building blocks of language are functionless. A case in point, cited by Hornstein (1990, p. 735) in the BBS debate, is (the principle of) structure-dependency.[11] Languages universally use structure-dependent rules; yet, structure-dependency does not seem to serve any function which is significant from the perspective of natural selection. Thus, Noam Chomsky (1988, pp. 46-47) – who first made the point about the functionlessness of structure-dependency – has repeatedly observed that structure-dependent rules are more complex, and consequently less highly valued, than structure-independent rules. Chomsky believes that a language using simpler, structure-independent, rules would be quite easy to construct. Such a language, in his view, would "function perfectly well for purposes of communication, expression of thought, or other uses of language". This means that in Chomsky's view structure-dependency, as a formal building block of language, is *not* required by the functions or uses of language. In turn, this means that on Pinker and Bloom's selectionist account of the evolution of language it is a mystery why language should have the property of structure-dependency.

Pinker and Bloom anticipate some of the threat posed by the functionlessness of certain formal properties of language and take certain steps to defuse it. First, they observe that:

> In their crudest form, arguments about the putative functionlessness of grammar run as follows: "I bet you can't tell me a function for Constraint X, therefore language is a spandrel". But even if it could be shown that one part of language had no function, that would not mean that all parts of language had no function. (Pinker and Bloom, 1970, p. 717)

This response of Pinker and Bloom's falls short, however, of addressing the threat which structure-dependency poses to their selectionist account. The functionlessness of structure-dependency is not taken to indicate that "all parts of language have no function". The point, rather, is that structure-dependency is such a fundamental formal feature of language that, on selectionist accounts of the evolution of language such as Pinker and Bloom's, one would expect it to have a function of the kind under consideration.

Second, Pinker and Bloom (1990, p. 717) suggest that what is taken to be a part of the language faculty may appear to be functionless since it "may not be a genuine part of the language faculty but just a description of one aspect of it ...". Thus, they (1990, p. 717) observe that "the recent history of linguistics provides numerous examples where a newly discovered constraint is first proposed as an explicit statement listed as part of the grammar, but is then shown to be a deductive consequence of a much wider ranging principle". They illustrate this point with reference to a filter ruling out [NP-VP] sequences (e.g. *John to have won is surprising*): at first it was proposed that these sequences were ruled out by a filter peculiar to English; in 1990, the ungrammaticality of such sequences is seen as a consequence of the Case Filter, a linguistic universal.[12]

Structure-dependency would, of course, have to be shown to be in fact an instance of the kind of constraint referred to by Pinker and Bloom. This is unlikely to be easy to do, however, for at least two reasons. On the one hand, unlike the above-mentioned filter, structure-dependency is one of the most fundamental formal features of language. On the other hand, as a fundamental feature of language, structure-dependency has proved to be relatively theory-neutral. Chomsky's theory of linguistic form has undergone numerous revisions – some quite radical – over the years; yet structure-dependency has retained the status of a fundamental property of language. In short, it would seem that structure-dependency remains an embarrassing formal feature from the perspective of selectionist condition (3)(b).

8.3.4 Arbitrariness. Pinker and Bloom's treatment of what may be problems of form-function fit within the framework of selectionist condition (3)(b) is less than adequate since they omit to draw certain fundamental conceptual distinctions in any explicit way. Specifically, instead of distinguishing in a deliberate way between dysfunctionality, non-uniqueness and functionlessness, they lump these together under the heading of "arbitrariness". As a consequence, they do not explicitly consider the question of whether all these kinds of form-function "misfit" are equally problematic from the perspective of selectionist condition (3)(b).

Particularly troublesome is the way in which functionlessness – Pinker and Bloom refer to it as "nonfunctionality" – and arbitrariness are interrelated. Pinker and Bloom consider features of language to be arbitrary if:

(6) (a) they are "not completely predictable" or cannot be "explained" in terms of an adaptive function (Pinker and Bloom, 1990, p. 716);

(b) there is "nothing necessary about them" (Pinker and Bloom, 1990, p. 717);

(c) they "could have been different" (Pinker and Bloom, 1990, p. 718);

(d) they are "nonoptimal" or if "there are alternative solutions that are better from the standpoint of some single criterion". (Pinker and Bloom, 1990, p. 717)

Clearly, the senses of "arbitrariness" alluded to in (6)(a)–(d) do not include a single one on which arbitrariness equals functionlessness: for a formal feature or structure to have no (communicative) function, obviously, is not the same as for a feature or structure to have a function that is "unpredictable" (6)(a), "inexplicable" (6)(a) or "nonnecessary" (6)(b), or for a feature or structure to serve a particular function in a nonoptimal way (6)(d). This means, then, that Pinker and Bloom cannot account for the functionlessness of features of language automatically, by mere appeal to considerations that can be used in explaining the arbitrariness of features. Their discussion of "nonfunctionality" or arbitrariness shows no awareness of this point, however, a fact that contributes to the conceptual fuzziness of selectionist condition (3)(b).

The main finding of Section 8.3, then is, that the concept of "function" in terms of which selectionist condition (3)(b) is stated not sufficiently discriminating. In particular, it conflates a number of distinctions that have to be drawn among such different kinds of form-function "misfit" as dysfunctionality, nonuniqueness and functionlessness. These kinds of form-function "misfit" are lumped together in Pinker and Bloom's concept of "arbitrariness". That is, Pinker and Bloom implicitly subscribe to the following (foundational) assumption:

(7) Dysfunctionality, non-uniqueness and functionless instantiate one and the same phenomenon.

As a consequence, the functionality requirement incorporated in selectionist condition (3)(b) cannot be applied in a non-arbitrary way to individual parts or features of language whose functionality appears to be problematic.

8.4 COMPLEX ADAPTIVE DESIGN

In terms of the second requirement included in selectionist condition (3)(b), language has to show signs of complex adaptive design in order to qualify for the evolutionary status of "having evolved by natural selection". But under what circumstances could language be considered to meet this requirement? To what extent is this a compound requirement, made up of less complex requirements for assigning entities the respective atomic properties of "being complex", "being adaptive" and "exhibiting design"? And is it possible for language as a whole and for individual parts or features of language to manifest complex adaptive design in one and the same way? That is, does it make sense to adopt a single, general requirement, which has to apply to both language as a unitary object and individual parts or features of language? The present section pursues these questions by analysing the concepts of "design", "complexity" and "adaptivity" that are central to Pinker and Bloom's selectionist account of language evolution. The aim of the analysis is to determine whether these concepts are sufficiently well constrained in content, to make it possible to assign a linguistic entity the property of complex adaptive design in a properly restrictive way.

8.4.1 Design. Pinker and Bloom attribute design both to language as a whole and to (the) specific parts of language. Specifically, they claim that:

(8) (a) Language shows signs of *design* for a communicative or mapping function. (cf. Pinker and Bloom, 1990, pp. 712, 726, 766, 767)
(b) Each of the many parts of language is *tailored* to the mapping function it serves. (cf. Pinker and Bloom, 1990, p. 713)

Claims (8)(a) and (b) clearly differ in content from claims (9)(a) and (b), respectively.

(9) (a) Language *has* a communicative or mapping function.
(b) Each of the many parts of language *has* a mapping function.

With reference to the parts of language referred to in (8)(a) above, claim (9)(b) can be fleshed out as (10)(a), which differs significantly in content from claim (10)(b):

(10) (a) The function of the major lexical categories noun, verb and adjective is to distinguish basic ontological categories such as things, events or states, and qualities.
(b) The major lexical categories of noun, verb and adjective are *tailored* to distinguish basic ontological categories such as things, events or states, and qualities.

Function claims such as (10)(a) differ in content from design claims such as (10)(b) in the following general way: something can serve a function without having been designed for it. Or, conversely, something could have been designed for a function, yet fail to serve it. These observations do not hold at a conceptual level only, but apply to biological function and natural design as well. This is shown by Allen and Bekoff, who observe that:

> Function ... is neutral with respect to the phylogenetic pathway by which a trait acquires a function. (Allen and Bekoff, 1995, p. 617)

They point out, moreover, that:

> A trait may have a biological function but not be naturally designed for that function (although it may be a product of natural design for some other function). (Allen and Bekoff, 1995, p. 617)

These considerations imply that showing that a particular trait was designed for a particular function requires more than showing that it serves that function. As Allen and Bekoff (1995, p. 617) put it, "showing design is more difficult than showing function".[13]

Pinker and Bloom do not in any explicit way draw a distinction between function claims such as (10)(a) and design claims such as (10)(b). And they seem to lack the conceptual basis needed for this. They do offer certain observations by Boorse and Cummins in an attempt to "characterize what is behind intuitions of design" of objects as wholes. Thus, according to Pinker and Bloom:

> The key features seem to be (1) a constant but heterogeneous structure: The parts or aspects of an object are unpredictably different from one another; (2) a unity of function: The different parts are organized so as to cause the system to achieve or maintain some special effect – special because it is improbable for systems lacking that organization that are otherwise physically similar to it, and special because it is

among the small set of states that we would antecedently recognize as beneficial to someone or something. (Pinker and Bloom, 1990, p. 767)

Pinker and Bloom's chosen characterization of the intuitions behind the design of objects as wholes does not, however, carry over to intuitions behind the tailoring of parts of objects. Clearly, the test of structural heterogeneity coupled with functional unity cannot be applied to a part of a whole: to do this would be to treat the part as if it were a whole. Pinker and Bloom offer nothing that serves as a clarification of the sense in which individual parts of language could be said to be tailored to their specific function(s). They lack an explicitly articulated and well-constrained concept of "the tailoring of a part of language" which is distinct from the concept of "the function of a part of language". This makes it impossible to apply the requirement of (complex adaptive) design – as a component of selectionist condition (3)(b) – to parts of language. Implicitly, therefore, they proceed from the untenable assumption that:

(11) Showing that some part of language (or UG) has a function is the same as showing that it exhibits design.

8.4.2 Adaptive complexity. Pinker and Bloom collapse the concepts of "complexity" and "adaptivity" into that of "adaptive complexity" which, on their view,

describes any system composed of many interacting parts where the details of the parts' structure and arrangement suggest design to fulfil some function. (Pinker and Bloom, 1990, p. 709)[14]

Both in the BBS debate and elsewhere, it has been argued that Pinker and Bloom's compound concept of "adaptive complexity" is flawed in that it is not sensitive to certain fundamental distinctions, to which we next turn.

A first distinction is that among different sources of complexity. In this connection David Pesetsky and Ned Block (1990, p. 751) point out that Pinker and Bloom allow for aspects of language not to be explained as adaptations "but as arbitrary features that are present because fixing on *some* communication protocol had an evolutionary advantage, even if there might have been far better alternatives". If arbitrariness characterizes language in a substantial way, a "serious problem" arises in Pesetsky and Block's (1990, p. 751) view: "How do Pinker and Bloom know that the arbitrary choices of which they speak don't increase complexity?"

Pesetsky and Block illustrate the point of this question with reference to the evolution of the locomotion of a crablike creature:

Suppose that in the evolution of a crablike creature, a change in environment creates a situation in which survival requires faster locomotion. There are many alterations that an engineer might think of, but evolution favours a quick and dirty approach. Thus, a mutant appears that does the trick by putting together already present behavioral patterns into an utterly shambolic combination of rolling, pushing, flipping, and sliding. If this arbitrary combination is preserved, it can lead to further complexities in later evolutionary change, some of which might themselves be adaptive, others not. (Pesetsky and Block, 1990, p. 751)

The application to language is "obvious" to Pesetsky and Block: the principle of parity plus the need for arbitrariness can result in the choice of "chimerical features of language that inculcate chimerical additions and encrustations down the road".[15]

The crucial question to Pesetsky and Block is "how much of the complexity that we see in language is there because of the needs of complex functional design, and how much is a by-product of arbitrary choices?" Pesetsky and Block proceed to argue that much of the complexity of language is a by-product of arbitrary choices, a conclusion which weakens Pinker and Bloom's selectionist view of linguistic complexity. The cause of the weakness here is that Pinker and Bloom have not made their concept of linguistic complexity sensitive to distinct sources of complexity, thereby implicitly subscribing to the following foundational assumption:

(12) Adaptive complexity need not be distinguished from the kind of complexity that arises from arbitrary choices.

Assumption (12) licenses the conflation of the complexity that arises from design and the complexity that arises from arbitrary choices. This introduces a considerable measure of arbitrariness in assigning language or parts of language the property of being adaptively complex within the framework of selectionist condition (3)(b). Pinker and Bloom, significantly, do not respond in a direct way to Pesetsky and Block's criticisms of their insufficiently well articulated concept of "complexity".

A second distinction to which Pinker and Bloom's concept of "adaptive complexity" is not sensitive is pointed out in the BBS debate by Richard Lewontin:

Pinker and Bloom's biological mistake is that it is not the complexity of language or its organs that is at issue, but the increase in complexity from the ancestral state. (Lewontin, 1990a, p. 740)

To flesh out his point, Lewontin (1990a, p. 740) observes that Broca's area and Wernicke's area were recruited from regions in the primate brain that served functions that were not in themselves linguistic. And he wishes to know: How much increase in complexity was involved in this recruitment, and was it credible without design? He suggests that Pinker and Bloom's concept of complexity does not capture the distinction between complexity and increase in complexity. And Lewontin (1990a, p. 741) maintains that we simply do not know how much change in the brain really had to take place "to make linguistic competence". This question is not addressed directly either by Pinker and Bloom in their response to Lewontin's commentary. They neither deny that they have proceeded from assumption (13) – the assumption attacked by Lewontin – nor offer a defence of it:

(13) Condition (3)(b) need not be sensitive to the destinction between complexity and an increase in complexity.

Which brings us to the third distinction that is collapsed in Pinker and Bloom's concept of adaptive complexity: that between the adaptive properties and the complex properties of an object. In this connection, Pesetsky and Block (1990, p. 750) have pointed out in the BBS discussion that Pinker and Bloom's selectionist account of the evolution of language is underpinned by the following assumption:

(14) The adaptive properties of language and the complex properties of language are the same.

This assumption can, in Pesetsky and Block's view, be falsified in both directions, since there is a mismatch of adaptive properties and complex properties. On the one hand, they observe, the properties of language considered adaptive by Pinker and Bloom are not judged to be complex by generative linguists:

> Their properties get scant mention in "linguistic practice" because they (unlike the structure of the human eye) are not complex enough to merit much discussion. (Pesetsky and Block, 1990, p. 750)

The properties of language referred to by Pesetsky and Block are those that have been exemplified in (4)(a)–(d) above. On the other hand, Pesetsky and Block maintain, the properties considered complex by linguists are not adaptive in Pinker and Bloom's sense:

> All or most of the complex properties of language fall in areas far removed from any currently adaptive function. (Pesetsky and Block, 1990, p. 750)

What compounds the problem of the mismatch of complex and adaptive properties, according to Pesetsky and Block, is that the complex properties discussed by linguists seem, despite their not being adaptive, to be deeply rooted in the human language faculty. These properties are, moreover, "detectable in any human language whose other properties do not inhibit the discovery of these facts".

How, then, do Pinker and Bloom respond to Pesetsky and Block's point about the mismatch of adaptive properties and complex properties? They (1990, p. 765) do commend Pesetsky and Block – as well as Ridley, Sober, and Tooby and Cosmides – for having presented "lucid arguments ... about the central role of adaptation in evolution ...". But as far as specifics are concerned, their response to Pesetsky and Block's point is tangential at best. As an illustration of the "complexities" that linguists study, Pesetsky and Block offer the following example amongst others:

Natural Selection in Language Evolution 109

linguists want to know why alongside passive nominals like *the city's destruction by the enemy* we do not find *the city's sight by the enemy*. And with reference to this example, they ask:

> Are the domains that linguists find complex also adaptive? What reproductive advantage is conferred on speakers because they do not fully accept *the city's sight by the enemy?* ... What function would be impaired if a speaker did accept *the city's sight by the enemy?* (We are ignoring the reproductive advantage to be gained by conforming with the rest of the local community. Such an advantage is independent of the complexity of the language that is shared.) (Pesetsky and Block, 1990, p. 751)

Pinker and Bloom's response to these questions by Pesetsky and Block reads as follows:

> We don't need to determine "the reproductive advantage ... conferred on speakers because they do not fully accept *the city's sight by the enemy"* because this is a datum about a bit of behavior, not a biological structure, and thus did not itself evolve; it's the language faculty, which gave rise to the judgment data, that evolved. (Pinker and Bloom, 1990, p. 771)

Pinker and Bloom's claim that the judgement in question is "a datum about a bit of behavior, not about a biological structure" is puzzling. On the standard generativist construal of the import of linguistic judgements, the judgement in question is taken to be ultimately a datum about a feature of the language faculty: the feature that causes speakers to consistently judge the utterance not (fully) acceptable. Underlying this construal of linguistic judgements is the following ontology:

(15) (a) (Intuitive) linguistic judgements are products of acts of language behaviour.
 (b) Acts of language behaviour are products of the use of, amongst other things, speakers' linguistic competence.
 (c) Speakers' linguistic competence is the product of the growth/maturation of (the initial state of) their language faculty.

In terms of this ontology, questions about linguistic judgements – such as the question being considered here – are questions about causal mechanisms forming part of speakers' linguistic competence and, ultimately, forming part of (the initial state of) their language faculty. What makes Pinker and Bloom's quoted response so puzzling is that they seem to realize this when they state that "it's the language faculty ... which gave rise to the judgment data". But, strangely, they do not draw the consequences of this position when responding to Pesetsky and Block's question about the reproductive advantage of speakers' judging *the city's sight by the enemy* unacceptable. That question clearly has to be understood as a question about the

110 *Unravelling the Evolution of Language*

reproductive advantage of the underlying mechanism – which is something biological – responsible for the judgement in question. It would be quite implausible to suggest that, in asking the quoted questions about the judgement under consideration, Pesetsky and Block wished to be understood in any other way. Which means that what Pinker and Bloom argue does not really address Pesetsky and Block's point about the non-adaptivity of the features of language judged complex by generative linguists.

Pinker and Bloom do not address that point either when they go on to observe that:

> **Pesetsky and Block**, by focusing on what linguists find "worth studying", state that the complex features of grammar play no role in allowing people to communicate, to express an infinite number of meanings using a finite number of lexical items, and so on. This claim is surprising. Wasn't it Chomsky who characterized a grammar as defining a mapping between sounds and meanings, and who said that a speaker can "make use of an intricate structure of specific rules and guiding principles to convey his thoughts and feelings to others, arousing in them novel ideas and subtle perceptions and judgments?" Don't linguists study such things as X-bar theory, word order parameters, inflectional morphology, segmental phonology, prosody, and so on, that are implicated every time we open our mouths to speak? (Pinker and Bloom, 1990, p. 771)

In terms of this line of argument, every feature of a grammar would, derivatively, have a function simply in virtue of being a part of a system that defines a mapping between sounds and meanings with the exception of ad-hoc devices that merely present summaries of unexplained phenomena, as Pinker and Bloom (1990, p. 772) put it. But if this were the case, how should one understand Pinker and Bloom's providing for the "ubiquity ... of arbitrary aspects of even the most obvious adaptations"? And why would they (1990, pp. 717-718) have to take the trouble to explain away certain functionless features of language as (part of) an inherent trade-off of utility within language? Or why would they (1990, p. 718) have to argue that arbitrariness is built into language? Derivatively assigning a function to what are believed to be functionless features of language, clearly cannot address Pesetsky and Block's point about the mismatch of complex properties and adaptive properties.

There is a certain line of argument that Pinker and Bloom could adopt in an attempt to counter the criticism that their concept of "adaptive complexity" is not sensitive to the distinction between the adaptive properties of the language faculty and its complex properties. They could argue that the notion of complex properties did not make sense, grounding this contention in their view that:

(16) It is not complexity per se that is at issue, but complexity of *design*. (Pinker and Bloom, 1990, p. 767)

Adopting (16), one could first observe that Pesetsky and Block, in criticizing some of the substantive claims made by Pinker and Bloom in terms of their concept of "adaptive complexity", refer to the (non-)complexity of "properties", "structures", "problems", "domains" or "facts". The (non-)complexity of these kinds of entities, one could then contend, is not the same phenomenon as complexity of *design*. For a design to be complex, the argument could run, ("facts" about) its properties, structures and so on are not required to be complex as well. Complexity of design can arise from the way in which noncomplex properties or structures are interlinked. The thrust of this line of argument would be, then, that Pesetsky and Block (and others) base their criticisms of Pinker and Bloom's claims about complexity of design on data that are irrelevant. In responding to the criticisms in question Pinker and Bloom themselves, however, do not develop any such argument explicitly. Curiously, they (1990, p. 771) seem to follow Pesetsky and Block in talking of "the complex features of grammar" (where on the ground of consistency one could have expected them to talk of "the complexity of design" of grammar.) Thereby, they effectively destroy the basis of this line of argument.

As a constituent of selectionist condition (3)(b), Pinker and Bloom's concept of "complex adaptive design," in sum, is not sufficiently well constrained in the sense that it fails to offer a basis for drawing some fundamental distinctions. These include the distinction between various sources of complexity, the distinction between complexity and an increase in complexity and the distinction between complex properties and adaptive properties. The non-drawing of these distinctions, of course, has a flip side which consists in implicitly making the assumptions (12), (13) and (14).

8.5 GENERAL PROBLEMS

It is time to bring the discussion of condition (3)(b) to a close. What this condition says is that it is correct to assign to language the evolutionary status of an adaptation by natural selection, if language shows complex adaptive design for some evolutionarily significant function. In closing, then, let us look at two general ways in which condition (3)(b) is problematic.

The first of these springs from (14): the assumption that the adaptive properties of language and its complex properties are the same. On Pesetsky and Block's (1990) analysis, though, this assumption is highly questionable – as we have seen above. The identification of what is adaptive with what is complex has recently been questioned by a number of other scholars as well. In responding to a letter by Pinker (1997a) in *The New York Review of Books,* Gould (1997b, p. 57) points out that Pinker in that letter has (again) failed to draw a distinction between "complex design" and "complex adaptive design". And he goes on to observe that—

[c]omplex design forms a much broader category than adaptive design – and has many other potential evolutionary causes. (Gould, 1997b, p. 157)

In similar vein, Grantham and Nichols (1999, pp. 51–52) refer to work by Kauffman (1995) and by Page and Mitchell (1999) which supports the view that "nonselective forces can create functional complexity." And Kirby (2000, p. 303) argues that the emergence of (complex) compositional syntax can be explained without its being viewed as an adaptation to natural selection pressures.

These remarks by Gould and the other authors – along with those by Pesetsky and Block – point to a risk in the use of a condition like (3)(b). Because it centrally involves a concept of "complex adaptive assign", using it could mislead one into assigning the evolutionary status of adaptations by natural selection to features that are complex but not adaptive. This is just the error that would occur if one were to adopt (14).

The second general way in which condition (3)(b) is problematic is, in a sense, the reverse of the first. It is this: using a selectionist condition at the centre of which there is a concept of "complex adaptive design" could mislead one into denying the evolutionary status of "adaptations" to features that in fact are adaptive. Conditions on adaptation at the centre of which there is a notion of "function" – as is the case with (3)(b) – are referred to as "teleonomic criteria" by Reeve and Sherman; the main problem with these, they maintain, is—

... that they are so conservative that many selectively favoured traits would not be recognized as adaptations. (Reeve and Sherman, 1993, p. 7)

The problem with strict teleonomic criteria, as Reeve and Sherman (1993, p. 7) see it, is this: only traits (or features) that have been under directional selection for the same function for a very long time would predictably be modified enough to meet such criteria. Various kinds of traits would not. These include, for example, newly arisen traits in which there has been no detectable fine-tuning; but then they equally include traits that have remained essentially unchanged since they first arose.[16] And so Reeve and Sherman (1993, p. 7) don't find it surprising that proponents of teleonomic definitions illustrate their concept of "adaptation" with "spectacular phenotypes whose complex forms suggest that they were indeed 'designed' to solve specific problems". Interestingly, they cite "the structure of the vertebrate eye" as one of the "spectacular phenotypes" used for this illustrative purpose. It has of course been used for just this purpose by Pinker and Bloom too.

We have seen above that, as a core component of condition (3)(b), a concept of "complex adaptive design" causes similar problems for Pinker and Bloom's adaptationist account of language evolution. First, as noted in Section 8.4.1, Pinker and Bloom's concept of "design" or "tailoring" does not carry over to parts of language that do not represent "spectacular phenotypes" – phenotypes that have the appearance of having been "designed" or "fine-tuned". Second, there is Pesetsky and Block's (1990, p. 750) observation – discussed in Section 8.4.2 – that properties of language considered adaptive by Pinker and Bloom are not judged to be complex by generative linguists, "because they (unlike the structure of the human eye) are not complex enough to merit much discussion". Pinker and Bloom obviously could not have rated these properties adaptive on the grounds of their appearing to have been "designed" or "tailored". This means that if Pinker and Bloom had good grounds for judging these properties to be adaptations by natural selection, they would have to amend condition (3)(b) by making it sensitive to those grounds as well. And they would have to modify the "crux" of their selectionist account of language evolution along the same lines.[17]

9

THEORIES OF EVOLUTIONARY PROCESSES

It will be useful to review here four main points from Chapters 6, 7 and 8. One: The characterizations used in some of the most detailed modern accounts of the processes by which language is claimed to have evolved are ad hoc and arbitrary in various ways. Two: This property of these characterizations has its main cause in the fact that they rest on informal assumptions about evolution which do not add up to a general theory of evolution that is restrictive enough and well enough founded. Three: A theory of evolution is restrictive to the extent that it makes it possible to distinguish in a non-arbitrary way between entities that are instances of a specific kind of evolutionary event, process or product and entities that are not. Four: Accounts of the processes by which language or other linguistic entities evolved will remain as ad hoc and arbitrary as they are at present, unless their informal foundational assumptions of what evolution is about are replaced by restrictive theories of co-optation, preadaptation or exaptation, and adaptation.

Gould and Vrba's (1982) theory of exaptation is an example – it was shown in Section 6.2 – of the kind of theory that has to be invoked in assigning to language or to other linguistic entities the evolutionary status of a by-product (the result of spandrel co-optation) or an exaptation (the result of function shift). Yet, even though it is one of the most fully articulated theories of its kind, this theory has been criticized for various alleged shortcomings, one of which is quite instructive here.[1] That is to say, Reeve and Sherman (1993, p. 3) have argued that, as set up in this theory, the distinction between adaptation and exaptation fails to make it possible to determine precisely where the one ends and the other begins. The reason for this, they hold, is that Gould and Vrba "did not specify how much the current function of a trait must differ from its original role for it to be classified as an exaptation".[2] Reeve and Sherman illustrate the point with reference to human ear bones, asking whether these bones are exaptations because, in addition to their original function, they now mediate social communication via telephones. According to Reeve and Sherman, the answer depends on how finely one subdivides roles or functions. If the original function is broadly defined – say, as being to facilitate detection of acoustic stimuli – then human ear bones, they find, are adaptations. If however it is narrowly defined – say, as being to facilitate detection of pre-Bell or prelinguistic acoustic stimuli – then, according to Reeve and Sherman, our ear bones are exaptations.

In essence, there are three points to the case that Reeve and Sherman are making. One: Gould and Vrba's characterization of the processes of adaptation and exaptation is not restrictive enough. Two: This is caused by the fact that their concept of "change in function" is insufficiently well developed: it leaves it unclear just how big or substantive a change in the function of a trait should be for it to be considered an exaptation as opposed to an adaptation. Three: In turn, this has the consequence that, where any trait has evolved as an adaptation, it is as a matter of principle not possible to assign it the evolutionary status of an exaptation.

Recall that Lieberman's preadaptive model of language evolution was found to be flawed in this way in Section 7.2.2. As we saw there, he (1990, p. 742) adopts Darwin's view that preadaptation is a "mechanism" whereby an "organ originally constructed for one purpose ... may be converted into one for a wholly different purpose". But if the notion of "a wholly different purpose" is not spelled out in a restrictive enough way – this too was shown in Section 7.2.2 – there is no non-arbitrary way of determining either whether the brain mechanisms involved in manual control were exapted for speech production or whether the brain mechanisms involved in speech production were at some later stage exapted for syntax. In the case of all three these things – manual control, speech production and syntax – the function of the brain mechanisms in question, in terms of Lieberman's model, is that of sequencing. Clearly, the notion of a "wholly different purpose" is not well enough articulated for Lieberman or others to be able to non-arbitrarily assign the evolutionary status of an exaptation to the brain mechanisms concerned with speech production or syntax.

This last point generalises to a large number of the core concepts that are used in modern accounts of the processes thought to have been central to the evolution of language or of features of language. Earlier sections have set out ample evidence to the effect that core concepts of such accounts do not derive from evolutionary theories that are restrictive and that give a basis on which to characterise the evolutionary history and status of linguistic entities in a non-ad hoc or non-arbitrary way. In the case of selectionist accounts, four of the concepts in question were seen to be "(dys)functionality", "design", "complexity" and "adaptivity". The upshot is clear: Assumptions that are ad hoc and that make use of poorly articulated concepts will have to give way to restrictive theories of the various evolutionary processes.

PART III

EVIDENCE AND ARGUMENTATION

Accounts of language evolution must, by their very nature, express claims of a historical sort: claims about why, when, where or how human language emerged and/or developed in some distant past. What is more, it is of the essence of those claims that they are put forward in the absence of direct historical evidence about the evolutionary events, biological processes, physical forces, environmental pressures, kinds of (pre)linguistic entities, and so on, that may or may not have been involved in the genesis of language. The lack of such direct historical evidence – that is, evidence derived from the data contained in natural or man-made records of these evolutionary events etc. – is generally seen as one of the most forbidding obstacles to doing work of scientific value on language evolution, as was pointed out in Chapter 1.

In modern work on language evolution, however, scholars have come up with strategies for solving, ameliorating or sidestepping the problem of evidential paucity, a major cause of which is the lack of direct historical evidence. These strategies include—

(1) (a) adopting a condition of testability for accounts of language evolution;
    (b) drawing evidence from new sources of data believed to bear indirectly on the truth of such accounts;
    (c) constructing arguments which invoke general non-empirical considerations of analogy, necessity, probability or ignorance in justifying, defending or criticizing such accounts;
    (d) having recourse to devices of a rhetorical sort;
    (e) telling plausible stories or creating fables about episodes in language evolution.

In this Part III, the present study looks into these strategies in some detail with a view to throwing light on their merits and limitations: Strategy (1)(a) in Chapter 10, strategy (1)(b) in Chapter 11, strategies (1)(c) and (d) in Chapter 12, and strategy (1)(e) in Chapter 13. Chapter 14 concludes the discussion of Part III by clarifying the nature of the theories – theories about the substance of science – by which these strategies should be underpinned. In doing this, it shows how the findings of Chapters 10 – 13 contribute to the core finding of this book, namely that a poverty of restrictive theory is the main obstacle to progress in finding out how language evolved.

10

TESTABILITY: A LITMUS TEST?

10.1 THE ROLE OF TESTABILITY

In much of the modern work on language evolution, the following is taken as a foundational assumption, often explicitly so:

(1) To be of scientific value, accounts of language evolution have to be testable, falsifiable or refutable.[1]

For example, Steven Pinker and Paul Bloom, and their critics along with them, adopt some version of assumption (1) as the basis of a fundamental criterion of adequacy; then, where any accounts of language evolution fail to meet that criterion, they dismiss them as "empty", "unscientific" and the like. In this connection, Pinker and Bloom observe for example that—

... lurking behind people's suspicions of natural selection is a set of methodological worries. Isn't adaptationism fundamentally untestable, hence unscientific, because adaptive stories are so easy to come by that when one fails, another can always be substituted? (Pinker and Bloom, 1990, p. 711)

Judging these "worries" unfounded, Pinker and Bloom maintain that—

[s]pecific adaptationist proposals are testable in principle and practice ... Supplementing the criterion of complex design, one can determine whether putatively adaptive structures are correlated with the ecological conditions that make them useful, and, under certain circumstances one can actually measure the reproductive success of individuals possessing them to various degrees ... (Pinker and Bloom, 1990, p. 711).

And they go on to argue that—

... it is nonadaptationist accounts that are often in grave danger of vacuity. Specific adaptationist proposals may be unmotivated, but they are within the realm of biological and physical understanding, and often the problem is simply that we lack the evidence to determine which account within a set of alternative adaptive explanations is the correct one. Nonadaptationist accounts that merely suggest the possibility that there is some hitherto-unknown law of physics or constraint on form – a "law of eye-formation", to take a caricatured example – are, in contrast, empty and nonfalsifiable. (Pinker and Bloom, 1990, p. 711)

Pinker and Bloom have not managed, however, to persuade all their BBS commentators that their selectionist account of the evolution of language is testable or refutable. Thus, Richard Lewontin (1990a, p. 741) suggests that Pinker and Bloom "often cannot know the basic facts on which the[ir] theory rests" – a suggestion which, if correct, would make this "theory" untestable in a specific sense. And Massimo Piattelli-Palmarini charges that it is impossible to "refute", or even to "substantially weaken", the adaptationist hypothesis offered by Pinker and Bloom because—

... they manage to render this approach utterly indefeasible (this is not meant to be a compliment ...) (Piattelli-Palmarini, 1990, p. 754)

Piattelli-Palmarini then makes this claim, much in the same spirit as Lewontin:

Resting their case on data that their own approach would have made impossible to collect, ... they proceed to construct an a posteriori, ad-hoc, irrefutable explanation. (Piattelli-Palmarini, 1990, p. 574)

So what does testability or refutability involve in the view of Pinker and Bloom or their critics? Regrettably, neither Pinker and Bloom nor their critics explicitly characterize what it is they take to be involved in the testability or refutability of an account (or theory) or its constituent claims (or hypotheses). As shown by the second quotation above, Pinker and Bloom do draw a distinction between testability-in-principle and testability-in-practice, though without explicating the assumptions on which it rests. For the purpose of the discussion here, it will be taken that their distinction is the conventional one, whose sense is as follows:

(2) (a) A theory (or hypothesis) is testable-in-principle if (a) precise test-implications can be derived from it and (b) the empirical data can be specified which, if they were available, would indicate that the test-implications are false.

(b) A theory (or hypothesis) is testable-in-practice if (a) it is testable-in-principle and (b) empirical data are in fact available with which its test-implications can be confronted.[2]

Over the years, at least two sets of things have been held to be harmful to the testability of a theory (or hypothesis).[3] One of these is to do with the effects and causes of obscurity in content. Obscurity in content or ontological import is seen as harmful to testability-in-principle in that it precludes the derivation of precise test-implications or the specification of the empirical data that would be needed for checking these implications. The things that cause theories (or hypotheses) to be obscure include reference to (parts of) entities or phenomena that cannot be identified uniquely, imprecise formulation and so on. The other set of things that may harm the testability-in-principle of a theory (or hypothesis) are devices that are adopted for the sole purpose of shielding it from the adverse impact of counterevidence. These devices include concepts, conceptual distinctions, auxiliary hypotheses and inferential strategies that allow defenders of the theory (or hypothesis) to interpret evidence that would have refuted it in such a way that this evidence is consistent with its test-implications.[4] In terms of conventional wisdom, the testability-in-practice of a theory (or hypothesis) is questioned if it is not possible to collect any of the evidence that would bear on the correctness of its test-implications.

If testability is adopted as a fundamental criterion of adequacy for modern accounts of language evolution, questions such as the following arise: To what extent is this criterion met by Pinker and Bloom's selectionist account of language evolution? Are the problems that arise in connection with the testability of this account typical of selectionist accounts of language evolution in general? These two questions are taken up in Section 10.2 below. Section 10.3 brings the discussion to a close by going into a more fundamental question: How good is the justification for the assumption that testability ought to be a fundamental criterion for accounts of language evolution?

10.2 CLAIMS EXPRESSED BY SELECTIONIST ACCOUNTS

To appraise the testability Pinker an Bloom's account of language evolution, it is necessary to distinguish among at least four categories of substantive claims expressed by it:[5]

(3) (a) claims about the function of language or of its components;

(b) claims about the design of language or of its components

(c) claims about the complexity of language or of its components; and

(d) claims about the historical process by which language or its parts actually evolved.

When considering the testability of these categories of claims, one should bear in mind that the first three – that is, 3(a)–(c) – embody what Pinker and Bloom have called "the crux of [their] argument" for the position that language evolved by means of natural selection.[6] The testability of these three categories of claims is examined in Sections 10.3–10.5 below. Claims of the fourth category – that is, claims about historical processes – have to be expressed not by selectionist accounts only but by nonselectionist ones as well. Some questions about the epistemological status of claims belonging to this fourth category are addressed in Section 11.3.1 below.

10.3 CLAIMS ABOUT FUNCTION

Recall that central to Pinker and Bloom's (1990, pp. 712-720, 726, 766, 767) selectionist account of the evolution of language is the claim that language shows signs of design for a particular function. As they characterize this function – we have seen in Section 8.3 above – it is that of "communicating propositional structures over a serial channel" (1990, p. 712) or, less formally, that of "mapping meanings onto pronounceable and recoverable sounds" (1990, p. 766). This communicative or mapping function is significant from an evolutionary and, more specifically, a selectionist perspective: by serving it, language increases according to Pinker and Bloom individuals' chances of surviving and reproducing. They assign a communicative function to language as a whole and also to certain components of language. As for these components, they anatomize the "linguistic function" into subfunctions which they assign to specific substantive linguistic universals, also labelled by them "the building blocks of grammar" or "the parts of language". As a result, Pinker and Bloom's selectionist account incorporates such specific claims about function as the following:

(4) (a) The function of the major lexical categories of noun, verb and adjective is "to distinguish basic ontological categories such as things, events or states, and qualities". (Pinker and Bloom 1990, p. 713)

(b) The function of phrase structure rules is that of providing "linear cues of underlying structure, distinguishing for example, *Large trees grow dark berries* from *Dark trees grow large berries"*. (Pinker and Bloom, 1990, p. 713)

(c) The function of mechanisms of complementation and control is to "allow the expression of a rich set of propositional attitudes within a belief–desire folk psychology, such as *John tried to come, John thinks that Bill will come, John hopes for Bill to come, John convinced Bill to come,* and so on". (Pinker and Bloom, 1990, p. 714)

Though some BBS commentators criticize Pinker and Bloom's selection of substantive universals,[7] the empirical nature or testability of individual function claims such as (4)(a)–(c) is not at issue in the discussion. These claims are taken to be amenable to criticism and falsification. What is considered a problem lies at a different level, springing from Pinker and Bloom's claim that

> ... each [of the many parts of language is] tailored to mapping a characteristic kind of semantic or pragmatic function onto a characteristic kind of symbol sequence ... (Pinker and Bloom, 1990, p. 713)

As various BBS commentators and other scholars have observed, however, many parts or features of language appear not to have any communicative or other adaptive function. Pesetsky and Block, for example, observe that:

> Linguists are fond of pointing out how nonfunctional many of the aspects of language that most interest them are. (Pesetsky and Block, 1990, p. 750)

And Hornstein concludes that:

> The position, then, that virtually all of the specific grammatical properties of NLs might well be there for reasons unconnected to adaptation is quite plausible for all we currently know. (Hornstein, 1990, p. 735)

The structure-dependence of grammatical rules – we have seen in Section 8.3.3 above – is often cited as an example of a fundamental property of grammar that does not seem to serve any function that can be accounted for in adaptationist terms.

It is now interesting that, in presenting their account, Pinker and Bloom (1990, p. 718) themselves make provision for the existence of *many* grammatical constraints that are "arbitrary" from the perspective of communicative function. And in their response to peer commentaries, they (1990, p. 705) express their gratitude to certain commentators for having drawn attention to "the ubiquity (and irrelevance) of arbitrary *aspects* of even the most obvious adaptations". Clearly, then, Pinker and Bloom admit that language or grammar has many parts or features which appear arbitrary from the viewpoint that the function of language is that of communicating (or mapping) propositional structures over a serial channel. Yet, equally they do not believe that such arbitrary parts or features provide evidence refuting their claim that *each* of the many parts of language has a characteristic semantic or pragmatic function in the mapping process. But, taken in conjunction with this admission of theirs, how could this claim of theirs be judged to be testable? To pursue this question, we have to examine the devices which Pinker and Bloom use for reconciling the existence of arbitrary features of grammar with the position that language evolved by natural selection as a means of communication.

10.3.1 Inherent trade-offs. In attempting to achieve the reconciliation mentioned above, Pinker and Bloom proceed from the following assumption amongst others:

> (5) No adaptive organ can be adaptive in every aspect because there are as many aspects of an organ as there are ways of describing it. (Pinker and Bloom, 1990, p. 717)

Having illustrated this assumption with an instance from "the recent history of linguistics",[8] Pinker and Bloom observe that:

> Because the mere appearance of some nonoptimal feature is inconclusive, we must examine specific explanations for why the feature exists. (Pinker and Bloom, 1990, p. 719)

And they proceed to identify trade-offs among conflicting adaptive goals as one source of explanation, since:

> Trade-offs among conflicting adaptive goals are a ubiquitous limitation on optimality in the design of organisms. (Pinker and Bloom, 1990, p. 717)

To illustrate this point, Pinker and Bloom, 1990, p. 717) use the example of a male bird for which "it may be adaptive to advertise his health to females by means of gaudy plumage or a long tail, but not to the extent that predators are attracted to it or flight is impossible".

Let us then examine the way in which Pinker and Bloom's use of assumption (6) affects the testability of the function claims expressed by their selectionist account of language evolution:

> (6) The existence of some arbitrary features of grammar can be explained with reference to trade-offs among conflicting adaptive goals of language users.

Pinker and Bloom (1990, p. 717) consider trade-offs in utility between, on the one hand, speakers' need for a large vocabulary allowing for concise and precise expression and, on the other hand, the need for all potential hearers to have the opportunity to learn each vocabulary item. They (1990, p. 717) believe that any shared system of communication will have to adopt a code that is a "compromise" among such conflicting demands. As a consequence, this code will appear to be "arbitrary from the point of view of any one criterion". This, they assert, applies to language as well:

> A given feature of language may be arbitrary in the sense that there are alternative solutions that are better from the standpoint of some single criterion. But this does not mean that it is good for nothing at all. (Pinker and Bloom, 1990, p. 716)

Against this background, Pinker and Bloom subsequently deal with the way in which Subjacency, as "a classic example of an arbitrary constraint", bears on their selectionist account. Their treatment of the arbitrariness of Subjacency illustrates one of the ways they use for reconciling the claim, on the one hand, that *each* of the parts of language has a function that is significant from an adaptionist point of view with the arbitrariness, on the other hand, of some of these parts.

Informally, Subjacency prohibits a dependency between a gap and its antecedent if the dependency spans certain combinations of phrasal nodes. It allows the formation of questions such as (7)(a); at the same time it rules out the formation of questions such as (7)b), which are semantically parallel but structurally nonparallel:

(7) (a) What does he believe they claimed that I paid?
    (b) What does he believe the claim that I paid?

In response to the questions "Why do languages behave in this way?" and "Why is extraction not allowed anywhere or nowhere?", Pinker and Bloom assert that:

> The constraint *may* [emphasis added – R.P.B.] exist because parsing sentences with gaps is a notoriously difficult problem and a system that has to be prepared for the possibility of inaudible elements anywhere in the sentence is a danger of bogging down by positing them everywhere. Subjacency has been held to assist parsing because it cuts down on the set of structures that the parser has to keep track of when finding gaps (Berwick and Weinberg, 1984). (Pinker and Bloom, 1990, p. 717)

Pinker and Bloom continue, however, as follows:

> This bonus to listeners is often a hinderance to speakers, who struggle with resumptive pronouns in such clumsy sentences as *That's the guy that you heard the rumour about his wife leaving him.* There is nothing "necessary" about the precise English version of the constraint or about the small sample of alternatives allowed within natural language. But by settling in on a particular subset of the range of possible compromises between the demands of expressiveness and parsability, the evolutionary process *may* [emphasis added – R.P.B.] have converged on a satisfactory set of solutions to one problem in language processing. (Pinker and Bloom, 1990, pp. 717–718)

From the perspective of the testability of their selectionist account, the explanation of the arbitrary nature of Subjacency offered by Pinker and Bloom is interesting in a number of ways. The first is that some of the crucial claims expressed in this explanation are hedged in regard to modality:

(8) (a) The constraint *may* exist ...
    (b) ... the evolutionary process *may* have converged on a satisfactory set of solutions ...

These claims are themselves not testable: what they assert can be reconciled with two mutually exclusive states of affairs, a "may" state and a "may not" state. To protect a theory from refutation by making claims that are not controvertible themselves is obviously harmful to the testability of this theory.

It is accordingly understandable that various participants in the BBS discussion have commented critically on the relative emptiness of Pinker and Bloom's claims about trade-offs. Hornstein, for example, argues that:

> ... one can look on subjacency as functionally related to parsing efficiency and thereby partially accounted for. To give an *adaptive* account, however, more is required: Under what environmental conditions is real time parsing adaptive? What was the selective pressure that weeded out the "slow" process? What costs were paid to effect this remarkable processing speed? (Hornstein, 1990, p. 736)

And he concludes:

> They further speculate, however, that subjacency "may" represent the best compromise given the demands of expressiveness and parsability. I agree it "may". But to show that there is strong reason to think it does one would have to spell out the environmental pressures that would make efficient parsing advantageous and the trading relations among the alternatives that would make subjacency the least costly way of meeting this demand. Despite the vigor of their discussions and many interesting observations along the way, Pinker and Bloom never provide a single detailed discussion of this type for a grammatical principle. (Hornstein, 1990, p. 736)[9]

Is the idea of trade-offs among conflicting demands, then a protective device whose use is generally harmful to the testability of selectionist accounts with the tenor of Pinker and Bloom's? Not necessarily. Referring to such trade-offs cannot be harmful if it involves making claims which are testable themselves. Minimally, such claims have to express in a factual modality non-empty assertions about the specifics of the conflicts and trade-offs or compromises which are postulated in explanations of so-called arbitrary features of language. In terms of the stronger requirement of testability-in-practice, there has to be, in addition, some evidence that can actually be brought to bear on the claims about such conflicts, trade-offs or compromises. Neither in their target article nor in their response to critics, however, do Pinker and Bloom give these desiderata any explicit consideration.

This brings us to the second way in which Pinker and Bloom's discussion of Subjacency as an arbitrary feature of language is interesting. Recall that they (1990, p. 717) discuss Subjacency as a "classic example" of a feature that is arbitrary "in the sense that there are alternative solutions that are better from the standpoint of some single criterion". The discussion of Subjacency forms part, however, of a section in which Pinker and Bloom would seem to be addressing criticisms of their selectionist account based on the "putative functionlessness of grammar". Thus, the introductory sentence of the paragraph reads:

In their crudest form, arguments about the putative functionlessness of grammar run as follows ... (Pinker and Bloom, 1990, p. 717, lines 10–12)

But, under the conventional interpretation of "functionlessness", Subjacency is not a functionless feature. Nor, indeed, is Subjacency an instance of a functionless feature in terms of Pinker and Bloom's own discussion of it. In their view, Subjacency has a function but does not serve this function optimally or, in negative terms, is not the best solution from the standpoint of a particular criterion. So even if Pinker and Bloom could provide an adequate explanation of why Subjacency does not serve its function optimally – that is, of why Subjacency is considered "arbitrary" – this explanation would not have any bearing on the threat which (putatively) functionless features pose to their selectionist account. What has happened is that Pinker and Bloom, in the course of their discussion, have made a conceptual switch from a notion of "the (putative) functionlessness of (features of) grammar" to a notion of "the arbitrariness of features of language". As identified in Section 8.3.4 above, the reason for this is that Pinker and Bloom do not distinguish among functionlessness, dysfunctionality and non-uniqueness as distinct forms of form-function "misfit". Instead, they rather lump these forms together under the heading of "arbitrariness". As a result, they create a concept of "arbitrariness" that allows them to make irrelevant use of a case of dysfunctionality – that is, the arbitrariness of Subjacency – to defuse (expected) criticisms couched in terms of (putative) nonfunctionlessness. Harmful to the testability of Pinker and Bloom's selectionist account, then, is their assumption that:

(9) Dysfunctionality and functionlessness represent one and the same form of form-function "misfit", namely arbitrariness.

Recall, in conclusion, that in Section 8.3.3 above it was shown that Pinker and Bloom (1990, p. 717), moreover, use an invalid form of argument to dismiss the threat posed by "putative functionless" features of grammar to their selectionist account.

10.3.2 Built-in arbitrariness. Using "arbitrary" in the sense of "what could have been different", Pinker and Bloom assume that there is a second basis on which the existence of arbitrary features of language can be explained:

(10) The nature of language makes arbitrariness of grammar itself part of the adaptive solution of effective communication *in principle.* (Pinker and Bloom, 1990, p. 718)

Following Liberman and Mattingly (1989), Pinker and Bloom assume that any communication system requires a coding protocol which can be arbitrary as long as it is shared or standardized. This requirement – the so-called requirement of parity – ensures that all the parties using the system are set to the same parity: a standardization which is essential for them to be able to communicate. According to Pinker and Bloom, such standardization is in fact far more important than any other adaptive feature possessed by one party.

Extending this line of thinking to language, Pinker and Bloom assume that:

(11) In the evolution of the language faculty, many "arbitrary" constraints may have been selected simply because they defined parts of a standardized communicative code in the brains of some critical mass of speakers. (Pinker and Bloom, 1990, p. 718)

To illustrate this assumption, Pinker and Bloom refer to Piattelli-Palmarini's observation that there is nothing adaptive about forming *yes-no* questions by inverting the subject and auxiliary as opposed to reversing the order of words in the sentence. But, they (1990, p. 718) maintain, "given that language must do one or the other, it is highly adaptive for each member of a community of speakers to be forced to learn to do it the same way as all the other members".

Pinker and Bloom (1990, p. 718), thus, attempt to reconcile their selectionist account with the existence of arbitrary features by (a) adopting the notion of "built-in arbitrariness" and (b) making assumptions (10) and (11). But how is the testability of their selectionist account affected by these steps? A first point to notice is that these steps cannot be used to reconcile Pinker and Bloom's account with the falsificatory threat posed by (putative) functionless features. These steps, after all, bear on features of grammar that are arbitrary in the sense of "capable of being different", not in the sense of "being without a communicative (or mapping) function".

A second point concerns the epistemological status of assumptions (10) and (11). They are couched in the form of factual claims, which implies that they have to be testable themselves. Pinker and Bloom, however, nowhere consider this implication and it is unclear what empirical evidence would be able to refute (10) and (11). In the case of (9), there is an additional problem, one arising from its modality: the use of *may* severely limits its content. Plugging holes with holes, (10) and (11), accordingly, can only lessen the testability-in-principle of the function claims which they serve to protect. Nothing in the nature of selectionist accounts of the evolution of language compels them, however, to make these assumptions. In other words, these assumptions do not point to a flaw that is inherent to such accounts.

A third point concerns a number of ways in which the concept of "built-in arbitrariness" is explicated insufficiently well by Pinker and Bloom. Their discussion of built-in arbitrariness fails, for instance, to offer explicit answers to questions such as the following:

(12) (a) How much built-in arbitrariness can language "tolerate" before, as a whole, it ceases to show sufficiently many signs of complex design for serving a communicative function?
 (b) How much built-in arbitrariness does language need in order to be sufficiently well standardized (or, equivalently, to meet the requirement of parity)?
 (c) Can (the category of) those features of language that are characterized by built-in arbitrariness be delimited in any way that is not post hoc?
 (d) Is it permissible to claim for any feature of language that it contributes to the standardization of the linguistic code without causing embarrassment to Pinker and Bloom's selectionist account?

The lack of explicit answers to these questions means that the concept of "built-in arbitrariness" can be used in such an unconstrained way that it effectively functions as a device for insulating Pinker and Bloom's selectionist account from the falsificatory threat of arbitrary features. That is, this concept can be used to convert what are false claims about the function of features of language into arbitrary features built into language.

Notice, in conclusion, that Pinker and Bloom's concept of "built-in arbitrariness" also gives rise to questions about the strength of their concept of "adaptation". For example: To what extent is this concept weakened by Pinker and Bloom's allowing built-in arbitrariness to be adaptive? And: Does such weakening entail that language cannot be adapted in the (strong) sense in which a physical structure such as the vertebrate eye is adapted? Or would Pinker and Bloom claim that the vertebrate eye has parts that exhibit a property "akin" to built-in arbitrariness too. Such questions are important in view of Pinker and Bloom's frequent recourse to arguments by analogy in defending their selectionist account, a matter to which we will return in Section 12.2 below.

10.4 CLAIMS ABOUT DESIGN

As noted in Section 8.4.1 above, Pinker and Bloom claim that:

(13) (a) Language shows signs of *design* for a communicative or mapping function. (cf. Pinker and Bloom, 1990, pp. 712, 726, 766, 767)

(b) Each of the many parts of language is *tailored* to the mapping function it serves. (cf. Pinker and Bloom, 1990, p. 713)

Claims (13)(a) and (b) clearly differ in content from claims (14)(a) and (b), respectively.

(14) (a) Language *has* a communicative or mapping function.

(b) Each of the many parts of language *has* a mapping function

In Section 8.4.1 it was noted, moreover, that something can clearly serve a function without having been designed for it. Or, conversely, something could have been designed for a function, yet fails to serve it. These considerations imply that showing that a particular trait was designed for a particular function requires more than showing that it serves that function.

How, then, do these considerations bear on the testability of Pinker and Bloom's claims about the design of language for a communicative function and on their claims about the tailoring of the parts of language for mapping functions? As for the latter claims, consider for the sake of concreteness (15)(a)–(c), which are the "design" equivalents of the function claims (4)(a)–(c).

(15) (a) The major lexical categories of noun, verb and adjective are *tailored* to distinguishing basic ontological categories such as things events or states, and qualities.

(b) Phrase structure rules are *tailored* to providing linear cues about underlying structure, distinguishing, for example, *Large trees grow dark berries* from *Dark trees grow large berries*.

(c) Mechanisms of complementation and control are *tailored* to allowing the expression of a rich set of propositional attitudes within a belief-desire folk psychology, such as *John tried to come, John hopes for Bill to come, John convinced Bill to come*, and so on.

Pinker and Bloom's (1990, pp. 712–721) discussion of "design in language" is problematic in that they conflate function claims and corresponding design/tailoring claims. Since they do not draw a distinction between these two categories of claims, they miss the point that function claims and corresponding design claims cannot be

Testability: a Litmus Test? 133

justified or tested with reference to one and the same body of evidence. The evidence used for justifying or testing the claim that language or a specific part or feature of language serves a particular function is insufficient for justifying or testing the claim that language or the part or feature in question was designed for this function.

Pinker and Bloom do not clarify the general nature and import of the evidence that would be required for testing claims about design or tailoring. What they do attempt is to rebut (anticipated) criticisms to the effect that "the argument for language design" is a "*just-so* story". Such a "story" comprises claims about the function(s) of a structure thought up in a post-hoc, circular way after an examination of the structure. The grounds on which Pinker and Bloom reject the criticism in question include the following:

(16) (a) The claims they make about substantive universals are not "particularly ingenious, contorted or exotic" but "could have been lifted out of the pages of linguistics textbooks". (Pinker and Bloom, 1990, p. 714)

(b) It is "not necessarily illegitimate to infer both special design and adaptationist origins on the basis of function itself. It all depends on the complexity of the function from an engineering point of view". (Pinker and Bloom, 1990, p. 714)

(c) Arguments that language is designed for the communication of propositional structures "are far from logical truths. It is easy to formulate, and reject, specific alternatives". (Pinker and Bloom, 1990, p. 714)

(d) The specific expressive abilities that are designed into language turn out to be "a well-defined set, and do not simply correspond to every kind of information that humans are interested in communicating". (Pinker and Bloom, 1990, p. 715)

(e) Though "these tests are difficult in practice", "convergent evolution, resemblance to man-made artefacts, and direct assessments of engineering efficiency are good sources of evidence for adaptation". (Pinker and Bloom, 1990, p. 715)

Suppose that (16)(a)–(e) are accepted as grounds for rejecting criticisms to the effect that Pinker and Bloom's "argument for design in language" is a "*just-so* story".[10] Does it then follow that these considerations provide evidence which bears on design claims such as (15)(a)–(c) in a way that makes these claims testable-in-principle or even testable-in-practice? What evidence can be derived from or via

(16)(a)–(e) for refuting the claims (15)(a)–(c) in the event that they are false? Pinker and Bloom do not consider questions such as these.

More seriously, they do not seem to be in a position to consider questions such as these. As we have seen in Section 8.4.1 above, Pinker and Bloom claim both that language as a whole was designed for its function and that each of the parts of language was tailored for its function. They do offer certain observations by Boorse (1973) and Cummins (1984) in an attempt to "characterize what is behind intuitions of design" of objects as wholes. Involving the structural heterogeneity and functional unity of such objects, these observations, however, do not carry over to the (tailoring of) their parts. As noted in Section 8.4.2, the test of structural heterogeneity coupled with functional unity cannot be applied to a part of a whole: to do this would be to treat the part as if it were a whole. Pinker and Bloom offer nothing that serves as a clarification of the sense in which individual parts of language could be said to be tailored to their specific function(s). As a consequence, it is not possible to determine what empirical data, if available, would indicate that specific design claims such as (15)(a)–(c) were false. What is clear, however, is that the considerations represented as (16)(a)–(e) cannot be straightforwardly understood as offering such data. We have here a further example of a problem created by the ambivalence of a Pinker and Bloom type of selectionist account. In regard to explanatory focus, it vacillates between the evolution of language as a whole and that of individual parts or features of language. Notions applying to the evolution of language as a whole, however, do not generalize without modification to the evolution of individual parts or features of language.

In sum: serious doubts exist about the testability of claims to the effect that parts of language were tailored to a particular mapping function. These doubts arise from the following two foundational assumptions made by Pinker and Bloom:

(17) (a) It is not necessary to draw from the perspective of testability a distinction between the claim that a particular part of language has a function and the corresponding claim that it was tailored to the function served by it.

(b) The tailoring of the parts of an object involve in essence the same as the design of the object as a whole.

Given these two assumptions, it is dubious that, within Pinker and Bloom's approach, there could be a body of evidence in virtue of which tailoring claims would be testable in principle. Both assumptions (17)(a) and (b), however, are untenable. But neither of these assumptions, has to be made by a selectionist account of language evolution. That is, what is questionable about the tailoring claims expressed in Pinker and Bloom's selectionist account are not necessarily flaws inherent to all selectionist accounts of language evolution.

10.5 CLAIMS ABOUT COMPLEXITY

Pinker and Bloom – we have seen in Section 8.4.2 above – do not attribute "mere" design or "mere" adaptivity to language and the parts or features of language known as substantive linguistic universals. Rather, what they attribute to language and to its parts is *complex* design (1990, p. 726, 767) or adaptive *complexity* (1990, p. 709), respectively. Complexity cannot be reduced to either function or design, which means that Pinker and Bloom's selectionist account incorporates a third category of claims, namely:

(18)(a) claims about the complexity of (the design of) language as a whole (cf. Pinker and Bloom, 1990, p. 709); and

(b) claims about the complexity of (the design of) substantive parts or features of language (cf. Pinker and Bloom, 1990, pp. 771-772).

The question, of course, is this: Can the complexity claims expressed in Pinker and Bloom's selectionist account be considered testable?

In this connection, various BBS commentators, including Lewontin (1990a, p. 740) and Piattelli-Palmarini (1990, p. 753), have commented on the absence of a measure or metric for judging linguistic complexity in an objective way. Pinker and Bloom's response is that:

... we do not need an exact mathematical description of complexity provided intuitive notions can be cashed out in particular cases. (Pinker and Bloom, 1990, p. 767)

This "cashing out", according to Pinker and Bloom, has three "components". One of these is that:

... we must show that intuitive assessments of complexity of design are widely shared among observers and not surreptitiously derived from some favoured explanation for it. (Pinker and Bloom, 1990, p. 767)

In terms of this view of Pinker and Bloom's, evidence for testing the complexity claims expressed by their selectionist account can be derived from intuitions which (certain) scholars have about complexity. This view is problematic, however: although the intuitive judgements which generative grammarians make about linguistic complexity clash with Pinker and Bloom's claims about the complexity of certain substantive linguistic universals, Pinker and Bloom appear unwilling to look upon the latter claims as refuted by the former judgements. Consider in this regard the following remarks by Pesetsky and Block:

Without an agreement on what complexity is supposed to be, the claim has not been sufficiently well formulated to be answerable. The only judgments of complexity we know of are those implicit in modern linguistics. We will argue that if these judgments are taken seriously, P&B's claims are probably false. (Pesetsky and Block, 1990, p. 751)

Elaborating on these remarks, Pesetsky and Block observe that:

Although there is no absolute metric of complexity, we might examine the judgment of linguistics on the *relative* complexity of facts about language. Here, too, it is hard to know how to proceed. By the standards that come to mind, P&B's list of properties stand much closer to the visors (and farther from the eyes) than do the properties commonly studied by linguists. Their properties get scant mention in "linguistic practice" because they (unlike the structure of the human eye) are not complex enough to merit much discussion. (Pesetsky and Block, 1990, p. 751)

In their response to Pesetsky and Block's commentary, Pinker and Bloom (1990, pp. 771–772) do not indicate that they accept the intuitive judgements by generative grammarians which contradict their own complexity claims. By not responding directly to Pesetsky and Block's remarks quoted above, Pinker an Bloom in effect indicate that they consider these intuitive judgements irrelevant, incorrect or flawed in some other way. Since they neither state nor argue this position explicitly, their seeming disregard of the judgements under consideration is obviously harmful to the testability of the complexity claims whose correctness is at issue: this seeming disregard discredits shared intuitive assessments of complexity of design as the only proposed source of evidence for testing complexity claims about the substantive parts or features of language. This, however, does not point to a limitation of selectionist accounts of the evolution of language in general. Proponents of such accounts could (a) accord intuitive judgements of complexity shared by practicing linguists the status of a legitimate source of evidence for testing complexity claims of the kind in question, and (b) give up those complexity claims which conflict with such intuitive judgements as "false". Or they could advance pertinent reasons for disregarding specific intuitive complexity judgements as evidence falsifying specific complexity claims. Complexity claims of the kind in question, therefore, need not be considered inherently untestable.

10.6 Testability Tested

The preceding sections looked critically at Pinker and Bloom's selectionist account of language evolution from the point of view of testability. Recall that this criterion has been adopted by Pinker and Bloom and by other scholars to ensure that accounts of language evolution are not "empty", "vacuous", "irrefutable", "unscientific" or the like. But let us now look critically at this criterion itself. How wise is it to use testability as a litmus test for assigning or denying an account of language evolution the attribute of "being scientific" or "saying something of scientific value"? For various reasons, the answer seems to be "not particularly".

To begin with, the idea that testability is the hallmark of scientific respectability – as it is articulated in for example Karl Popper's falsificationist methodology – is untenable. Thus in his appraisal of this methodology Imre Lakatos (1971, pp. 111–113) has argued that this idea is "falsified" by "basic appraisals of the scientific elite". For example, important ideas of Bohr and Dirac, among others, were not falsifiable in Popper's sense, yet were not for this reason appraised negatively by the "scientific elite" of the time. To reject these ideas out of hand on account of their being "unfalsifiable" would have been extremely unwise. What is more, the history of science offers many counter-examples for the idea that the contribution of a theory to the solution of scientific problems or to the understanding of the world depends primarily on the extent to which it is testable. Galileo made use, for instance, of various means for protecting the Copernican thesis from refutation in a way that was harmful to its falsifiability.[11] In so doing he won some "breathing space", though, for what turned out to be a profound scientific insight.

To be of "scientific value" – it has been argued – an idea or theory accordingly need not be (fully) falsifiable. Indeed, even scientifically worthless ideas can be falsifiable. Thus Larry Laudan (1996, p. 219) points to a range of examples of (bodies of) "crank claims" which are falsifiable in making ascertainably false assertions and, thereby, could lay claim to the attribute of "being scientific/scientifically respectable". As he puts it,—

> ... flat earthers, biblical creationists, proponents of laetrile or orgone boxes, Uri Geller devotees, Bermuda Triangulators, circle squarers, Lysenkoists, charioteers of the gods, *perpetuum mobile* builders, Big Foot searchers, Loch Nessians, faith healers, polywater dabblers, Rosicrucians, the-world-is-about-to-enders, primal screamers, water diviners, magicians, and astrologers all turn out to be scientific on Popper's [falsificationist – R.P.B.] criterion – just so long as they are prepared to indicate some observation, however improbable, which (if it came to pass) would cause them to change their minds. (Laudan, 1996, p. 219)

Falsifiability (of the Popperian brand) fails in Laudan's (1996, pp. 219–220) view to explicate the paradigmatic usages of "scientific" because it is unwilling to link scientific status to any evidential warrant. On older traditions, given ideas or theories had to be worthy of belief in order to be scientific. And assessing the belief-worthiness of ideas or theories requires retrospective judgement of how they stood up to empirical scrutiny and how much evidential support they have. Laudan (1996, p.

220) concludes that, as the basis of a demarcation criterion, falsifiability thus reveals itself a largely toothless wonder, in that it does not serve to explicate the paradigmatic usages of "scientific" (and its cognates) nor does it manage to carry out the crucial chores of stable cleansing that it was originally meant for.

And he (1996, p. 221) argues that it is probably futile to seek a single criterion for distinguishing between what intuitively is considered to be scientific and what is not. The reason for this he finds in the epistemic heterogeneity of the activities and beliefs that are customarily seen as scientific. Thus:

> Some scientific theories are well tested; some are not. Some branches of science are presently showing high rates of growth; others are not. Some scientific theories have made a host of successful predictions of surprising phenomena; some have made a few if any such predictions. Some scientific hypotheses are ad hoc; others are not. Some have achieved a "consilience of inductions"; others have not. (Laudan, 1996, p. 221)

Neither testability nor any of the many other criteria that has been proposed can, in Laudan's (1996, p. 220) view, be a necessary and sufficient condition for something to count as "science" as this term is customarily understood.

So how is one to respond to the insistence by Pinker and Bloom and various other scholars that accounts of language evolution have to be "testable", "falsifiable", "refutable" or the like? First: for the reasons given above, testability – in its various forms – cannot be used as a necessary and sufficient condition for discriminating between accounts of language evolution that are "(of) scientific (value)" and those that are not. Second: what matters is the well-foundedness of such accounts as reflected by a variety of converging considerations. The following are just some of them: (a) the extent to which such an account is supported by empirical evidence, (b) the extent to which it is consonant with (well-founded) ideas or theories proposed in other areas of linguistics as well as such fields as evolutionary biology, palaeontology, neuroanatomy, anthropology and so on, (c) the success with which it has stood up to critical scrutiny, (d) its heuristic fruitfulness, and (e) its conceptual soundness. In this context, Laudan (1996, p. 222) observes that through certain vagaries of history two quite distinct questions came to be conflated. The first of these is, "What makes a belief well founded (or heuristically fertile)?" The second is, "What makes a belief scientific?" In Laudan's view, the first question is interesting and tractable, the second one – to judge by its chequered past – is not.

Pinker and Bloom and other like-minded scholars working on language evolution may, of course, be fully au fait with the problems of assigning to testability the status of a fundamental criterion for "scientific value". But they need to address the issues explicitly. It would be especially ironical if selectionist or other accounts of language evolution were rejected for failing a criterion of scientific respectability that ought not to have been adopted in the first place. Suppose that Pinker and Bloom or others succeeded in overcoming the problems of testability discussed above and elsewhere. Then, of course, they would still have to respond to criticisms to the effect that their account of language evolution is untestable in specific ways. These criticisms – including those offered in Sections 10.3–10.5 above – are, after all, the results of bringing to bear a criterion which they themselves adopt.

11

INDIRECT EVIDENCE

11.1 NEW SOURCES OF DATA

The strategies for alleviating the paucity of factual evidence for accounts of language evolution include one that has at its centre this assumption:

(1) There are various (untapped) sources of data that provide indirect evidence for such accounts.

A first category consists of data which are also of a historical sort. For instance, Wendy Wilkins and Jenny Wakefield (1995) argue from palaeoneurological data for their "scenario" of the emergence in *Homo habilis* of certain preconditions for a Chomskyan language faculty. A second category is made up of data of a nonhistorical sort. Thus, when Steven Pinker and Paul Bloom (1990) put forward their selectionist account of the evolution of a Chomskyan language faculty, the data that they argue from include data about the reliance on lexical association by right-handed people who have a family history of left-handedness. Which brings us to the general question that will be the focus of this chapter: How tenable is assumption (1)?

In order to constitute evidence for or against an account of language evolution, the data of any specific kind have of course to meet certain requirements. Central among these is a requirement of relevance that may be stated in the form of a general question:

(2) Under what conditions are data about phenomena in domain X relevant to the truth of (the claims expressed by) accounts of the evolution of linguistic entities occurring in domain Y?

In what follows, I will go into this question first as it applies to the way in which Wilkins and Wakefield (1995) use palaeoneurological data as evidence for their reappropriationist scenario for the emergence of the neural preconditions for language in *Homo habilis* (Section 11.2). And then as it bears on Pinker and Bloom's (1990) use of nonhistorical data as evidence for certain claims expressed by their selectionist account (Section 11.3). Question (2), of course, came up in the discussion of Calvin and Bickerton's exaptationist theory (Section 7.4.2) and Carstairs-McCarthy's co-optationist scenario (Sections 7.5.3 and 7.5.4).

It perhaps needs to be stressed what the central aim of this chapter is not: it is not to give a critical appraisal of the use of data about phenomena in any specific domain as indirect evidence for or against accounts of language evolution. Positively put, however, this central aim is twofold. On the one hand, it is to show why question (2) applies to the use of any kind of indirect evidence for or against accounts of language evolution. On the other hand, it is the central aim to identify, in so doing, (i) the ways in which foundational assumption (1) is problematic and (ii) a way in which (some of) these problems may be solved. If successful, this analysis should then make it possible to judge how much substance there is to Pinker and Bloom's (1990, p. 727) view that there is a wealth of respectable scientific information that is relevant to the evolution of language but that has not been exploited.

Sections 11.2 and 11.3, in addition, serve to move forward the discussion of questions that have been taken up in earlier chapters. Thus Section 11.2 throws some more light on the nature and limitations of the case which Wilkins and Wakefield have built for their claim that Broca's Area and the POT emerged in *Homo habilis* by a process of reappropriation (see Section 7.3.2 above). And Section 11.3 looks further into the matter of the testability of the claims expressed by Pinker and Bloom's selectionist account about the historical process by which language – or some of its parts – evolved (see Section 10.2 above).

11.2 INDIRECT HISTORICAL EVIDENCE

Central to Wilkins and Wakefield's scenario of the emergence of the neurological preconditions for language – we have seen in Section 7.3.1 above – is the claim that:

(3) The neuroanatomical structures associated with Broca's area and the POT were reappropriated in *Homo habilis* for a new function: that of processing sensory input into conceptual structures that are amodal and hierachically ordered.

Having conceptual structure, in Wilkins and Wakefield's view, is not the same as having language; it does, however, offer the hierarchical ordering necessary for modern syntax and phonology. Wilkins and Wakefield (1995, p. 795), moreover, equate *Homo habilis's* having the reappropriated neuroanatomical structures in question with *Homo habilis's* having the capacity for language. In short, the entity with whose emergence they are concerned is the cognitive entity called "the human language capacity".

Of interest to us is what Wilkins and Wakefield do to justify claim (4), which is:

(4) ... to infer cognitive capacity from admittedly scant information about neuroanatomical structure that can be gleaned from the available (and often) imperfect endocasts. (Wilkins and Wakefield, 1996, p. 795)

An endocast – on Ralph Holloway's (1983, pp. 215, 219) characterization – is a mold of the interior table of cranial bone on which surface details of the cerebral cortex might have been impressed. The resulting impressions appear as bumps or ridges on endocasts of which there are two kinds, natural and artificial ones. Whereas natural endocasts are models of the brain formed by geological processes acting on a skull case, artificial endocasts are generally latex models of the brain molded by scientists with the aid of a fossil skull case.[1]

So what is the paleoneurological evidence adduced by Wilkins and Wakefield for the emergence by reappropriation of the POT and Broca's area? As evidence for the reappropriated POT, Wilkins and Wakefield (1995, p. 171) cite observations which Tobias and Falk made on the basis of an examination of endocasts prepared from the reconstructed skulls of an "individual" of the *Homo habilis* genus and an "individual" of the robust form of *Australopithecus*. In essence: On the basis of fronto-orbital sulcus and overall basic shape, the australopithecine brain is taken to exhibit pongid-like organization. The habiline endocast, in contrast, is believed to reveal distinctive frontal, parietal, and overall shape features that clearly differentiate the brain of *Homo habilis* from that of *Australopithecus*.[2]

Which brings us to the paleoneurological data considered by Wilkins and Wakefield (1995, p. 171–172) to furnish evidence for the emergence of Broca's area in *Homo habilis*. These data, represent observations by Falk to the effect that the australopithecine endocasts in her 1980 study are pongid-like in their overall frontal lobe morphology, and that the Koobi Fora specimen is so in overall shape as well as by fronto-orbital criteria. In contrast, the fronto-orbital sulcus is absent in the Koobi Fora *Homo habilis* brain.[3] These data suggest, according to Wilkins and Wakefield (1995, p. 171), that language-relevant frontal cortex (pars opercularis and pars triangularis) is present in the habiline brain (as a consequence of preferential expansion of the inferior frontal gyrus).

Having furnished what they consider to be "fossil evidence" for the emergence of POT and Broca's area as neuroanatomical structures underlying "language capacity", Wilkins and Wakefield (1995, p. 172) in addition "note" that there is "supporting evidence in the fossil record" that bears on the phenomena of cerebral lateralization and handedness. This evidence is taken to indicate that lateralization and handedness – which Wilkins and Wakefield (1995, p. 172) and others believe to be human traits that are highly correlated with language – first appeared in *Homo habilis* as well. Given the aims of this chapter, however, it is not necessary to go here into the specifics of the "fossil evidence" in question. Of interest to us, rather, are the doubts which have been expressed about whether the paleoneurological data cited by Wilkins and Wakefield do indeed constitute evidence for their claim that the human language capacity or its neuroanatomical substrate emerged in *Homo habilis*.

11.2.1 Doubting the data. What, then, are the reasons why scholars – BBS discussants to begin with – have doubted whether Wilkins and Wakefield's paleoneurological data constitute evidence for the claim that the POT and Broca's area emerged as (pre)linguistic areas in *Homo habilis*? There are essentially two. The first – which has been argued robustly by Holloway in particular – is that the data in question simply don't exist. Thus, as early as 1976 he has maintained that—

... there is no good paleoneurological evidence as yet from the fossil hominid record that either proves or disproves when this or that hominid acquired the capacity for language. (Holloway, 1976, p. 333)

And with reference to the endocast data cited by Wilkins and Wakefield as evidence for the emergence of the POT in *Homo habilis*, Holloway maintains that—

The authors make the "facts" regarding brain endocasts look so clear and simple. Unfortunately, the evidence is fraught with problems, as the following will indicate. Bluntly, the ugly fact is that there is not one single well-documented instance of paleoneurological evidence that unambiguously demonstrates a relative expansion of the parietal-occipital-temporal (POT) junction in early *Homo*. (Holloway, 1995, p. 191)

Holloway (1995, pp. 191–193) justifies this view by raising a number of penetrating questions about the accuracy of the observations by Falk and others from which Wilkins and Wakefield have derived the evidence in question. In their response, Wilkins and Wakefield regrettably make no attempt to counter the technical specifics of Holloway criticisms. Thereby they have done nothing to remove the doubt about whether what investigators claim to have observed in crania of fossil skulls or endocasts is indeed present in them in the form of physical features.

A second doubt is even more interesting. Suppose that investigators were to agree that certain "bumps", "ridges", "bulges", "dimples", "furrows", "impressions" and the like did indeed exist as physical features of particular endocasts or crania. It can then still be doubted whether the data about these features had any bearing whatsoever on claims to the effect that the human language capacity – or its neuroanatomical substrate – did or did not emerge in *Homo habilis* or some other early hominid species. This has actually been done by some BBS commentators, including Elizabeth Whitcombe (1995) and Merlin Donald (1995). For illustrative purposes, it is sufficient to consider here Donald's (1995, p. 188) view that—

> Hominid-like morphology in habiline cranial endocasts does not necessarily imply the presence of language capacity. (Donald, 1995, p. 188)

Much earlier, Holloway has of course maintained in even stronger terms that—

> It must be obvious that paleoneurology, or even the broader study of human origins, paleoanthropology, cannot prove when and how language originated. (Holloway, 1983, p. 105)

It is clear from the context that Donald does not use the expression "necessarily imply" in a strong formal sense; had he done so his view would have been uninterestingly true. Similarly, Holloway does not use "prove" in the technical sense accorded to it in formal logic.

11.2.2 The relevance condition. Why, then, can it be doubted whether paleoneurological data of the kind under consideration are properly relevant to claims about the presence or absence of a human language capacity in *Homo habilis* or some other hominid species? A general reason derives from the fact that fossil skulls and the language capacity belong to different ontological domains: fossil skulls are material entities; the language capacity is a functionally-defined, cognitive entity. Clearly, it cannot be simply assumed or stipulated that physical features of fossil skulls or endocasts correlate in some simple way with properties of the human language capacity. Being the kind of thing they are, fossil skulls or endocasts do not necessarily contain information about cognitive linguistic entities, being the different kind of thing they are. That is to say: nothing at all makes it obvious that data about impressions on the interior of a fossil skull or corresponding bumps or ridges on the exterior of an endocast furnish evidence about the presence or absence of a language capacity located somehow in a brain that was once contained in such a skull. The core of the problem is this: features of fossil skulls or endocasts, which are properties of material entities, and properties of a language capacity, which are properties of a cognitive entity, belong to different ontological domains. And for data about features of material entities to be able to bear on (the truth of) claims about properties of a cognitive entity, the gap between these domains has to be crossed in a nonarbitrary way.

The question, accordingly, is: How have Wilkins and Wakefield dealt with this gap? A reconstruction of their reasoning and of that of some BBS commentators shows that the attempt by Wilkins and Wakefield to cross this gap involves the use of two kinds of devices: inferential jumps and bridge theories. So let us consider the functions and properties of inferential jumps and bridge theories.

11.2.3 Inferential jumps. As is implicit in Wilkins and Wakefield's position quoted in (4) above, they do not attempt to bring paleoneurological data about features of fossil skulls or endocasts directly to bear on claims about the presence or absence of the language capacity. Rather, they take a series of smaller inferential jumps, including the three listed in (5):

(5) (a) From data about certain physical features of fossil skulls or endocasts inferences are drawn about the sulcal pattern of the ancestral brains (that were once) contained in them.
 (b) From the inferences about ancestral brains' sulcal pattern drawn as in (5)(a), further inferences are drawn about the ancestral brains' neuroanatomical organization.
 (c) From the inferences about the ancestral brains' neuroanatomical organization drawn as in (5)(b), further inferences are drawn about the ancestral brains' functional organization in general and about the presence of the language capacity in particular.

Wilkins and Wakefield thus attempt to cross the ontological gap between certain physical features of fossil hominid skulls or endocasts on the one hand and properties – including the property of being present – of the language capacity on the other hand by making the inferential jumps identified in (5)(a)–(c) one after the other. This series of inferential jumps is represented schematically in (6):

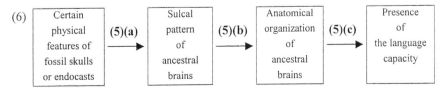

The schema in (6), it should be stressed, offers a reconstructed version of the structure of Wilkins and Wakefield's reasoning; they do not themselves present their reasoning in such an explicit way.

11.2.4 Bridge theories. Which brings us to the question of the validity of the inferential jumps (5)(a)–(c): Why should the individual inferential jumps (5)(a)–(c) be considered valid at all? That is, what are the warrants that license these inferential jumps? This is where the second device mentioned above comes into play. The inferential jumps in question have to derive their validity from (sets of) assumptions which specify how properties of entities of one ontological domain connect with properties of entities of another ontological domain. The different domains of entities are represented by the boxes in (6). An internally coherent set of assumptions which explicitly interlink properties of entities of one ontological domain with properties of entities of another ontological domain functions as a bridge theory. That is, bridge theories are theories about the nature and extent of the covariation of properties of entities which belong to ontologically distinct domains. Underlying – and warranting or licensing – each of the inferential jumps (5)(a)–(c), there ought to be a distinct bridge theory. The question, of course, is whether those bridge theories actually exist.

Consider Wilkins and Wakefield's first inferential jump, (5)(a). To be valid, it has to be licensed by a bridge theory which specifies how impressions on the interior surface of fossil skulls – or corresponding bumps and ridges on the exterior surface of endocasts – covary with sulci on the surface of human brains. Wilkins and Wakefield do not offer such a theory, probably because the correlations in question appear to them to be evident. The same correlations, however, are all but evident to Whitcombe who maintains that—

> An adequate anatomical record of the surface of the hemispheres cannot be read from the endocast because it cannot be written into the inner surface of the skull. Some record of the pattern of events of gyrification may be impressed on the inner table of the growing skull by the pulsatile expansion of the growing brain in normal development up to approximately 10 years of age. In the normal adult, cerebral expansion is buffered by cerebrospinal fluid. Neither the depth nor the ramifications of so conspicuous a landmark as the Sylvian fissure are reflected in the contour of the inner table of the mature cranial vault, still less the pattern of perisylvian gyri, so fundamental to conventional interpretation of language organization (du Boulay, 1965; pers. comm., 1994) (Whitcombe, 1995, p. 204)

Wilkins and Wakefield's response to these remarks is quite instructive:

> ... Whitcombe asserts that the pattern of sulci on the surface of the brain "cannot be read from the endocast because it cannot be written into the inner surface of the

skull". This would seem antithetical to the concerns of Holloway, insofar as there does exist a field of paleoneurology, a field in which he is a primary contributor. We leave the validation of the field as a whole to those who are most familiar with the data. (Wilkins and Wakefield, 1995, p. 218)

These remarks by Wilkins and Wakefield clearly do not offer the bridge theory which is required for licensing the inferential jump (5)(a), i.e., the inference of properties of the sulcal pattern of ancestral brains from data about physical features of fossil skulls or endocasts. Their reference to the "concerns" of Holloway, moreover, is curious since, as we have seen above, he does not believe that there is paleoneurological evidence bearing on the appearance of the language capacity.

Let us turn next to (5)(b), the second inferential jump taken by Wilkins and Wakefield. From (inferences about) the sulcal pattern of ancestral brains, they draw inferences about the neuroanatomical structure of these brains. Specifically, they (1995, p. 161) infer the existence of an "incipient Broca's region" which they (1995, p. 163) locate in the posterior position of the third frontal convolution, lying anteriorly adjacent to the motor cortex. And they infer the existence of the POT which they (1995, p. 161) describe as "a configurationally unique junction of the parietal, occipital, and temporal lobes of the brain". The question, of course, is whether Wilkins and Wakefield have a bridge theory which licences these inferences by specifying how properties of the sulcal pattern of human brains are correlated with features of their neuroanatomical organization. They do indeed offer a theory – to which they refer as "the mechanics of deformation" which function as a bridge theory. Fundamental to this theory is the assumption that—

> The deformational behavior of any solid, including the brain ... is determined by its mechanical attributes, which, in turn are determined in large part by microstructural properties of the material (strength of atomic bonds, packing order of molecules larger constituents, etc.). (Wilkins and Wakefield, 1995, pp. 165–166)

Having presented some specifics of the theory of the mechanics of deformation, Wilkins and Wakefield (1995, p. 166) derive from it the inference license represented as (7):

(7) Systematic shifts in the placement of primary sulci during primate evolution may legitimately be taken to be evidence of systematic shifts in underlying architectonic boundary conditions.

The assumption expressed in (7) is not directly criticized in the BBS discussion; rather, the existence of the kind of sulcal evidence presupposed by (7) is denied – for example, by Holloway:

one of Baldwinian evolution (adding mechanisms useful for marking the new structures with grammatical morphemes and making them more readily processable). (Calvin and Bickerton, 2000, p. 148)

Bickerton's earlier theory, thus, expresses the claim that the emergence of syntax was not a gradual process comprising a series of several events but rather that it took the form of one catastrophic step. In support of this claim, Bickerton presents what he calls "five independent lines of argument". The gist of these lines of argument is that there is no evidence bearing out the expectations created by the "alternative claim", namely that the emergence of syntax was indeed a gradual process comprising a series of several events. These expectations, on Bickerton's construal, are the following:[18]

(11)(a) Cognition evolved (or "grew") gradually over the 2-million-plus years of hominid development (but had virtually no effect on behaviour or technology). (Bickerton, 1998, p. 354)

(b) There should be synchronic varieties of language intermediate between protolanguage and fully developed human language.[19] (Bickerton, 1998, p. 354).

(c) We should find a "stable level" of syntax between "true language" and protolanguage across the wide range of aphasic and dysphasic syndromes, cryptolects, stages of first and second language acquisition and other atypical manifestations of the human language faculty. (Bickerton, 1998, p. 355).

(d) It should not be "beyond human ingenuity" to hypothesize what the intermediate states between protolanguage, the initial stage, and (full) language, the final state would have been like (in the event that these latter stages might have permanently self-destructed and be irrecoverable today). (Bickerton, 1998, p. 355).

(e) The properties that distinguish language from protolanguage must be dissociable in the sense that the existence of one does not depend on the existence of another. (Bickerton, 1998, pp. 355–357)

Let us assume for the sake of argument that Bickerton is right in considering (11)(a)–(e) to be (test-)implications of the claim that syntax emerged gradually in a series of steps. Let us moreover assume, again for the sake of argument, that Bickerton is right in claiming that there is no evidence which bears positively on (11)(a)–(e). Interestingly, then, the lack of such evidence bears negatively also on Calvin and Bickerton's new theory on which syntax developed in two stages. For, given the way in which Bickerton (1998) reasons, this theory has test-implications – or gives rise to "expectations" – which are parallel to those of the theory that the emergence of syntax was a gradual process comprising a series of several events. Thus, on Calvin and Bickerton's theory:

(12)(a) There should be two stages in the evolution of cognition over the 2-million-plus years of hominid development: a first stage of abrupt appearance and a second stage of gradual step-wise evolution. (See (11)(a) above.)

(b) There should be synchronic varieties of language between protolanguage and fully developed human language: one of these varieties should correspond to poorly parsable syntax, the other should represent more parsable levels of syntax that came between poorly parsable syntax – or "language"– at the one extreme and fully parsable syntax – or "true language" – at the other extreme. (See (11)(b) above.)

(c) One should find one or more stable levels of syntax between protolanguage and "true language" across the wide range of aphasic and dysphasic syndromes, cryptolects, stages of first and second language acquisition and other atypical manifestations of the human language faculty. (See (11)(c) above.)

(d) It should not be "beyond human ingenuity" to hypothesize what the intermediate states between poorly parsable syntax – or "language" – and fully parsable syntax – or "true language" – were. (See (11)(d) above.)

(e) The properties that distinguish protolanguage from language – characterized by poorly parsable syntax – and those that distinguish language from "true language" – characterized by fully parsable syntax – must be dissociable. (See (11)(e) above.)

Bickerton, of course, has claimed that there is no evidence which bears out the expectations (11)(a)–(e). But this implies that there is no evidence bearing out the expectations (12)(a)–(e) either. And if there were evidence which bore out the latter expectations, this evidence would automatically bore out some of the expectations created by a theory on which the emergence of syntax was a gradual process comprising a series of several events as well. Calvin and Bickerton, regrettably, do not consider the question of why Bickerton's (1998) "five independent lines of argument" against a theory on which syntax emerged gradually in a series of several events are not "lines of argument" against their new theory as well. It would have been interesting to see how they reconciled the gradualist claims implicit to the role assigned to organic selection with the absence of the evidence in question. The existence of "language", characterized by poorly parsable syntax, should of course

Indirect Evidence 149

... without a lunate sulcus (LS) to delineate primate visual striate cortex (area 17) or even an interparietal sulcus (IP) (posterior end) to suggest where it might have been, there is simply *no* brain endocranial evidence for a POT reorganization in early *Homo*. (Holloway, 1995, p. 191).[4]

In the absence of the required sulcal evidence, the anatomical boundaries assigned by Wilkins and Wakefield to the POT are unclear. For example, Jacobs and Horner (1995, p. 194) find it unclear how much of the superior temporal gyrus is included in the POT, believing as they specifically do that the POT excludes much of Wernicke's area.

As for the third inferential jump, (7)(c): various BBS commentators see it as the most problematic one of the three. To be valid, this jump has to be licensed by a bridge theory which correlates functionally defined cognitive entities with physically demarcated neuroanatomical ones. Wilkins and Wakefield adopt a neurolinguistic bridge theory – a variant of the Wernicke/Geschwind theory – central to which is the following assumption:

(8) Linguistic capacity is localized in the two neuroanatomical areas known as a "Broca's area" and the "POT".[5]

Recall that Wilkins and Wakefield (1995, p. 175) takes the function of the POT to be that of processing human sensory input in association cortex whereby it loses its modality specific character. As for the function of Broca's area, they (1995, p. 175) assume that by virtue of its "influence" on the POT the amodal representations are "subject to hierarchical structuring".[6]

How good, then, is the localizationist neurolinguistic theory adopted by Wilkins and Wakefield for licensing the inferential jump (6)(c), i.e., for inferring functional linguistic organization – and specifically the presence of a language capacity in *Homo habilis* – from the neuroanatomical organization of ancestral brains? This theory has proven to be highly controversial, as is clear from such critical comments as those made by BBS commentators. Consider, for example, the following ones of which the first three express general criticisms and the last three more specific ones:

(9) (a) The functional anatomy of human brains is not known in the sort of detail presupposed by Wilkins and Wakefield's theory. (Jerison, 1995, p. 195; Whitcombe, 1995, p. 204)

(b) Cognitive functions are not "localized" anatomically in the simple way presupposed by Wilkins and Wakefield's theory. (Donald, 1995, p. 188; Lieberman, 1995, p. 198)

(c) There is no reliable neuroanatomical map of the sort required by Wilkins and Wakefield's theory for the association of functions with neuroanatomical areas. (Whitcombe, 1995, p. 204)

(d) Broca's area and the POT have non-linguistic functions too. (Donald, 1995, p. 188).

(e) Linguistic functions are associated with various neuroanatomical areas other than Broca's area and the POT. (Donald, 1995, p. 185; Jacobs and Horner, 1995, p. 194)

(f) Research involving neuroimaging techniques casts doubts on the functions assigned by Wilkins and Wakefield to Broca's area and the POT. (Dingwall, 1995, pp. 187–188)

These comments converge in indicating that Wilkins and Wakefield's inferential jump from properties of neuroanatomical organization to the existence of a language faculty is not warranted.[7] They lack the means – a well-founded neurolinguistic theory – in terms of which data about neuroanatomical organization can be made properly relevant to the truth of claims about (the existence of) an ancestral language capacity.

Under what conditions, then, may paleoneurological data be legitimately brought to bear on the truth of a theory of language evolution which claims for instance that a particular hominid species was the first to have the capacity for human language. From the preceding sections, two general points have emerged. First, the relevance requirement imposes the necessity of bridge theories for licensing or warranting the various inferential jumps that need to be taken to cross the ontological gap between properties of fossil skulls or endocasts on the one hand and properties of the language capacity on the other hand. Second, the strength of such warrants or inference licences depends on the closeness of the correlations – i.e., the strength of the bridges – established by such theories. Cryptically, these are the points that "bridges are a must" and that "bridge strength sets licence strength".

11.3 INDIRECT NONHISTORICAL EVIDENCE

In modern work – it was noted in Section 11.1 above – data of a nonhistorical sort have been offered as evidence for accounts of language evolution as well. This is illustrated by Pinker and Bloom's (1990, p. 721) attempt to show that "what we do know from the biology of language and evolution makes each of the [i.e., Pinker and Bloom's – R.P.B.] postulates [about the process of language evolution – R.P.B.] quite plausible". What they attempt to do in this regard is interesting from the perspective of the conditions that data have to meet to be properly relevant to the truth of the claims expressed by accounts of language evolution. It, moreover, sheds some light on the question of the testability of these "postulates" which represent a fourth category of claims expressed by Pinker and Bloom's selectionist account.[8] So let us take a look at how they argue in attempting to bring data of this sort to bear on the postulates in question.

11.3.1 "Postulates" about the evolution of language. For universal grammar or the initial state of a Chomskyan language faculty to could have evolved by natural selection, Pinker and Bloom (1990, p. 721) assert, it is not enough that "it be useful in some general sense". The actual process by which it evolved must, in addition, have had certain characteristics. About this process, Pinker and Bloom (1990, pp. 721–726) make a number of claims in the form of "postulates" such as the following:

(10) (a) "There must have been genetic variation among individuals in their grammatical competence". (Pinker and Bloom, 1990, p. 721)
 (b) "There must have been a series of steps leading from no language at all to language as we find it …". (Pinker and Bloom, 1990, p. 721)
 (c) "… each step [must have been] small enough to have been produced by a random mutation or recombination …". (Pinker and Bloom, 1990, p. 721)
 (d) "… each step [must have been] useful to its possessor". (Pinker and Bloom, 1990, p. 721)
 (e) "Every detail of grammatical competence that we wish to ascribe to selection must have conferred a reproductive advantage on its speakers". (Pinker and Bloom, 1990, p. 721)
 (f) "… this advantage must be large enough to have become fixed in the ancestral population". (Pinker and Bloom, 1990, p. 721)
 (g) "… there must be enough evolutionary time and genomic space separating our species from nonlinguistic primate ancestors". (Pinker and Bloom, 1990, p. 721)

Before examining the way in which Pinker and Bloom "argue" for these "postulates", it is necessary to get some clarity about the nature of the claims expressed by them. Formulated in a "must be/must have been" modality, these postulates do not express simple historical claims which collectively offer a reconstruction of the actual process by which language evolved. Yet, by observing that "various people" have claimed each of (10)(a)–(g) to be "false" and by defending them against this criticism, Pinker and Bloom (1990, p. 721) indicate that they consider these postulates falsifiable or testable, though they observe that "[t]here are no conclusive data on any of these issues". Let us consider, then, the nature of the data which Pinker and Bloom furnished in defence of postulate (10)(a).

11.3.2 Evidence for genetic variation. One of the criticisms expressed by Philip Lieberman (1989) of Chomskyan universal grammar is that—

> A true nativist theory must accommodate genetic variation. A detailed genetically transmitted universal grammar that is identical for every human on the planet is outside the range of biological plausibility. (Lieberman, 1989, p. 223)

In defence of postulate (10)(a), Pinker and Bloom now claim that—

(11) (a) "... there does exist variation in grammatical ability". (Pinker and Bloom, 1990, p. 721)

(b) "At least some of this variation is ... suspected to be ... genetic ...". (Pinker and Bloom, 1990, p. 721)

In support of (11)(a), Pinker and Bloom assert that—

(12) "... we all know some individuals who habitually use tangled syntax and others who speak with elegance, some who are fastidious conformists and others who bend and stretch the language in various ways". (Pinker and Bloom, 1990, p. 721)

In support of (11)(b), Pinker and Bloom refer to

(13) (a) "... experimental data [collected by Bever et al. (1989) – R.P.B.] showing that right-handers with a family history of left-handedness show less reliance on lexical analysis and more reliance on lexical association than people without such a genetic background." (Pinker and Bloom, 1990, pp. 721–722)

(b) data about "documented genetically transmitted syndromes of grammatical deficits". (Pinker and Bloom, 1990, p. 722)

The argument used by Pinker and Bloom to show that postulate 10(a) is "quite plausible" can be reconstructed schematically as follows, with the arrows representing relations of support:

Indirect Evidence 153

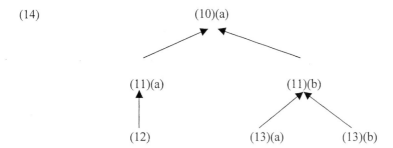

One of the interesting properties of this argument is that the supporting claims and the supported claims are not claims about the same kind of entities or phenomena, i.e., entities or phenomena belonging to the same ontological domain. Thus, postulate (10)(a), the main claim in need of support, expresses an assertion about a property – genetic variation – of entities – the grammatical competence of individuals – that existed at a certain time, namely a time in the past. (Let us refer to these entities as "GC_{past}"). Supporting claims (11)(a) and (b), however, express assertions about a property – genetic variation – of entities – namely, the grammatical ability of individuals – that exist at a different time, a time in the present separated from the former time in the past by tens of thousands of years. (Let us refer to the latter entities as "$GA_{present}$"). What claims (11)(a) and (b) assert about $GA_{present}$ is relevant to what postulate (10)(a) asserts about GC_{past} only if certain assumptions are made about differences and similarities between GC_{past} and $GA_{present}$. These assumptions have to bridge the ontological gap between the properties of GC_{past} and $GC_{present}$ and include the following two:

(15) (a) Though there may be many differences between $GA_{present}$ and GC_{past} – differences caused by processes through which $GA_{present}$ evolved out of GC_{past} – $GA_{present}$ is still identical to GC_{past} in regard to a number of fundamental properties.

(b) Genetic variation is a property in regard to which $GA_{present}$ is identical to GC_{past} and which, consequently, $GA_{present}$ did not acquire in the process by which it evolved out of GC_{past}.

Without making these bridge assumptions – which might look obvious but which are not necessarily true – (11)(a) and (b) do not bear on the truth of postulate (10)(a) at all. I have assumed above that Pinker and Bloom use the expressions "grammatical competence" and "grammatical ability" as synonyms: if this assumption is false, they will have to make additional bridge assumptions warranting an inference from the properties of one entity, namely grammatical competence, to the properties of another, distinct entity, namely grammatical ability.

154 *Unravelling the Evolution of Language*

As for the justification of claim (11)(a): to be able to offer (12) in support of (11)(a), certain bridge assumptions have to be made as well since the respective claims of (11)(a) and (12) do not express assertions about the same kind of entity. (11)(a) expresses a claim about grammatical ability, which (presumably) is the entity also referred to by means of the expressions "grammatical competence" or "tacit knowledge of (the grammar) of language". By contrast, (12) clearly refers to a distinct entity and this distinct entity may be either that known as "linguistic performance" or that known as "the ability to use language". It is not clear which of these two entities Pinker and Bloom have in mind. Within the linguistic ontology developed by Noam Chomsky, linguistic ability in the sense of "linguistic competence", linguistic performance and the ability to use language belong to three distinct ontological domains.[9] And to be able to legitimately bring data about (say) the ability to use language to bear on the correctness of a claim about variation in grammatical competence, it is necessary to make bridge assumptions that warrant the inferential jump in question.

Which brings us to what is involved when the data alluded to in (13)(a) are offered in support of the claim about genetic variation expressed in (11)(b). These data concern that way in which a certain category of people – right-handers with a family history of left-handedness – actually process utterances. The claim, by contrast, asserts something about the nature of the variation in a certain state of an abstract mental faculty. The data are not data about this entity and, as such, are not directly relevant to the correctness of claims about it unless additional assumptions are made. At an appropriate level of specificity, these assumptions have to characterize the way in which a certain kind of processing – the kind engaged in by right-handers with a family history of left-handedness – is systematically interrelated with variation in grammatical ability. Understandably, these additional assumptions must themselves be supported by actual evidence. The gap between the relevant properties of the processing under consideration and those of the grammatical variation at issue, obviously, cannot be bridged in a purely speculative or arbitrary way. The same applies to bridging the gap between the properties of this variation and the properties of the grammatical deficits referred to in (13)(b).

In their defence of postulate (10)(a), Pinker and Bloom do not dwell on the make-up of their argument reconstructed in (14) above. And, even more pertinent, they do not spell out the various bridge assumptions which have to be made in order to bring the data referred to in (12), (13)(a) and (b) to bear, via claims (11)(a) and (b), on the correctness of postulate (10)(a). Their blanket qualification "There are no conclusive data on any of these issues" says very little indeed.

Which brings us to the testability of postulate (10)(a). To show that it is testable in the sense that it can be confronted with data about processing or language deficit,

Pinker and Bloom would have to show what the test-implications are that it has in these domains. And, important, they would have to make clear whether they would consider this postulate falsified, if, for example, data about the processing performed by right-handers with a family history of left-handedness were such that these data contradicted (some of) its test-implications. And, whether they would be willing to consider postulate (10)(a) falsified if there were data about grammatical deficits that clashed with some of its test-implications. If Pinker and Bloom were not willing to assign such processing and deficit data – which in their own view are not "conclusive" – the status of potentially falsifying evidence, it is unclear how it could be maintained that postulate (10)(a) expresses a testable claim. The question which they do not address, of course, is: How can a claim be falsifiable in the absence of (sufficiently) "conclusive data" about the "issue" on which it bears? These considerations apply to Pinker and Bloom's other process postulates – i.e., (10)(b)–(g) – as well.

11.4 BUILDING BRIDGES

Recall now assumption (1), in terms of which there are various (new) sources of data that provide evidence for accounts of language evolution. From the discussion in earlier sections, it is clear that associated with this assumption there is a second one which is submerged in some of the best modern accounts of language evolution:

(16) It is not necessary to show for any specific source of data that it can indeed yield evidence which is properly relevant to the truth of the claims about language evolution on which the data are believed to bear.

In fact, however, assumption (16), holds for only one source of data, namely historical data contained in natural or man-made records of what actually happened in (some phase of the evolution of (some aspect of) language. Assumption (16) is incorrect in the case of all other putative sources of data that may bear on language evolution. On the one hand, there **are not** any man-made records of the kind in question; on the other hand, language **does not** fossilize. Richard Lewontin extends these points to "high cognitive function" in general:

> When we consider other evidence of high cognitive function – language, planning, political organization, technology beyond stone tools – we have absolutely no evidence. (Lewontin, 1990b, p. 239)

Or, as Jerry Fodor (1988, p. 100) puts it: "Cognition is too soft to leave a paleontological record".

To show that data about some phenomenon or entity do provide evidence which is relevant to the truth of claims about some aspect of language evolution one cannot make do with some act of arbitrary stipulation. Rather, good grounds have to be given for taking data about a specific phenomenon or entity to have a bearing on the truth of such claims. The source of such grounds was shown in earlier sections to lie in bridge theories. What is more, Section 11.2.4 establishes two points – "Bridges are a must." and "Bridge strength sets licence strength." – which apply to data of any kind that are thought to be evidence bearing on the truth of claims about what actually happened in language evolution. Consequently, every account of language evolution that expresses such historical claims needs to involve one or more bridge theories in addition to the "theory", "model" or "scenario" of language evolution proposed in it.[10] Yet, even though bridge theories are compulsory as components of (historical) accounts of language evolution, those so far invoked in modern work are on the whole neither well enough articulated nor well enough justified. This means then that, to make significant progress, work on language evolution must begin to include the constructing of better bridge theories.

A last question: Why is it that in so much of modern work on language evolution there is such limited appreciation of the need for well-articulated bridge theories? A reason which suggests itself is that in this work, the distinction among data, facts and evidence is on the whole not upheld in any deliberate way. In brief, here is how this threefold distinction is conventionally drawn. The data about an entity E are bits of raw information about E. Those data that accurately represent what is the case with E are facts about E. Those facts about E that bear on the truth of a claim C about E – or some other entity – are evidence for or against C. In essence, then, facts are data that satisfy a condition of correctness, whereas evidence is a fact or facts that meet a condition of relevance.

If one does not make a clear distinction between data or facts on the one hand and evidence on the other hand, one in effect allows data or facts to acquire automatically the status of "evidence". As a consequence, one is unable to contemplate in a non-accidental way the possibility that data or facts about phenomena in a particular domain could not constitute evidence for claims about phenomena in a different domain. That is, one forfeits the conceptual means of doubting whether data or facts about phenomena in a particular domain are indeed relevant to the truth of claims about phenomena in a particular other domain. Which is to say that one cannot have a problem to whose solution the idea of bridge theories would be pertinent! But, of course, the belief that there is no relevance problem to be solved is a consequence of subscribing to a flawed foundational assumption, namely that—

(17)   Data, facts and evidence are one and the same kind of thing.

This assumption is completely non-restrictive. That is, it does not allow one to discriminate, on the basis of what they are about, between data/facts that are evidence for an account and data/facts that are not evidence for it.[11]

12

NON-EMPIRICAL ARGUMENTATION

12.1 SOME CONSEQUENCES OF EVIDENTIAL PAUCITY

In the target article in which they put forward their selectionist account of language evolution, Steven Pinker and Paul Bloom (1990) have this to say about its goal and conclusion:

> In one sense our goal is incredibly boring [R]. All we argue is that language is no different from other complex abilities such as echolocation or stereopsis [A], and that the only way to explain the origin of such abilities is through the theory of natural selection [N]. One might expect our conclusion to be accepted without much comment by all but the most environmentalist of language scientists [R] ... On the other hand, when two such important scholars as Chomsky and Gould repeatedly urge us to consider a startling contrary position [R], their arguments can hardly be ignored ... Furthermore, a lot is at stake if our boring conclusion is wrong [R]. (Pinker and Bloom, 1990, p. 708)

These remarks illustrate some of the consequences of the paucity of the empirical evidence that bears on accounts of language evolution. Those consequences include the use of arguments in which considerations of a non-empirical sort are brought to bear on claims whose (empirical) correctness is at issue – considerations that are to do with analogy (marked by the "A" that I have added to the passage) and with necessity (marked by the "N"). The consequences also include the use of rhetorical devices (marked by the "R's") for purposes like persuasion and derision.

Sections 12.2 – 12.4 below offer a critical examination of a number of such non-empirical arguments – arguments from analogy, necessity, probability and ignorance. The focus, throughout is on the assumptions – often of an implicit sort – which underpin the use of these arguments. Section 12.5 shows how rhetoric has been used

158   *Unravelling the Evolution of Language*

for the purpose of presenting, justifying, criticizing or defending modern accounts of language evolution. But how does the discussion of this chapter relate to the core finding of the book, namely that a poverty of restrictive theory is the main impediment to progress in work on language evolution? The answer to this question is given in Section 12.6 and in Chapter 14.

12.2   ARGUMENTS FROM ANALOGY

Considerations of analogy are regularly invoked in presenting, justifying and defending modern accounts of language evolution. A good example is the way in which Pinker and Bloom (1990) make use of the vertebrate eye analogy. At the centre of this analogy there is the following assumption:

(1) Language – in the sense of the language faculty – shows signs of design for a communicative function in the same way that the vertebrate eye shows signs of design for the purpose of seeing. (cf. Pinker and Bloom, 1990, pp. 708–210, 712)

This assumption plays a dual role in the case made by Pinker and Bloom for their selectionist account of language evolution. On the one hand, they take it to indicate that—

(2) [l]anguage evolved by the same process, namely natural selection, as the vertebrate eye.

On the other hand, they use assumption (1) as the basis of a test for "blunting" a certain category of criticisms of their selectionist account:
> Among those that attempt to show that the human language faculty is not an adaptation, we ask whether the criteria employed would also rule out the vertebrate eye being an adaptation. (Pinker and Bloom, 1990, p. 765)

In terms of this test, Pinker and Bloom reject a criticism if it is based on criteria by which the vertebrate eye would not be granted adaptation status.

The vertebrate eye analogy, then, takes up a central place in Pinker and Bloom's selectionist account. But how much can it contribute to the case for this account? To be able to answer this question, one has to look for dissimilarities between relevant features of language and of the vertebrate eye. There are two dissimilarities that are of particular significance: the first we inspect directly below; the second we turn to in Section 12.4.

As for the first dissimilarity, recall that Pinker and Bloom (1990, p. 718) start out from the assumption below.

(3) There are arbitrary features built into grammar as part of the adaptive solution of effective communication in principle.

But what about the vertebrate eye? Is it characterized by a similar kind of arbitrariness? Or does this represent a basic way in which language and the vertebrate eye are dissimilar? Pinker and Bloom do not address questions such as these. David Pesetsky and Ned Block, however, draw the following conclusion:

> Though Pinker and Bloom might adopt extreme adaptationism with respect to the eye, they cannot be extreme adaptationists with respect to language. (Pesetsky and Block, 1990, p. 751)

On the characterization by Pesetsky and Block (1990, p. 751), extreme adaptationism is the view that every feature of a system that an engineer might take to be a design feature was shaped by natural selection. When Pinker and Bloom attribute built-in arbitrariness to language, though, they are in fact adopting a weaker view of the adaptedness of language – a view that is referred to by Pesetsky and Block as "strong adaptationism". On this weaker view, many of the most salient features of a system that an engineer might take to be design features were shaped by natural selection. From a selectionist stand, therefore, it is significant that language seems to differ from the vertebrate eye in incorporating arbitrary features. In this dissimilarity, Pinker and Bloom's vertebrate eye analogy breaks down in a major way. The dissimilarity thus places a significant limitation on what the analogy could contribute to the strength of the case for Pinker and Bloom's selectionist account.

Clearly, arguments from analogy depend for their force on a tacit premise that there is a large enough amount of similarity or isomorphism between the entities that are being claimed to be analogical.[1] Pinker and Bloom haven't gone into the requirement involved here; and it is not clear whether they have a non-ad hoc idea about what would and what would not constitute a sufficient measure of similarity between the vertebrate eye and human language for their analogical inference to be properly warranted. The problem with assumption (1), in short, is that it takes for granted some more fundamental assumptions about how similar language and the vertebrate eye should be. And Pinker and Bloom have assumed in an essentially arbitrary way that language is sufficiently similar to the vertebrate eye, a point for which further evidence will be put forward in Section 12.4 below.

12.3 ARGUMENTS FROM NECESSITY AND PROBABILITY

12.3.1 The "onliness" of natural selection. To complement the analogical argument examined above, Pinker and Bloom advance an argument from necessity for their claim that the "physical process" by which language evolved must have been natural selection. In essence, here is how they put that argument [emphases added – R.P.B.]:

(4) (a) It would be natural, then, to expect everyone to agree that human language is the product of Darwinian natural selection. The **only** successful account of the origin of complex biological structure is the theory of natural selection ... (Pinker and Bloom, 1990, p. 708)

(b) All we argue is that language is no different from other complex abilities such as echolocation or stereopsis, and that the **only** way to explain the origin of such abilities is through the theory of natural selection. (Pinker and Bloom, 1990, p. 708)

(c) The essential point is that **no** physical process **other than** natural selection can explain the evolution of an organ like the eye. The reason for this is that structures that can do what the eye does are extremely low-probability arrangements of matter. (Pinker and Bloom, 1990, p. 710)

(d) Natural selection ... is the **only** physical process capable of creating a functioning eye, because the criterion of being good at seeing can play a causal role. (Pinker and Bloom, 1990, p. 710)

(e) Natural selection is not just a scientifically respectable alternative to divine creation. It is the **only** alternative that can explain the evolution of a complex organ like the eye. The reason that the choice is so stark – God or natural selection – is that structures that can do what they do are extremely low-probability arrangements of matter. (Pinker, 1994, pp. 360–361)

For the purpose of further discussion, the core of Pinker and Bloom's argument from necessity may be represented as below:

(5) *Premise 1:* Biological structures that exhibit complex design are extremely low-probability arrangements of matter.

Premise 2: Natural selection is the only physical process that can create complex design manifested in low-probability arrangements of matter.

Premise 3: Language – like the vertebrate eye – exhibit complex design manifested in a low-probability arrangement of matter.

Conclusion: Natural selection is the only physical process that could have created language.

The assumption stated in *Premise 2* of this argument has been questioned by various critics of Pinker and Bloom's selectionist account. Underlying this argument, moreover, there are various general assumptions which have turned out to be controversial; (6)(a) and (b) are two cases in point.

(6) (a) Arguments from necessity can be used for justifying new hypotheses in empirical inquiry.

(b) Low-probability arrangements of matter can be detected straightforwardly in empirical inquiry.

Below, we will be looking first into the criticisms of the assumption expressed in *Premise 2* and in (6)(a) and (b) and then into Pinker and Bloom's response to these criticisms.

12.3.2 "God's-eye" estimate of probability. In the BBS discussion of Pinker and Bloom's selectionist account, both assumptions (6)(a) and (b) are questioned by Massimo Piattelli-Palmarini. With respect to the former assumption, he maintains that—

[a]n explanation through natural selection, just like another scientific explanation, can *only* be a piece of induction. A bet not a necessity. (Piattelli-Palmarini, 1990, p. 753)

Pinker and Bloom, regrettably, do not attempt to show that this view of the status of necessity arguments in empirical science is untenable.

As regards assumption (6)(b), Piattelli-Palmarini argues that Pinker and Bloom incorrectly create the impression that probabilities – as well as complexities – are "sculpted into matter itself", there "for any sane mind to see". His position is that—

[t]he growth of knowledge incessantly leads to probability reassessments and to more nuanced explanations. There is no God's-eye estimate of absolute low-probability, just as there is no God's-eye estimate of an objectively high complexity. (Piattelli-Palmarini, 1990, p. 753)

Piattelli-Palmarini, moreover, maintains that Pinker and Bloom mistakenly proceed as if there were "a universal, objective, interest-independent and background-knowledge-independent probability metric".

In their response to peer commentary, Pinker and Bloom do react to Piattelli-Palmarini's point – also made by Lewontin (1990a, p. 740) – about the way in which the growth of knowledge has caused reassessments of what is (physically) probable. They (1990, p. 767) agree that "the kinds of effects that we view as physically improbable will be revised as our knowledge of physics and development progress". They (1990, p. 767) maintain, however, that complexity of design is not a variable about which there can be a physical law. Their remarks on the matter are as follows:

Complexity of design is not a variable that there can be a[n as yet undiscovered – R.P.B.] physical law about. It depends crucially on events at much higher levels of interaction involving the internal and external environments. It is simply not reasonable to expect that some currently unknown chaotic process will result in the formation of transparent lens-shaped tissue just in case it is in front of a light-sensitive diaphragm (as opposed to behind the kneecap) or in the formation of fin-shaped structures just for systems that develop in trees. (Pinker and Bloom, 1990, p. 767)

It is not clear how these remarks by Pinker and Bloom are meant to counter Piattelli-Palmarini's criticisms. These remarks, moreover, presuppose that Pinker and Bloom's articulation of the concept of "complex design" is unproblematic and that their vertebrate-eye analogy has sufficient force. Both of these presuppositions, however, are questionable, as has been shown in earlier sections.[2]

12.3.3 "Ultra-Darwinism". The assumption – expressed in *Premise 2* of the necessity argument (5) – that natural selection is the only physical process that can create complex design has been challenged by various scholars. For example Noam Chomsky, referring to the notion of "good design", has criticized this assumption as follows:[3]

> Natural selection can't work in a vacuum; it has to work within a range of options, a structured range of options; and those options are given by physical law and historical contingency. The ecological environment is in a certain state and it is going to impose constraints: you could imagine a planet in which you have different ecological conditions and things would work in a different way. So, there are contingencies and there's physical law and within that range natural selection finds its way, finds a path through it; but it can never be the case that natural selection is acting on its own ... When you read these excited pronouncements about "show me good design and I'll find natural selection," ... "God or natural selection" – taken literally, it's worse than Creationism. (Chomsky, 2000, p. 22)

Chomsky (1997, 2000, p. 22) judges the "either or" view of evolution – "God or natural selection" – to the both incoherent and irrational. It is "incoherent" in assuming that some selectional process can take place in a vacuum – that is, outside a physical channel. And it is "irrational" in that it assumes that the evolution of everything or every property of an organism can be explained in terms of natural selection.[4] The question, according to him, is this: To what extent is the channel functioning to determine the output? It has to be more than zero and in some cases it may approach 100%, in Chomsky's view.[5]

The view that all aspects of organismic design could be explained satisfactorily through natural selection alone has been dysphemistically referred to by Niles Eldredge (1995, p. 36) as "ultra-Darwinism".[6] Darwin, it is often pointed out, did not hold this view. Steven Gould (1998, p. 25) is "confident", for instance, "that Darwin would have eschewed ultra-Darwinism", believing that Darwin was "in near despair" when he wrote as follows in the last edition of *The Origin of Species*:

> As my conclusions have lately been much misrepresented, and it has been stated that I attribute the modification of species exclusively to natural selection, I may be permitted to remark that in the first edition of this work, and subsequently, I placed in a most conspicuous position – namely at the close of the Introduction – the following words: "I am convinced that natural selection has been the main, but not the exclusive means of modification." This has been of no avail. Great is the power of steady misinterpretation. (Darwin, 1872, pp. 25–26)

Over the years, various factors – in addition to physical law, historical contingency and natural selection – have been claimed to play a role in the evolution of organisms, co-determining their properties.[7] In fact, as those opposed to "ultra-Darwinism" see it, "the real task" of giving a scientific account of some evolutionary phenomenon is to tease out the relative contributions of all the factors at work – "genetic, physical, developmental, or whatever, including natural selection". (Jenkins 2000, p. 185)

12.3.3.1 Professing pluralism. This brings us to Pinker and Bloom's response to the criticism that they hold an "ultra-Darwinian God or natural selection" view of the evolution of language. In essence, there are two sides to this response. First, they deny that they believe that natural selection is the only factor involved causally in the evolution of language. Here is how they put it:

> Although Chomsky does not literally argue for any specific evolutionary hypothesis, he repeatedly urges us to consider "physical laws" as possible alternatives to natural selection. But it is not easy to see exactly what we should be considering. It is certainly true that natural selection cannot explain all aspects of the evolution of language. But is there any reason to believe that there are as yet undiscovered theories of physics that can account for the intricate design of natural language? (Pinker and Bloom, 1990, p. 720)

In a more general vein, there is also the response by Pinker to Gould's (1997b, p. 50) claim that "the much publicized doctrine" of evolutionary psychology has fallen into the "ultra-Darwinian trap". In that response, Pinker has this to say.

> Gould claims his targets [i.e., "ultra-Darwinians" – R.P.B.] invoke selection to explain everything. They don't. Everyone agrees that aspects of the living world without adaptive complexity – numbers of species, nonfunctional features, trends in the fossil record – often need different kinds of explanations, from genetic drift to wayward asteroids. So, yes, we all should be, and are, pluralists. (Pinker, 1997a, p. 55)

In turn, however, Gould (1997c, p. 57) rejects Pinker's denial that evolutionary psychology is "ultra-Darwinian", arguing that Pinker (still) fallaciously equates complex design with complex adaptive design. "Complex design", Gould (1997c, p.

57) points out, "forms a much broader category than adaptive design – and has many other potential evolutionary causes".[8]

12.3.3.2 Improbable complexity. In the paragraph just above, mention was made of a second side to Pinker and Bloom's response to Premise 2 of the necessity argument (5). In this side of their response, they argue that what is to be explained by an account of the evolution of language – as by one of the vertebrate eye – is not that it exhibits signs of **good** design. Rather – as they (1990, p. 766) emphasize – it is that it exhibits signs of **complex** design. For the complexity of this design to have come about by some process other than natural selection is, as they see it, quite improbable. Pinker argues in like vein when he responds to Chomsky's view that factors other than natural selection – physical laws, in particular – could have played an important role in the evolution of complex biological structures. He puts it like this.

> ... structures that can do what the eye does are extremely low-probability arrangements of matter. By an unimaginably large margin, most objects thrown together from generic stuff, even generic animal stuff, cannot bring an image into focus, modulate incoming light, and detect edges and depth boundaries. (Pinker, 1994, pp. 360–361)

Pinker responds, too, to Chomsky's view that a physical law, namely gravity, acting on mass can be invoked to explain why flying fish fall back into the ocean. Here, he argues as follows:

> Gravity alone may make a flying fish fall into the ocean, a nice big target, but gravity alone cannot make bits of flying fish embryo fall into place to make a flying fish eye. When one organ develops, a bulge of tissue or some nook or cranny can come along for free, the way an S-bend accompanies an upright spine. But you can bet that such a cranny will not just happen to have a functioning lens and a diaphragm and a retina all perfectly arranged for seeing. It would be like the proverbial hurricane that blows through a junkyard and assembles a Boeing 747. (Pinker, 1994, p. 361)

Extending this line of reasoning to the evolution of language, Pinker maintains that—

> [i]f language is a complex system involving many finely interacting parts that collectively do something interesting (as Chomsky himself has shown), then by the laws of probability you would not expect one random mutation to give some fortunate ancestor all of the necessary neural modifications in one thunderclap. (Pinker 1997b, pp. 115–116)

It is clear that the argument from necessity by Pinker and Bloom depends crucially on probability considerations. This is interesting, for it means that in fact they are arguing in terms of a notion of "qualified necessity".

So what is the upshot? Is Pinker and Bloom's argument from necessity (5) undermined, then, by the view that there are various factors that can contribute to "good design" or "eminently workable design"? Not inevitably. It depends on whether they can draw a principled distinction between "good design" or "eminently workable design" and "complex design". It may be, after all, that factors that contribute to the former kind of design do not automatically contribute to the latter kind of design as well. But, as has been shown in Section 8.4 above, Pinker and Bloom have not succeeded in giving a satisfactory characterization of what complex design may involve in the case of language. Their defence of the claim that natural selection is the only physical process that can create complex design depends, moreover, on various probability considerations which – even if correct – weaken the notion of necessity which enters into their argument. The first of these probability considerations, as was noted above, embodies the controversial assumption that probabilities are "sculpted into matter itself" and "are there for everyone to see". The second one involves the idea that it is highly improbable that factors other than natural selection can create design of a complex kind. In addition, as the analysis by Lyle Jenkins shows, the alleged analogy between the creation of the flying-fish eye and the assembly of a Boeing 747 breaks down:

> Neither the flying fish eye nor the language faculty arose full blown, analogous to a Boeing 747 being assembled from junk, by either natural selection or a hurricane. This is because neither natural selection nor other physical, genetic and developmental constraints act apart from one another, but only through intricate mutual interactions, as played out in evolution. (Jenkins, 2000, p. 190)

Finally – and very much to the point for our concern with non-empirical arguments – an argument from ignorance has been put forward in support of the view that complexity of design need not have arisen through natural selection in the case of cognitive systems. We turn to this argument directly below.

12.4 ARGUMENTS FROM IGNORANCE

Jerry Fodor (1998, pp. 208–209, 2000, pp. 87–89, 2001, pp. 627–628) has put forward an interesting argument from ignorance against the view that "there is no way except evolutionary selection for nature to build a complex adaptive system".[9] He (1998, p. 208) suggests that there is indeed an alternative to natural selection as a source of complexity of cognitive systems. This is so because, according to him, it is common ground that the evolution of our behaviour was mediated by the evolution of our brains. As a consequence, what matters in the question of whether the mind is an adaptation is not how complex our behaviour is. Rather, in Fodor's view, what matters is how much change in an ape's brain would have been required to produce the cognitive structure of a human mind. And, he maintains,—

> ... about this, exactly nothing is known. That's because nothing is known about how the structure of our minds depends on the structure of our brains. Nobody even knows *which* brain structures our cognitive capacities depend on. (Fodor, 1998, p. 208)

Fodor (1998, p. 209) points out too that, unlike our minds, our brains are, by any gross measure, very similar to those of apes. This shows, he takes it, that relatively small alterations of brain structure must have brought on large behavioural discontinuities in the transition from ancestral apes to us. And, if that is so, Fodor (1998, p. 209) asserts, then "... you don't have to assume that cognitive complexity is shaped by the gradual action of Darwinian selection on prehuman behavioral phenotypes".

In an alternative, but equivalent, formulation of his Fodor puts it like this:

> Since psychological structure (presumably) supervenes on neurological structure, genotypic variation affects the architecture of the mind only via its effect on the organization of the brain. And, since nothing at all is known about *how* the architecture of our cognition supervenes on our brains' structure, it's entirely possible that quite small neurological reorganizations could have effected wild psychological discontinuities between our mind's and the ancestral ape's. This really is *entirely* possible; we know nothing about the mind/brain relation with which it is incompatible". (Fodor, 2000, p. 89)

Fodor (2000, p. 89) emphasizes two points that are of interest here. First point: Darwinism can work only if or only where there is some organic parameter in the case of which small, incremental variations produce corresponding small, incremental variations in fitness. Second point: according to Fodor, it is "entirely unknown" whether alterations to brain structures and alterations to cognitive structures meet this condition of incremental linearity.

Analogies in which the evolution of cognitive structures such as language is likened to that of "organic" structures break down in respect to the condition of incremental linearity. Fodor puts the point as follows:

> Analogies to the evolution of organic structures, though they pervade the literature of psychological Darwinism, actually don't cut much ice here. Make the giraffe's neck just a little longer and you correspondingly increase, by just a little, the animal's capacity to reach the fruit at the top of the tree. So it's plausible, to that extent, that selection stretched giraffe's necks bit by bit. But make an ape's brain just a little bigger (or denser, or more folded, or, who knows, grayer) and it's anybody's guess what happens to the creatures' behavioral repertoire. Maybe the ape turns into us. (Fodor, 1998, p. 209)

It is clear that Fodor's view of the way in which the evolution of cognitive structures differs from that of "organic" structures has a direct bearing on the soundness of the vertebrate eye analogy – examined in Section 12.2 above. It is a view, after all, that points to yet another nontrivial dissimilarity between (the) language (faculty) and the vertebrate eye. This, in turn, weakens the associated argument by analogy still further.

The purpose of Fodor's argument from ignorance is, of course, to undermine Pinker and Bloom's assumption that natural selection is "the only way" to build complex adaptive structures (or complex design). In the case of language, that assumption is bound up with the following, more fundamental, compound one:

(7) In the evolution of the brain there is a parameter that is characterized by small, incremental, variations. These cause the complexity of (the) language (faculty) to increase by small increments. These, in their turn, cause small increments in (behavioural) fitness.

Assumption (7) is dubious because of our ignorance of how the structure of humans' minds depends on the structure of their brains. Fodor's argument from ignorance is supplemented by an implausibility argument. That is, in terms of what is known (a) about the differences between humans' brains and apes' brains and about (b) the associated differences between humans' cognitive structures, and apes' cognitive structures, it is not plausible for there to be a parameter of the sort referred to in assumption (7). As Fodor (1998, p. 209) puts it: "Unlike our minds, our brains are, by any gross measure, very similar to those of apes". Ignorance, of course, is something that is being chipped away at all the time, as is evidenced by the history of scientific inquiry. This means that Fodor's argument from ignorance could lose its power overnight.[10]

The reasoned nature of Fodor's argument from ignorance makes it one of the better arguments of its kind to have been offered for or against claims about language evolution. To bring this out more clearly, let us compare the argument by Fodor with the following one by Chomsky for the nongradual emergence of features of language [emphasis added – R.P.B.].

> These skills [e.g., learning a grammar or the ability to handle the mathematical system – R.P.B.] may well have arisen as a concomitant of structural properties of the brain that developed for other reasons. Suppose that there was selection for bigger brains, more cortical surface, hemispheric specialization for analytic processing, or many other structural properties that can be imagined. The brain that evolved might well have all sorts of special properties that are not individually selected; there would be no miracle in this, but only the normal workings of evolution. **We have no idea at present, how physical laws apply when 10^{10} neurons are placed in an object the**

size of a basketball, under the special conditions that arose during human evolution. (Chomsky, 1982b, p. 321)[11]

Chomsky's argument is similar to Fodor's in that both are based on the assumption that nothing is known about a specific state of affairs. The two arguments differ, though, in a significant way. Fodor sets out some considerations – relating to differences between humans and apes – which make it plausible that what could be discovered about the way in which minds depend on brains would support his questioning of the view that natural selection is "the only way" for nature to build complex adaptive design. Chomsky, however, does not offer any analogous considerations as to whether what might be discovered about neuron packaging would support his view on the role of physical constraints in the evolution of language. Clearly, arguments from ignorance do not all have the same force.

12.5 RHETORIC

There are non-accidental reasons why rhetorical devices are used in discussions on questions of language evolution. First, and above all, there is – as we have seen – the paucity of the empirical evidence that is properly relevant to the truth of the claims made by accounts of language evolution. Second, the use of rhetoric is favoured by the limited extent of the power that inheres in arguments from general non-empirical considerations such as – for instance – analogy, necessity, probability and ignorance. Third, questions about human evolution continue to be highly "politicized", as pointed out by Fodor (2000, p. 90). As he sees it, this explains why "pretty appalling" arguments about psychological Darwinism are so widely influential. But now, for illustration, let's have a look at some instances of the rhetorical means that have been used in recent discussions of language evolution.

A first example is to be found in the use that Pinker and Bloom make of the expression "(incredibly) boring" when they argue for their claim that natural selection is "the only way" to explain the origin of a complex ability such as language. Their "goal" in arguing for this claim they (1990, p. 708) characterize as "incredibly boring". And the conclusion of their argument they (1990, p. 708) portray as "boring" as well. Pinker and Bloom's use of the expression "(incredibly) boring" has evoked the following response from Piattelli-Palmarini:

> This rhetoric is suspicious, because it can be anything but "boring" to discover that "the only way" to explain the origins of a structure (in this case the central properties of UG) is by applying a doctrine that went out of its way (and often out of its depth) to deny the very meaningfulness of the search for that structure. Those of us who are familiar with the rhetoric, and the (otherwise excellent) writings of Richard Dawkins

(notably in Dawkins, 1983, 1986), from whom Pinker and Bloom have derived much inspiration, will recognize the ploy. "Boredom" is caused by the impression these authors have of arguing for the recognition of a *necessary* truth. Because they maintain that for any sane and unprejudiced mind the process of natural selection is the only explanation of "extremely low-probability arrangements of matter" (Pinker and Bloom, after Dawkins, Section 2.2, par. 3), those who resist the inevitable appear to them as boringly irrational. (Piattelli-Palmarini, 1990, pp. 752–753)

The expression "(incredibly) boring" is by no means the only rhetorical device used by Pinker and Bloom. To give just two more examples: within a single short passage, they (1990, p. 710) speak of a certain margin as being "unimaginably large" and dismiss a certain idea as being "absurdly improbable".[12]

As regards the use of rhetoric in the BBS debate, it is not possible to draw a distinction between "nonselectionist good guys" and "selectionist bad guys". Thus Carlos Otero (1990, pp. 745–750), an outspoken defender of Chomsky's non-selectionist conception of language evolution, diagnoses Pinker and Bloom's views of the interaction between "nature" and "nurture" as "an unfortunate regression ... to the environmentalism of Rousseau's Hobbesian discussion of the origin of language back in 1755", "[a] cultural regression [which] is anything but small". And he concludes his commentary by observing that:

> The target article offers abundant proof that along some dimensions the intellectual advance of the last 20 years, at least in some quarters, has not been that spectacular. (Otero, 1990, p. 750)

Responding to Otero's charge that Descartes, Goethe, and Humboldt would have been dismayed by their article – because it would have put them in mind of the ideas of Aristotle, Rousseau, and Hobbes – Pinker and Bloom (1990, p. 770) sarcastically "admit that we have no defense against these criticisms".

Turning now to rhetorical devices of a different sort, recall that in Chapter 10 we looked into the way in which a testability condition has been used in an attempt to draw a distinction between work on language evolution that is of "scientific value" and work that isn't. Notions of "testability", "falsifiability" or "refutability" may also, however, be used for purely rhetorical purposes alone. In this regard, Laudan (1996, p. 217) points out that demarcation criteria are typically used by rival camps as *machines de guerre* in polemical battles over the scientific status of ideas or theories:

> It is well known, for instance, that Aristotle was concerned to embarrass the practitioners of Hippocratic medicine, and it is notorious that the logical positivists wanted to repudiate metaphysics and that Popper was out to "get" Marx and Freud. (Laudan, 1996, p. 217)

In each of these cases, Laudan maintains, the "attacking" scholars used a demarcation criterion of their own devising as a means to discredit their opponents.

The quotations given in Section 10.1 above clearly show how selectionists and nonselectionists have been faulting one another for holding ideas or proposing accounts which are branded "untestable", "non-falsifiable", "utterly indefensible", "irrefutable" and the like. Pinker and Bloom, for example, have made the following charge:

> Nonadaptationist accounts that merely suggest the possibility that there is some hitherto-unknown law of physics or constraint on form – a "law of eye-formation", to take a caricatured example – are, in contrast [to adaptationist accounts – R.P.B.], empty and nonfalsifiable. (Pinker and Bloom, 1990, p. 711)

And here is Piattelli-Palmarini, "returning" the "compliment":

> They [i.e., Pinker and Bloom – R.P.B.] manage to render this approach utterly indefeasible (this is not meant to be a compliment ...) (Piattelli-Palmarini, 1990, p. 754)

The condition of testability, of course, was not "devised" by Pinker and Bloom or by Piattelli-Palmarini to get at one another. But one cannot fail to notice how they use it as a polemical *machine de guerre* in conjunction with caricature and such turns of phrase as "manage to", "not meant to be a compliment" and so on.

The use of the rhetorical devices in question is symptomatic of the relative poverty of the objective means that are available for presenting, justifying, criticizing or defending accounts of language evolution.[13] Fortunately, many of the scholars working on this topic refrain from the use of such non-objective means – a line of conduct by which they make a notable contribution to the respectability of modern work on language evolution.

12.6 ARGUMENT CLUSTERS

Non-empirical arguments are typically used in clusters for the purpose of justifying, criticizing or defending accounts of language evolution. Thus in support or defence of their selectionist account, Pinker and Bloom have combined arguments from analogy, necessity and probability. It may accordingly be maintained that what matters is not how strong each of the individual arguments is. What counts, rather, is the power of a cluster of interlinked arguments. That is, whereas the arguments making up a cluster might individually not be particularly strong, collectively they could add up to a cluster that gave a considerable measure of support for a specific account or claim. This would be a valid point if the way in which the individual arguments in a cluster relate to one another were taken into consideration.

Consider a simple case in which two arguments, A and B, form a cluster that is being put forward for or against a claim, C. A and B may, in principle, relate to one another in one of two ways: they may either complement or supplement one another. In the case of complementation – shown schematically as (8) – A and B offer independent, but converging, considerations for or against C.

(8)   Claim C

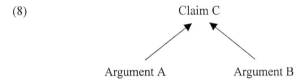

        Argument A   Argument B

In the case of supplementation, by contrast, A and B do not both bear directly on C. Rather, the function of the one (say B) is to support a claim representing a premise of the other (say A). Schematically, the second way in which A and B may be interrelated can be shown as below:

(9)   Claim C

        Argument A

        Argument B

In assessing the power of a cluster of arguments for or against a specific claim about language evolution, it is crucial to determine how the constituent arguments hang together. If they are interlinked in terms of complementation, the cluster as a whole will bear more strongly on the claim in question than any of the constituent arguments. If, however, the individual arguments form a chain in which some have the function of providing justification for premises of others, the cluster will be as strong as its weakest component.

This may be illustrated with reference to Pinker and Bloom's argument from necessity – represented above as (5) – for the claim that natural selection is the only physical process that could have created language. Invoking a consideration of necessity, this argument appears to furnish powerful support for the claim under consideration. However, as shown in Section 12.3.3.2, *Premise 1* of this argument – let us call it A – requires support from further arguments – let us call them B, C and D – which invoke considerations of probability and analogy. These considerations, we have seen, are all controversial. Collectively, arguments A (that is, (5)), B, C and D accordingly do not make up a cluster which is powerful in that it furnishes converging, complementing considerations for the claim that natural selection is the only physical process that could have created language. Rather, A is the only argument bearing directly on this claim and one of its premises requires support from supplementing arguments all of which are relatively weak. In sum, what matters is not the sheer number of the (non-empirical) arguments for or against a specific claim about language evolution. Rather, it is the way in which the various arguments are interlinked. And, if they are interlinked in terms of supplementation, it is the power of the weakest individual supplementing argument that matters.

What matters ultimately, of course, is whether the concepts of "analogy", "necessity", "probability" and "ignorance" that underpin such non-empirical arguments are characterized in a sufficiently restrictive way. If they were, it would be possible to make judgements such as the following in a non-arbitrary way:

(10)(a) Argument W can be properly accorded the status of "argument from probability".
   (b) Argument X cannot be properly accorded the status of "argument from necessity".
   (c) Argument Y is a strong argument from ignorance.
   (d) Argument Z is a weak argument from analogy.

On the whole, however, the concepts of "probability", "necessity", "ignorance" and "analogy" that are invoked in work on language evolution are of an intuitive sort. That is – as we have seen in earlier sections – they do not articulate the considerations which are required for any systematic justification of discriminating judgements such as (10)(a)–(d).

13

PLAUSIBLE EVOLUTIONARY STORIES

13.1 INTRODUCTION

In the absence of sufficient evidence about what actually happened in the evolution of a biological entity, some scholars resort to telling stories or creating fables about what might have happened there. These stories have been referred to as "evolutionary stories", "plausible stories" or "adaptive stories". They have also been called by a derogatory name, "*Just-so* stories". This reflects the judgement that what they do is to account for the evolution of an entity or trait by making use of natural selection in a facile way.

There are accounts of the evolution of language that have been made out to be (or to tell) *Just-so* stories. Two prime examples are Steven Pinker and Paul Bloom's (1990) selectionist account and Noam Chomsky's (1998) abstraction of instantaneous language evolution. The present chapter goes into the question of how plausible – "not plausible (at all)", "(only) just plausible", "highly plausible", "(not) more implausible (than)" – these two "stories" are. And it puts forward an assessment of their (potential) contribution to work on language evolution. It does this in Sections 13.3 and 13.4 against the backdrop of Section 13.2, where the nature of *Just-so* stories is first characterized in general terms. The findings of this chapter are related in Chapter 14 to those of the other chapters of Part III.

13.2 *JUST-SO* STORIES

As noted by Niles Eldredge (1995, p. 41), the expression "*Just-so* story" or "*Just So* Story" was originally used by Rudyard Kipling to refer to his fables or narratives recounting how the elephant got its trunk, the rhino its wrinkly skin or the leopard its spots. The expression has in addition been used to refer to the explanations given by Voltaire's Dr Pangloss of why things are as or where they are, have the purpose that they do have and so on. According to one of Dr Pangloss's stories, for example, "[e]verything is made for the best purpose. Our noses were made to carry spectacles, so we have spectacles". And – to give one more example – referring to the great Lisbon earthquake of 1755, Dr Pangloss pronounces: "All this is a manifestation of the rightness of things, since if there is a volcano at Lisbon, it could not be anywhere else. For it is impossible for things not to be what they are, because everything is for the best".

As stories about the evolution of biological entities, *Just-so* stories have, on Eldredge's analysis, two main ingredients: an account of how some structure works and a "homily" about its evolution by natural selection:

> A study of how some structure works was followed by a flat-out assertion that the complex functioning of structures are carefully fashioned through natural selection. For instance, a woodpecker manages to blast into a tree with such rapidity and force without scrambling its brains because the bones and muscles of a woodpecker's head are built through natural selection precisely to avoid brain scrambling. The functional anatomical analysis would often be elegant, but the evolutionary homily at the end, presented as a "conclusion", was in reality nothing but a statement of the underlying assumptions brought to the research in the first place. (Eldredge, 1995, p. 41)

The criteria for appraising such evolutionary stories are relatively lax. Thus, according to Eldredge, there are only two in the case of evolutionary biology:

> Plausibility and consistency with the basic tenets of population genetics provide the sole criteria for evaluating these historical reconstructions. In the typical just-so evolutionary tale, there was little of the "rigor" justly so revered by scientists. There was no way, in other words, to verify the truth of any version – to test the hypothesis. (Eldredge, 1995, p. 42)

On some analyses, the criteria for such stories are even less strict. Stephen Gould and Richard Lewontin (1979, p. 588), for example, remark in this regard that "[o]ften evolutionists use *consistency* with natural selection as the sole criterion and consider their work done when they concoct a plausible story". The criterion of "having to be plausible", moreover, has on occasion been weakened to "having to be not less plausible than" or "having to be not more implausible than", as will be shown in Section 13.4.6 below. From this it follows that evolutionary stories are not all equally good or equally bad. Their merit co-varies with the number, variety and strictness of the criteria they meet. This is why, at the one end of the spectrum there may be *Just-so* stories of the crudest Panglossian kind, while, at the other end, there may be evolutionary stories that are (much more) highly plausible. In fact, since plausibility considerations take up so central a place in their assessment, the evolutionary stories at issue could have been discussed under the heading of "arguments from plausibility" in the preceding chapter. They are dealt with separately here, however, in view of the special status that they have acquired in the technical literature.

13.3 PINKER AND BLOOM'S SELECTIONIST "STORY"

13.3.1 Some charges. The label of "*Just-so* story" has been used, as Pinker and Bloom observe, to ridicule adaptationist accounts of the evolution of cognitive entities:

> In many discussions with cognitive scientists, we have found that adaptation and natural selection have become dirty words. Anyone invoking them is accused of being a naive adaptationist, or even of "misunderstanding evolution". Worst of all, such a person is open to easy ridicule as a Dr. Pangloss telling Just-so stories! (Premack's 1986 reply to Bickerton, 1986, is typical). (Pinker and Bloom, 1990, pp. 710–711)

Pinker and Bloom (1990, p. 711) hold, however, their selectionist account is not a *Just-so* story, since it is "testable in principle and in practice". And, with reference to specific selectionist proposals they comment as follows:

> Supplementing the criterion of complex design, one can determine whether putatively adaptive structures are correlated with the ecological conditions that make them useful, and, under certain circumstances, one can actually measure the reproductive success of individuals possessing them to various degrees ... . (Pinker and Bloom, 1990, p. 711)

It would seem, though, that not everyone agrees with Pinker and Bloom's view of the epistemological status of their selectionist account.

In a recent review of a collection of papers on evolutionary psychology, for example, Jerry Fodor maintains in a general vein that[1] —

> I'm aware that nothing that I say about this book (or about anything else) will succeed in slowing the outpouring of just-so stories by which the mainstream of evolutionary psychology is very largely constituted. Practitioners will continue to speculate hopelessly in advance of the facts, they will continue to hold conferences at which they air these speculations and they will continue to publish the proceedings of these conferences; world without end. (Fodor, 2001, p. 627)

In Section 12.4 above, it was noted that in Fodor's (2000, p. 89) view we know nothing about how the structure of our minds depends on the structure of our brains. And that just such knowledge is taken for granted by Pinker and Bloom's selectionist account. Notice what this reduces their account to, in Fodor's terms: first, their account is simply speculation of the sort that he calls "hopelessly in advance of the facts"; and thereby, second, their account is simply one more of the *Just-so* stories that form the bulk of mainstream evolutionary psychology.[2]

In regard to the nature of Pinker and Bloom's selectionist account, Norbert Hornstein has claimed in a more specific vein that—

> ... despite Pinker and Bloom's sensitivity to providing "just-so" stories in section 3.1, that is indeed all they provide." (Hornstein, 1990, p. 736)

In support of this criticism – as we saw in Section 10.3.1 above – Hornstein argues that Pinker and Bloom do not give even the outlines of an account of what specific environmental pressures specific grammatical properties are responses to, let alone evidence that these pressures ever impinged on our ancestors. Nor, he points out, do Pinker and Bloom suggest what sort of trade-offs might have led to natural selection choosing some specific principle of grammar.

Lyn Frazier (1990, p.732) has been equally critical of Pinker and Bloom's assumption that the various functions of language place conflicting demands on the grammatical system and that the properties of grammar that were actually chosen, therefore, never look finely tailored to the needs or demands of any particular function. She argues that the claims made by Pinker and Bloom about such choices or trade-offs are not testable. She argues, too, that—

> Pinker and Bloom's case would be much stronger if they demonstrated that these demands conflict with each other, rather than merely assuming that they do. (Frazier, 1990, p. 732)

In Frazier's view, the fit between grammar and function should be loose only where clearly distinct needs can be demonstrated for learners versus perceivers versus producers.

For Gould and Lewontin, the way in which an adaptive account of (language) evolution puts the idea of trade-offs to use is crucial to that account being or not being a *Just-so* story. Thus, on their (1979, p. 585) analysis, if an adaptationist account cannot show for specific traits of an organism that they are optimal, then in effect it acknowledges interaction among these traits via the dictum that an organism cannot optimize each part without imposing expenses on others:

> The notion of "trade-off" is introduced, and organisms are interpreted as best compromises among competing demands. (Gould and Lewontin, 1979, p. 585)

And the idea that such trade-offs may cause the parts to be less than optimal makes it possible to maintain the claim that the parts are adaptations. That is, in Gould and Lewontin's (1979, p. 585) view, this idea discourages one from even entertaining the thought that such parts might be something other than "the immediate work of natural selection". This they see as a truly Panglossian way to explain how a thing comes to have the properties it has:

As Dr Pangloss said in explaining to Candide why he suffered from venereal disease: "It is indispensable in the best of worlds. For if Columbus, when visiting the West Indies, had not caught the disease, which poisons the source of generation, which frequently hinders generation, and is clearly opposed to the great end of Nature, we should have neither chocolate nor cochineal". (Gould and Lewontin, 1979, p. 585)

13.3.2 An assessment. The question, then, is this: Does Pinker and Bloom's selectionist account of language evolution really come down to at most a *Just-so* story? The answer must be, "No" – not if a *Just-so* story is distinguished solely by its meeting criteria (1)(a) and (1)(b):

(1) (a) being plausible and consistent with the basic tenets of population genetics (cf. Eldredge, 1995, p. 42); and
    (b) being consistent with natural selection (cf. Gould and Lewontin, 1979, p. 588).

In earlier sections, we have seen that Pinker and Bloom adopt stricter criteria than (1)(a) and (1)(b) for selectionist accounts of the evolution of language. Their criteria include—

(2) (a) exhibiting signs of complex (adaptive) design (see Section 8.4 above);
    (b) being testable in principle and in practice (see Section 10.1 above); and
    (c) having postulates that are plausible in view of what is known about the biology of language and evolution (see Section 11.3 above).

We have moreover seen that Pinker and Bloom attempt to justify their selectionist account by presenting non-empirical arguments which draw on—

(3) (a) considerations of analogy (see Sections 12.2 and 12.4 above);
    (b) considerations of necessity (see Section 12.3 above); and
    (c) considerations of probability (see Section 12.3 above).

It is clear that a selectionist account for which criteria (2)(a) - (c) are adopted, and in support of which considerations (3)(a) - (c) are adduced, goes well beyond a *Just-so* story as defined by Gould and Lewontin (1979) or Eldredge (1995).

In preceding sections, however, we have also seen that Pinker and Bloom's articulation and use of criteria (2)(a) - (c) are quite problematic: Section 8.4.2 gives details of ways in which their notion of "complex (adaptive) design" is flawed; Chapter 10 pinpoints various limitations on the testability of their selectionist account; and Chapter 11 questions the soundness of their arguments drawing on evidence from biology and evolution. Hornstein (1990) and Frazier (1990) are right to argue that Pinker and Bloom's use of the notion of "inherent trade-offs" is harmful to the testability of their selectionist account. But their arguments do not warrant the unqualified conclusion that Pinker and Bloom's account is made up of no more than *Just-so* stories in the sense of (1)(a) - (b) above.

We have seen too that, as they are used by Pinker and Bloom, the non-empirical considerations listed in (3)(a)–(c) can be questioned in various ways. Thus, Sections 12.2 and 12.4 identify dubious aspects of their arguments from analogy, and Section 12.3 does the same in regard to their arguments from necessity and probability. From these arguments, therefore, Pinker and Bloom's selectionist account gains some – limited, but more than negligible – amount of support.

In short, then, Pinker and Bloom's selectionist account comes down to much more than a mere *Just-so* story. It is true that, in view of the problems with criteria (2)(a)–(c) and with considerations (3)(a)–(c), their account cannot be considered to be highly plausible. Yet it has nevertheless made a major contribution to modern work on language evolution in at least two respects. For one thing, it has made it possible to identify and discuss in a focused way a variety of factual and conceptual questions that have to be solved if such work is to make any substantial progress. For another thing, it has set itself up as a benchmark for comprehensive selectionist accounts of language evolution: any such account would have to be better than Pinker and Bloom's in a significant way in order to qualify as representing an advance over it.

13.4 CHOMSKY'S "FABLE" OF INSTANTANEOUS LANGUAGE EVOLUTION

13.4.1 An unlikely story-teller. Noam Chomsky – as we saw in Section 1.1.3 above – has been sceptical all along about any possibility of finding out the truth about how human language actually arose. In a recent interview, he (2000, p. 25) speaks in positive terms of Lewontin's view that there is no way of finding out how language and cognition in general originated. Referring then to "others" who, by contrast, "feel that they can do something" by telling stories, he comments as follows:

> But telling stories is not very instructive. You can tell stories about insect wings, but it remains to discover how they evolved – perhaps from protuberances that functioned as thermoregulators, according to one account. A famous case is giraffes' necks, that was the one case that was always referred to as the obvious example of natural selection with a clear function; giraffes get a little bit longer neck to reach the higher fruits, and they have offspring and so giraffes have long necks. It was recently discovered that this is apparently false. Giraffes don't use their necks for high feeding, end of that story. You have to figure out some other story: maybe sexual display like a peacock tail or some other story, but the point is that the story doesn't matter. You

can tell very plausible stories in all sorts of cases but the truth is what it is. (Chomsky, 2000, pp. 25–26)

As regards the evolution of language, Chomsky (2000, p. 24) observes that we all assume it is the result of biological evolution and goes on to ask, "But what kind of result of biological evolution?" His answer is this:

> We can make up a lot of stories. It is quite easy ... for example, take language as it is, break it up into fifty different things (syllable, word, putting things together, phrases and so on) and say: "OK, I have the story: there was a mutation that gave syllables, there was another mutation that gave words, another one that gave phrases ..." Another that (miraculously) yields the recursive property (actually, all the mutations are left as miracles). OK, maybe, or maybe something totally different; the stories are free and, interestingly, they are for the most part independent of what the language is. So if it turns out that language has a head parameter, same story; if it doesn't have a head parameter, same story. The story you choose is independent of the facts, pretty much. (Chomsky, 2000, p. 24)

From these remarks it might be thought that Chomsky himself would hardly be eager to engage in telling "plausible stories" about the emergence or evolution of language. Yet, interestingly, he has done just that in a recent paper, making up what on his (1998, p. 17) own characterization is a "Just So Story" and three other "fables" about the way in which language might have emerged. In the sections below, we examine these fables in some depth, looking first at the context in which he tells them.[3]

13.4.2 On the perfection of language. Chomsky (1998) presents his fables about the emergence of language in a discussion of the perfection of language design. According to him, it has become possible in the Minimalist Program to ask "new" and "far-reaching" questions about the design of language, some of which he phrases as follows:

(4) (a) How close does language come to what some super-engineer would construct, given the conditions that the language faculty must satisfy? (Chomsky, 1998, p. 6)

(b) How closely does language resemble what a superbly competent engineer might have constructed, given certain design specifications? (Chomsky, 1998, p. 15)

(c) How 'perfect' is language, to put it picturesquely? (Chomsky, 1998, p. 6)[4]

Chomsky's (1998, p. 7) short answer to the third question is: "surprisingly perfect".[5]

To justify this answer, Chomsky (1998, pp. 17–18) does two things that merit close inspection. He first makes up his fables about how language got to be such a "perfect system". Central to these fables is the abstraction of instantaneous language evolution. Next Chomsky offers an argument from analogy in support of this abstraction: he points out a "resemblance" between this new abstraction or idealization and the well-known abstraction of instantaneous language acquisition.

But what are the specifics of Chomsky's fables? What does the abstraction of instantaneous language evolution involve? How sound is the analogy invoked in support of the abstraction? What are the benefits and costs of adopting this abstraction? In particular, how much does it contribute to our understanding of language design and/or language evolution? Before we turn to these questions, however, it is necessary to consider the conditions or specifications which, in Chomsky's view, the design of language has to meet.

13.4.3 Specifications for the design of language. Chomsky (1998, p. 15) draws a distinction between two categories of conditions or specifications which the design of language has to meet. The first category includes conditions he characterizes as "internal and general, having to do with conceptual naturalness and simplicity".[6] The conditions belonging to the second category are, on Chomsky's (1998, p. 15) characterization, "external and specific, having to do with the conditions imposed by the systems of the mind/brain with which the faculty of language interacts". Central among these external or "performance" systems, are the sensory-motor system and the conceptual or language use system. A language constructs representations which have to be interpreted or "read" by these systems as instructions for action and thought. If it is to be usable at all, language must accordingly be designed to meet what Chomsky (1998, p. 18) has technically called "legibility conditions" or "bare output conditions". In Chomsky's (1998, p. 18) view, language represents a "good solution" to the legibility conditions imposed by the external systems mentioned above. In more "picturesque" terms, Chomsky's (1998, p. 15) conclusion is that it "might turn out that language is very well designed, perhaps close to 'perfect' in satisfying external conditions".

13.4.4 The fables. Chomsky (1998, p. 15) considers the conclusion that language is perhaps close to perfect in satisfying external conditions to be "rather surprising". On the one hand, it contradicts according to him (1998, p. 15) the widely held assumption that languages are "complex and defective objects" that require "regimentation, or replacement by something quite different, if they are to serve some purpose other than the confused and intricate affairs of daily life". On the other hand, the conclusion that language is close to perfection is surprising to Chomsky in that it is not in accord with what one expects to find about the design properties in biological systems. Evolving over long periods through incremental changes under complicated accidental circumstances, biological systems do not exhibit the near perfect design attributed by Chomsky to language. If language is a biological system, as Chomsky takes it to be, it would be unsurprising to find it a messy entity invented by opportunist tinkering with accidentally available materials.

The question, then, is how the near perfection of language can be reconciled with its being a (complex) biological system. Or, equivalently, how could language have evolved, given its near perfection? Chomsky (1998, pp. 17–18) addresses this question in four steps. First, he stresses our lack of understanding of language evolution:

> Human language lies well beyond the limits of serious understanding of evolutionary processes, though there are suggestive speculations. (Chomsky, 1998, p. 17)

This remark has a pre-emptive function: it cautions potential critics not to expect too much from answers to the question of how the near perfection of language may be reconciled with its being a biological system.

Second, Chomsky (1998, p. 17) adds "another suggestive speculation" comprising three "suppositions" to which he subsequently refers as "fables":

(5) (a) ... there was an ancient primate with the whole human mental architecture in place, but no language faculty. (Chomsky, 1998, p. 17)[7]

(b) ... a mutation took place in the genetic instructions for the brain, which was then reorganized in accord with the laws of physics and chemistry to install a faculty of language. (Chomsky, 1998, p. 17)

(c) ... the new system was ... beautifully designed, a near-perfect solution to the conditions imposed by the general architecture of the mind-brain in which it is inserted ... (Chomsky, 1998, p. 17)

Supposition (5)(b) is of special importance: it represents the core of the abstraction of instantaneous language evolution which should offer a basis for reconciling the near perfection of language with its being a biological system. If it is assumed that language was inserted instantaneously into the mind-brain, there is no tension between the near perfection of language and its being a biological system.

Third, Chomsky (1998, p. 17) attempts to clarify the epistemological status and function of suppositions (5)(a) – (c). As for their status, he remarks:

> To be clear, these [suppositions – R.P.B.] are fables. Their only redeeming value is that they may not be more implausible than others, and might even turn out to have some elements of validity. (Chomsky, 1998, p. 17)

The fables seem to derive the "elements of validity" from their function. Thus Chomsky observes that:

> The imagery serves its function if it helps us pose a problem that could turn out to be meaningful and even significant: basically, the problem that motivates the minimalist

program, which explores the intuition that the outcome of the fable [of instantaneous language evolution – R.P.B.] might be accurate in interesting ways. (Chomsky, 1998, p. 17)

What Chomsky seems to say here is that the fables allow him to pursue an "intuition" – namely that language is near perfect in design – which is implausible from an evolutionary perspective.

Fourth, Chomsky (1998, p. 18), makes an attempt at justifying the adoption of the abstraction or fable of instantaneous language evolution. He attempts this justification because he is well aware of the fact that "the faculty of language was not inserted into a mind-brain with the rest of its architecture intact". This justification is offered in the form of a skeletal argument by analogy drawing on a "resemblance" between the abstraction of instantaneous language evolution and the earlier adopted abstraction of instantaneous language acquisition:

> Notice a certain resemblance to the logical problem of language acquisition, a reformulation of the condition of explanatory adequacy as a device that converts experience to a language, taken to be a state of a component of the brain. The operation is instantaneous though the process is plainly not. (Chomsky, 1998, p. 17)

To Chomsky (1998, p. 17), the "serious empirical question" is how much distortion is introduced by the abstraction of instantaneous language acquisition. It seems to him, surprisingly, that little if any distortion is introduced by it, a point which he uses in developing the analogy under consideration:

> The issues posed by the minimalist program are somewhat similar. Plainly, the faculty of language was not instantaneously inserted into a mind/brain with the rest of its architecture fully intact. But we are now asking how well it is designed on that counterfactual assumption. How much does the abstraction distort a vastly more complex reality? We can try to answer the question much as we do the analogous one about the logical problem of language acquisition. (Chomsky, 1998, p. 18)

To determine how well-justified or "valid" Chomsky's abstraction of instantaneous language evolution is, it is necessary to determine how close the analogy between this abstraction and the one of instantaneous language acquisition is. Clearly, if this analogy turned out to be weak or incomplete in important ways, the abstraction of instantaneous language evolution would lack the measure of justification accorded to it by Chomsky. As a consequence, his intuition about the perfection of language would be hard to reconcile with what is known about the imperfect nature of complex biological systems which – as he notes – evolved gradually in opportunistic ways.

13.4.5 The analogy. To be able to judge the closeness of the "resemblance" or the strength of the analogy between instantaneous language acquisition and instantaneous language evolution, these abstractions have to be compared in a systematic way.

13.4.5.1 Basic problem. The abstraction of instantaneous language acquisition was adopted by Chomsky and others to enable them to solve a particular "basic problem". This problem is stated by Chomsky in the skeletal form of (6)(a) and the fleshed out form of (6)(b).

    (6) (a) How is knowledge of language acquired? (Chomsky, 1986, p. 3)
        (b) ... the basic problem is that our knowledge [of language – R.P.B.] is richly articulated and shared with others from the same speech community, whereas the data available are much too impoverished to determine it by any general procedure of induction, analogy, association, or whatever. (Chomsky, 1986, p. 55)

It is in the form of (6)(b) that this "basic problem" has been referred to by Chomsky and others as "the logical problem of language acquisition".[8]

So what would be the counterpart of the logical problem of language acquisition in the context of language evolution or design? That is, for the solution of which analogous "basic problem" is it necessary to adopt the abstraction of instantaneous language evolution? Chomsky has not offered an explicit statement of this problem which, presumably, may be referred to as "the logical problem of language evolution." Speculatively, (7)(a) and (b) could be considered evolutionary counterparts of (6)(a) and (b) respectively:

    (7) (a) How did language evolve (or, equivalently, How was language designed)?
        (b) ... the basic problem is that language is so perfect(ly designed), whereas complex biological systems which evolved gradually in an accidental/opportunistic way are such complex and "imperfect" objects.

(7)(a) and (b), however, are clearly not fully analogous to (6)(a) and (b) respectively, for reasons which we will now consider.

13.4.5.2 Poverty of the evidence. The logical problem of language acquisition arises from a tension that exists between the properties of two entities. On the one hand, there is the richness of the acquired knowledge of language; on the other hand, there is the poverty of the data, evidence or experience on the basis of which such knowledge is acquired. But what would be the analogous tension from which "the logical problem of language evolution" arose? One could speculate that corresponding to the richness of acquired knowledge of language, there could be the perfection of evolved language, as is done in (7)(b). But would it make sense, within the framework of the analogy in question, to say that corresponding to the poverty of the data etc. in the case of language acquisition, there is the imperfection of a complex biological system which evolved gradually in an opportunistic way? What would clearly not make sense is to say that corresponding to the poverty of the former data, there is the poverty of scientific data about the way in which language actually evolved.[9]

13.4.5.3 States of a faculty. The solution to the logical problem of language acquisition proposed by Chomsky (1986, pp. 3–4, 24–25, 52) involves the postulation of a language faculty that has two significant states, as we have seen in Section 2.3 above. The first is the initial state (S_0): a state that incorporates a genetic language programme, or genetically encoded linguistic principles, representing the child's innate linguistic endowment or knowledge. The language faculty is in its initial state in a child that has not had any linguistic experience in the sense of having been exposed to utterances of or data about his/her language.[10] The second significant state of the language faculty is an attained, steady or stable state (S_s): it represents the "richly articulated knowledge" which a linguistically mature speaker has of his/her language. This steady state develops or "grows" out of the initial state under the "triggering and shaping" influence of the child's limited experience of the language.[11]

In a nutshell, Chomsky's solution to the logical problem of language acquisition is that much of what a speaker/hearer knows of his/her language is not acquired or learned in a conventional sense: part of this knowledge is innate and part of it is the result of biological growth or maturation.

So, what in the case of language evolution would be the entities that corresponded to the initial and the attained steady state of the language faculty as they feature in language acquisition? Chomsky has not explicated the analogy in the detail required by a nonspeculative answer to this question. Presumably, the attained state in the case of language evolution would be the genetic language programme. But it is hard to even speculate on what the initial state would be in the case of language evolution. That is, it is quite unclear what to Chomsky the input to the mapping operation of instantaneous language evolution might be a point noted in Section 6.4 above as well.

13.4.5.4 Factors abstracted away from. The way in which the initial state S_0 of the language faculty develops or grows into the steady state S_s is described as follows by Chomsky:

> The initial state of the language faculty, S_0 incorporates the primitive operations, the format for possible rule systems and the evaluation metric. Given experience, the language faculty in the state S_0 searches the class of possible languages, selecting the

highest valued one consistent with the data and entering the state S_1, which incorporates the rules of this language. Given new data, the system enters S_2, and so forth, until it enters a state S_s in which the procedure terminates, either because of some property of S_s or because the system has reached a state of maturation that does not permit it to proceed. At each step, the learner's mind selects the highest valued ("simplest") language consistent with the newly presented evidence and its current state. (Chomsky, 1986, p. 52)

Elaborating on this description, Chomsky (1986, p. 52) suggests. As an "empirical hypothesis", that order of presentation of data is irrelevant, so that learning is "as it were instantaneous" as if S_0 maps the data directly to S_s. More formally, he states this "empirical hypothesis" as follows:

Suppose we regard S_0 as a function mapping a collection of data E to a state attained. If E is the totality of data available to the language learner, then the steady state S_s attained is $S_0(E)$, the result of applying the principles of S_0 to E. (Chomsky, 1986, p. 52)

Referring to his description of the way in which the initial state S_0 of the language faculty develops or grows into the steady state S_s, Chomsky (1986, p. 53) remarks that "this model depends crucially on the legitimacy of the idealization of instantaneous learning", that is on the "correctness of the empirical assumption" stated above. Accordingly, he considers it important to be clear what is and what is not implied by the abstraction (or idealization) of instantaneous language acquisition. To clarify this point, Chomsky (1986, pp. 52–54) mentions a wide range of empirical possibilities that are consistent with the empirical hypothesis in question. He thereby identifies a range of factors from which the hypothesis abstracts away, including the following:

(8) (a) the fact that the child receives the evidence about the language piece by piece over a period of time;

(b) the possibility that, because of memory limitations etc., only simpler parts of the evidence that leads to attainment of the steady state are available to the child at early stages of language acquisition;

(c) the possibility that intermediate states attained by the child may change the principles available for interpretation of data at later stages in a way that affects the state attained;

(d) the possibility that an option permitted by UG (represented in S_0) is fixed in one manner at an early stage of acquisition, and the choice is reversed at a later stage on the basis of evidence not available or unused at the earlier stage;

(e) the possibility that some of the principles of S_0 are available to the language learner only at a late stage of language acquisition and that the language faculty matures through childhood making various principles available at a particular stage of the process.

Chomsky sums up (8)(a)–(e) by observing that:
> What the empirical hypothesis asserts is that irrespective of questions of motivation, order of presentation, or selective availability, the result of language acquisition is as if it were instantaneous: In particular, intermediate states attained do not change the principles available for interpretation of data at later states in a way that affects the state attained. (Chomsky, 1986, p. 54)

The factors abstracted away from by the hypothesis of instantaneous acquisition fall within the scope of the so-called psychological problem of (real-time) language acquisition: How does a child acquire its language in stages over a period of time, the earlier stages influencing the later ones?[12]

Turning to instantaneous language evolution again: What are the factors from which this abstraction or idealization abstracts away? Chomsky has not identified these factors as explicitly and systematically as those involved in the abstraction of instantaneous language acquisition. Some, however, can be identified in his discussion of language design (Chomsky, 1998). A first and fairly obvious factor is that of time. In this regard, Chomsky remarks that:
> Plainly, the faculty of language was not instantaneously inserted into a mind/brain with the rest of its architecture fully intact. (Chomsky, 1998, p. 18)

While Chomsky has spelled out the specifics of non-instantaneity in the case of language acquisition, he has not done so in the case of language evolution.

The "plainly" remark quoted above alludes to a second factor from which the idealization of instantaneous language evolution abstracts away: the probability that the faculty of language and certain components of the "rest" of the architecture of the mind/brain evolved together. In particular, it is hard to imagine that the language faculty and the two external systems – the articulatory-perceptual system and the language use or conceptual system – evolved in isolation from each other. It seems reasonable to allow for the possibility that the properties of the external systems were codetermined by the way in which these systems interact with the internal language system. In this connection, it is significant that Chomsky observes that:
> The external systems are not well understood and, in fact, progress in understanding them goes hand-in-hand with progress in understanding the language system that interacts with them. (Chomsky, 1998, p. 18)

This observation obviously applies to the evolution of the external systems as well. Someone whose work focused on the design of the external systems could even transpose Chomsky's question about the perfection or optimality of the design of language to the design of these systems, asking: To what extent are the external systems a good solution to the linguistic conditions posed by (the) language (faculty)?

As third set of factors from which the idealization of instantaneous language evolution abstracts away relates to Chomsky's (1998, p. 17) position that the "design [of language was – R.P.B.] determined by natural law rather than bricolage through selection". Bricolage through selection is a gradual process in terms of which

... evolution is an opportunist, an inventor that takes whatever materials are at hand and tinkers with them, introducing slight changes so that they might work a bit better than before. (Chomsky, 1998, p. 17)

A critical difference between the factors abstracted away from in the abstraction of instantaneous language acquisition and the factors abstracted away from in the abstraction of instantaneous language evolution is of a "meta" sort. It concerns the availability of relatively reliable data about the factors abstracted away from. In the case of instantaneous language acquisition there are ample data about the factors which make real-time acquisition the complex phenomenon it actually is. As has been stressed by Chomsky himself, however, there is very little evidence of a direct sort about the factors involved in language evolution. This means that in the case of instantaneous language evolution, unlike that of instantaneous language acquisition, it is not really known what the abstraction involves in regard to specifics. This is one of the most critical ways in which the analogy between the two abstractions breaks down, a way that underlies the one to which we next turn.

13.4.5.5 Function and epistemological status. Initially, the abstraction of instantaneous language acquisition was adopted by Chomsky and others as a conceptual tool for meaningful investigation of a phenomenon considered too complex for "realistic study":

... there is another, much more crucial, idealization implicit in this account. We have been describing acquisition of language as if it were an instantaneous process. Obviously, this is not true. A more realistic model of language acquisition would consider the order in which primary linguistic data are used by the child and the effects of preliminary "hypotheses" developed in the earlier stages of learning on the interpretation of new, often more complex, data. To us it appears that this more realistic study is much too complex to be undertaken in any meaningful way today and that it will be far more fruitful to investigate in detail, as a first approximation, the idealized model outlined earlier, leaving refinements to a time when this idealization is better understood. (Chomsky and Halle, 1968, p. 331)

Initially, then, the abstraction of instantaneous language acquisition had the function of heuristic device. As noted above, over the years Chomsky has changed his stance on the function of this abstraction: he now considers it to be more than a mere means for fruitfully investigating a phenomenon which is too complex to be studied in detail in a realistic way. Rather, Chomsky (1986) now assigns this abstraction the epistemological status of "empirical hypothesis" (pp. 52-54), "empirical assumption" (p. 53), or "working hypothesis" (p. 53). This hypothesis or assumption is on Chomsky's (1998, p. 53) view capable of being "empirically correct" or "incorrect".

Moreover, as for its actual status, Chomsky considers the hypothesis of instantaneous language acquisition to be "rather credible, perhaps surprisingly" (1986, p. 53), and to introduce "little if any distortion" (1998, p. 17). In addition, on Chomsky's judgement, "the empirical evidence seems to support [this hypothesis]" (1998, p. 17), and it "capture(s) real properties of a complex reality" (1998, pp. 17–18).

Turning to the function of the abstraction of instantaneous language evolution: According to Chomsky (1998, p. 17), it "serves its function if it helps us pose a problem that could turn out to be meaningful and even significant." And concerning the epistemological status of this abstraction, Chomsky states that:

(9) (a) [its] only redeeming value is that [it] may not be more implausible than [other fables or speculations about the evolution of language] (Chomsky, 1998, p. 17);

(b) [intuitively] the outcome of the fable might be accurate in interesting ways. (Chomsky, 1998, p. 17)

Chomsky, however, indicates neither how these two statements are to be reconciled with each other nor how they – individually or collectively – should be reconciled with his judgement that the abstraction in question expresses a counter-factual claim:

Plainly, the faculty of language was not instantaneously inserted into a mind/brain with the rest of its architecture fully intact. (Chomsky, 1998, p. 18)

In addition, Chomsky refrains from giving an explicit answer to the question "How much does the abstraction distort a vastly complex reality"?

In regard to function and epistemological status, then, the abstraction of instantaneous language evolution is quite obscure in comparison to the abstraction of instantaneous language acquisition. The underlying reason for this may be the lack of data about the actual, "real-time" evolution of language, as was noted above. Paradoxically, the absence of such data may in a perverse sense be beneficial to the former abstraction. If the abstraction of instantaneous language evolution were assigned the status of "empirical hypothesis" – as has been the abstraction of instantaneous language acquisition – it might be found to be incorrect. What is beyond doubt, though, is that the "resemblance" or "similarity" seen by Chomsky to

Plausible Evolutionary Stories 189

exist between the two abstractions is of a quite nebulous sort in the case of their function and epistemological status.

In summary: the analogy – "resemblance" or "similarity" – between the abstraction of instantaneous language evolution and that of instantaneous language acquisition is not particularly strong. On the one hand, it is obscure in certain ways. That is:

(10) It is not clear what it is, in the case of instantaneous language evolution, that corresponds to—
   (a) the logical problem of language acquisition,
   (b) the poverty of the evidence, and
   (c) the various states of the language faculty in the case of instantaneous language acquisition.

On the other hand, there is disanalogy in other respects:

(11)(a) In the case of instantaneous language acquisition there is ample data about the factors abstracted away from; in the case of instantaneous language evolution virtually no data about the corresponding factors have been offered by Chomsky.
   (b) The abstraction of instantaneous language acquisition is considered an empirical hypothesis supported by evidence; the abstraction of instantaneous language acquisition has not been accorded this epistemological status by Chomsky.

The adoption of the abstraction of instantaneous language evolution, accordingly, cannot be justified by alluding to ways in which it resembles the abstraction of instantaneous language acquisition.

13.4.6 Appraisal. Which brings us to some of the negative consequences of adopting the abstraction of instantaneous language evolution in its present form. This abstraction, it will be recalled, has been adopted by Chomsky as the basis of a solution for a particular problem. On the one hand, Chomsky believes that language is close to perfect in satisfying the legibility conditions of two external systems with which it interacts. On the other hand, it is known that biological systems which have evolved gradually under complicated and accidental circumstances typically do not exhibit the near perfection in their design attributed by Chomsky to language. By adopting the abstraction of instantaneous language evolution, it becomes possible for Chomsky to eliminate this tension: if it is assumed that language evolved instantaneously, it could be explained why it is free from the kind of imperfections which would expectedly result from accidental and opportunistic evolution taking place in a gradual way. If, however, the abstraction of instantaneous language evolution were to lack the required justification, the perfection attributed by Chomsky to the design of language would be something very unreal, a truly fable-like attribute of language.[13]

Adopting the abstraction of instantaneous language acquisition in its present form has other consequences that are unattractive. This is clear from an examination of the life history of the abstraction of instantaneous language acquisition. As shown above, this abstraction was initially adopted by Chomsky and Halle, to study in a "meaningful way" a phenomenon, namely real-time language acquisition, that was considered "much too complex" for "more realistic study". Scholars who have been studying real-time language acquisition within a Chomskyan framework would be able to cite strong evidence indicating that the adoption of this abstraction has indeed led to significant progress in this study. But does this carry over to the abstraction of instantaneous language evolution? It is not clear in what way the study of "real-time" language evolution could benefit from this abstraction. By assuming that language evolution is instantaneous, the potential role of bricolage through selection in the evolution of language is excluded from the focus of serious work on language evolution. If language is in fact a complex biological system, this assumption places a potentially serious restriction on work on language evolution. Suppose for the sake of argument that bricolage through selection were not a central force in the evolution of language. This would be a truly significant – and, some would say, surprising – fact about language evolution. But it would be impossible to discover this fact, were it one, by assuming on a priori grounds that language evolution was instantaneous. The adoption of the abstraction of instantaneous language evolution in its present form, then, may well be a hindrance to the "meaningful study" of the complex phenomenon of language evolution.[14]

Finally, adopting the abstraction of instantaneous language evolution involves a weakening of the criterion that evolutionary stories or fables have to be plausible. Recall, in this connection that, having candidly stated that suppositions (5)(a)–(c) are "fables", Chomsky (1998, p. 17) remarks that "[t]heir only redeeming value is that they may not be more implausible than others ...". So how plausible has an evolutionary fable to be in order not to be more plausible than others that might not be all that plausible to begin with? The answer to this question clearly presupposes a restrictive theory of what plausibility involves in the domain of biological evolution. This theory has to offer a basis for discriminating in a non-arbitrary way between evolutionary fables or stories that are plausible, ones that are implausible and so on.

14

THEORIES OF THE SUBSTANCE OF SCIENCE

Let us begin this chapter by seeing how it ties in with what has gone before. Previously, it has been shown that the scientific substance – or "value" – of modern accounts of language evolution depends on amongst other things the strategies which they adopt for overcoming the problem of the paucity of factual evidence about the evolution of language. It has been shown too, however, that these strategies make use of assumptions which are problematic in various ways – in being obscure in terms of content, and/or insufficiently well-articulated, and/or ad hoc or arbitrary in some other way, and/or insufficiently restrictive. It has accordingly been suggested that these assumptions should be replaced by theories whose function it is to ensure that accounts of language evolution have the desired scientific substance. These theories, to be able to do their job, should be free – needless to say – from the kinds of flaws that mar the assumptions whose place they are taking. The present chapter considers in retrospect the main (kinds of) theories about scientific substance that provision was made for in Chapters 10 to 13.

First, a general theory of science is needed in place of the problematic assumptions which enter into the adoption of a condition of testability for accounts of language evolution. These assumptions – as we saw in Chapter 10 – include those about –

(1) (a) the criteria on the basis of which a distinction can be drawn between good science on the one hand and bad science or non-science on the other hand; and

(b) the role that testability should (not) play in the constructing of scientific accounts of language evolution.

Of course, a candidate theory of science would not serve the purpose if it included discredited ideas about what good science was once believed to be. Likewise, it should not be a set of assumptions mustered for the sole purpose of being a *machine de guerre* in getting the upper hand in controversies about the evolution of language. It should, on the contrary, be non-ad hoc in the sense of also applying to the study of evolutionary events and phenomena in domains other than that of language.

Second, the problematic assumptions underlying the use of indirect evidence for or against accounts of language evolution have to make way for a principled theory of indirect evidence and for various bridge theories of the sort discussed in Chapter 11. The former theory has to replace obscure or ad hoc assumptions about such matters as—

(2) (a) the conditions which data about phenomena that are distinct from language evolution should meet to be indirect evidence for or against accounts of language evolution; and

(b) the factors that determine the strength of the various kinds of indirect evidence that bear on accounts of language evolution.

The theory of indirect evidence has to be complemented by bridge theories that warrant those (chains of) inferences by means of which data that are in the first place about phenomena that are distinct from language evolution are brought to bear on claims about language evolution as well. The theory of indirect evidence is by its very nature a metascientific theory; by contrast, bridge theories – as was shown in Chapter 11 – express empirical claims about the interrelatedness of phenomena that belong to different ontological domains.

Third, the unclear or otherwise questionable assumptions involved in the use of non-empirical considerations for or against accounts of language evolution should be given up in favour of an explicit theory of non-empirical argumentation. As we saw in Chapter 12, the former assumptions express claims about, amongst other things –

(3) (a) the nature of the various non-empirical considerations that can or cannot be invoked for or against accounts of language evolution;

(b) the relative strength of the non-empirical considerations that can be brought to bear on accounts of language evolution.

To be able to say well-founded things about the considerations referred to in (3)(a) and (b), the required theory would, to begin with, have to offer a restrictive characterization of the concepts of "analogy", "necessity", "probability" and "ignorance" that are central to them.

Fourth, the strategy of telling plausible evolutionary stories or fables about language evolution presupposes a non-ad hoc theory of the considerations which add to or subtract from the plausibility of such stories or fables. As used by many scholars, however, this strategy sets out from obscure or arbitrary assumptions about, inter alia—

(4) (a) the conditions that a story or fable about the evolution of language should meet in order to be considered "plausible";
(b) the factors that make some stories/fables about the evolution of language "plausible stories/fables" and others "less than plausible "stories/fables" or "implausible stories/fables".

At the core of a theory of the former conditions and the latter factors would have to lie a restrictive conception of what plausibility involves in the domain of biological evolution.

Crucially, in order to ensure that accounts of language evolution have the desired scientific substance or "value", the theories listed above have to share a particular property. All have to be restrictive in the sense of offering a basis for distinguishing in a non-arbitrary way between entities that do have a certain desirable attribute and entities that do not have this attribute: in the case of the general theory of science, between accounts of language evolution that do represent good science and accounts that do not; in the case of the theory of indirect evidence, between kinds of data that do offer indirect evidence for or against such accounts and kinds of data that do not; in the case of the theory of non-empirical argumentation, between non-empirical considerations that do add to or subtract from the merit of such accounts and non-empirical considerations that do not; and in the case of the theory of evolutionary plausibility, between accounts that do have some specific measure of plausibility and accounts that do not have it. It is to the extent that they are suitably restrictive that these theories will be able to impart scientific substance or "value" to such accounts.

Theories of what it entails for scientific work to have sufficient substance or "value" form part of the fabric of mature sciences. Determinants of or conditions on such substance are even occasionally a topic in discussions that are taken part in by scientists and philosophers alike, as witness the recent remarks on the criterion of testability for evolutionary theories.[1] This means that scholars will not have to start from scratch if they set out to construct the theories that are needed for making sure that modern work on the evolution of language will have the scientific substance wished for.

15

CAPSTONE

15.1 CLOSING THE ARGUMENT

If work on the evolution of language is to grow in substance rather than mere volume, it will have to make a shift – so the preceding chapters argue – to a specific kind of theoretical work. In particular, poorly developed assumptions about entities of various sorts should be replaced by theories that are explicitly articulated and that characterize those entities in a restrictive way. To bring the argument for this claim to a close, the present chapter shows how it applies to some recent work by Ray Jackendoff (1999, 2002) on the evolution of language.

Jackendoff offers an account of the evolution of modern language in terms of which it emerged in "nine partially ordered steps" (1999, p. 273). What is more, he (1999, p. 272) claims to have found "a new source of evidence on the issue", so-called language "fossils". In view of the paucity of factual evidence about the evolution of language, this is a very interesting claim. Below, however, the case for it will be shown to be weak in that it presupposes restrictive theories of a range of things – theories which Jackendoff has so far failed to offer.

15.2 "STEPS" IN THE EVOLUTION OF LANGUAGE

In a review of work on language evolution, Jackendoff (1999, p. 727) argues that "the emergence of modern language [can be broken down – R.P.B.] into nine partially ordered steps, each of which contributes to the precision and variety of expression". He (1999, p. 272) claims, too, to have found "traces" of these steps "in degraded forms of modern language". It is to such traces that he assigns the status of "fossils"; it is such fossils that he sees as a new "source of evidence". And what this evidence indicates to him (1999, p. 272) is that "the language capacity can be conceived of as having evolved incrementally, rather than appearing all at once in an undecomposable bloc."

In his recent book, Jackendoff (2002, p. 238) offers the diagrammatic representation (1) of the partially ordered steps that he discerns in the emergence of language. (Logically sequential steps are ordered top to bottom by him; logically independent steps he presents side by side.)

(1)

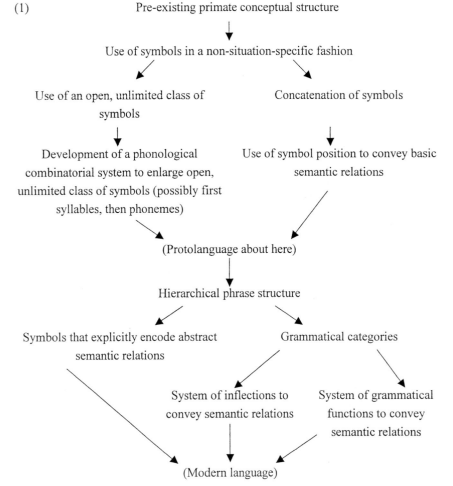

For the purpose of what follows below, this diagram is largely self-explanatory of what was involved in the individual steps.[1] The step – or "stage" – referred to as "protolanguage", however, calls for some elucidation. In describing the properties of this stage, Jackendoff (1999, pp. 275-276) draws both on Bickerton's notion of "protolanguage" and on Klein and Perdue's (1979) notion of "The Basic Variety" (BV). In terms of Bickerton's notion, protolanguage is characterized by short structureless strings of words, resembling "an early stage pidgin without any formal structure – just handfuls of words or gestures strung together".[2] The notion of BV, by contrast, is used by Klein and Perdue for identifying a "stage of linguistic competence" attained in a target language by a specific category of second-language learners – adult immigrant workers who did not receive explicit instruction. The features of BV that Jackendoff (1999, p. 275) sees as relevant are these: (1) lexical competence, (2) absence of inflectional morphology, (3) absence of sentential subordination, and (4) single, largely semantically based principles of word order. Why does Bickerton assign to protolanguage a less stable word order than that of BV? This may, in Jackendoff's (1999, p. 276) view, be "partly because his evidence comes from pidgins, which are heavily influenced by the native language(s) of their speakers". Jackendoff assigns various BV principles of word order to that stage in the emergence of the language capacity which he has labeled "protolanguage" (more on those below).

15.3 SOME LANGUAGE "FOSSILS"

How, then, are language "fossils" used by Jackendoff as evidence for (claims about) the existence and/or properties of stages of language evolution? A typical example focuses on the way in which the linear order of concatenated symbols serves to express semantic relationships among them. In terms of just symbol concatenation, Jackendoff (1999, p. 275) observes, it is not clear whether the string *hit Fred tree* means "Fred hit the tree" or "the tree hit Fred". The pragmatics of the concatenated words alone does not select one of these meanings over the other. Jackendoff (1999, p. 275) now argues that there is no need to advance to full generative syntax in order to improve the situation. This is because—

> [m]odern languages display some robust principles that are in some sense prior to syntax, and that reveal themselves more clearly in less fully developed situations.
> (Jackendoff, 1999, p. 175)

And Jackendoff (1999, p. 275) looks upon BV as such a "situation" in that it exhibits two semantically based principles of word order, namely:

(2) (a) Agent First: Agent is expressed in subject position.
    (b) Focus Last: The informationally focal element appears last.

According to Jackendoff (1999, p. 275) the string *hit tree Fred* would mean one thing only to a speaker using Agent First: "the tree hit Fred". This principle enables a speaker to disambiguate a large proportion of "utterances involving two characters". Focus Last, in turn, is taken by Jackendoff (1999, p. 276) to be an element in the discourse coding of given and new information. For example, in the utterance *In the room sat a bear*, the subject appears at the end for focal effect.

Jackendoff (1999, p. 275) asserts that, in addition to occurring in BV, Agent First "seems to be observed" in home signs invented by deaf children of non-signing parents and in pidgin languages. Agrammatic aphasics also "fall back" on Agent First "to some degree", as their errors on reversible passives (*The boy was hit by the girl*) and object relatives (*The boy who the girl kissed is tall*) seem to indicate. Against this background, Jackendoff suggests that—

> ... Agent First and Focus Last are "fossil principles" from protolanguage, which modern languages often observe and frequently elaborate. Like the features Bickerton discusses, they often survive in degraded forms of language, which may serve as evidence for their evolutionarily more primitive character. (Jackendoff, 1999, p. 276)

These two "fossil principles" – along with the "fossil feature" of modern language that he calls "Grouping" and the "protolinguistic fossil" of noun compounding in English – make up what Jackendoff judges to be "a plausible step between raw concatenation and full syntax".[3]

But how valid are the inferences about stages in the emergence of (the) language (faculty) drawn by Jackendoff from data about features of "degraded" forms of modern language? That is, what conditions would make it proper for data about "degraded" forms of language to be used as evidence for or against claims about the existence or properties of such evolutionary stages? Below we consider three of these conditions.

15.4 A Theory of "Degraded" Language

The first condition calls for clarity on the nature of what Jackendoff refers to as "degraded (forms of) language". The pertinent questions in this regard is:

(3) What is it that makes language or a form of language "degraded"?

Jackendoff (1999, 2000) does not anywhere offer a characterization of what "degradedness" involves. This omission is unfortunate in itself; it implies, too, that he is ignoring some crucial further questions. One: How is it to be determined in a non-arbitrary way whether a particular linguistic phenomenon does or does not represent "(a) degraded (form of) language"? Two: How is it to be determined in a non-arbitrary way that a given linguistic phenomenon has the property of "degradedness" and not that of simplicity or the like.[4] Three: Must the features associated with every form of language pathology, deficit or abnormality be taken as a manifestation of "degradedness"?

Jackendoff does not address these questions in a systematic way. What he (1999, pp. 275-276) does do is to offer an ad hoc list of examples of "degraded forms of language". His list seems to have the following five as definite members: "home signs" invented by deaf children of non-signing parents, pidgin languages, the "language" of agrammatic aphasics, BV, and the language used "early" by children. Perhaps, however, the following two are also members of the list: the "competence attained by Genie" and the "(linguistic) achievements of language-trained apes".

One of the consequences of this arbitrary and ad hoc way of listing "degraded forms of language" is to make of "degraded language" an entity or phenomenon that is artificial and poorly demarcated. Another is that characterizing a language "fossil" as something which exists to the extent that it is manifested in "a degraded form of language" is to make of it something that is equally nebulous. If it can be stipulated what does and what does not constitute "(a) degraded (form of) language", it can be stipulated too what is and what is not a language "fossil" and, ultimately, it can be stipulated what was and what was not a stage in the evolution of language. But the way of such stipulation is not the way of science. Science would require us to keep clear of mere ad hoc stipulation; it would require us, instead, to travel the road of theory formation. Specifically, it would require us to try to develop a well-articulated theory of degraded language. Such a theory has to offer a restrictive characterization of what degraded language is – a characterization on the basis of which questions such as those posed above can be answered.

But, for argument's sake, let us assume that it is possible to characterize "degraded language" in a non-ad hoc and restrictive way and, consequently, that it is possible to distinguish in non-arbitrary way between linguistic phenomena that do represent "degraded forms of language" and linguistic phenomena that don't. That is, let us take it for granted that the first of the three conditions mentioned above has been met. Then the second condition – to which we next turn, – comes into play.

15.5 A Bridge Theory

The second condition which data about characteristics of "degraded" (forms of) language have to meet in order to qualify as evidence for or against claims about the existence or properties of stages in the emergence of the language faculty is a relevance condition. Here is this condition, put in the form of a question:

(4) Why would data about a "degraded (form of) language" – being the kind of entity it is – bear on claims about a stage in the evolution of the language faculty – being the different kind of entity it is?

This is one more question that Jackendoff does not explicitly go into.

The answer to question (4) has to be a theory that gives a licence whereby claims about features of stages in language evolution may properly be inferred from data about characteristics of "degraded (forms of) language". Such a licence will take the form of a bridge theory whose hypotheses state how features of "degraded forms of language" are interlinked with properties of stages in the evolution of language. Clearly, it will not do to just stipulate ad hoc that a given feature of a given "degraded form of language" is a sign that some stage occurred in the evolution of language or that this stage was marked by such-and-such a property. In the absence of a theory that is general, that is well founded and that states how features of "degraded (forms of) language" and properties of stages in the evolution of language are interrelated, such stipulation is a mere terminological game, empty of scientific substance.

Here again, let us make an assumption for argument's sake. Let us take it for a fact that, as is claimed by Jackendoff (1999, p. 276), the principles of Agent First and Focus Last occur in "degraded forms of language". Then, why does this fact make them evidence for the existence of protolanguage? Why does the mere fact of their occurrence in "degraded forms of language" give them what Jackendoff calls "their evolutionarily primitive character"? Would every feature of every "degraded form of language" be "evolutionarily primitive" and, thereby, be evidence for the existence of some stage in language evolution or a property of it? If not, what (kind(s) of) features would not? These are examples of the questions that the required bridge theory should be able to answer in order to provide a licence or warrant for inferences from features of "degraded forms of language" to the existence or properties of stages in the evolution of language.

15.6 A THEORY OF LANGUAGE "FOSSILS"

Violating the third condition referred to above, the way in which Jackendoff uses "fossil" evidence for claims about stages in the evolution of language is problematic in other ways as well. Thus, for some of his "fossils", he fails to furnish any evidence showing that they occur in "degraded forms of language". The principle of Grouping is a case in point. On Jackendoff's (1999, p. 276) characterization, Grouping is a purely semantically-based principle stating that modifiers tend to be adjacent to what they modify. Using this principle, a speaker would interpret the utterance *dog brown eat mouse* as meaning "the brown dog ate the mouse" and not "the dog ate the brown mouse". Interestingly, though Jackendoff refrains (1999, p. 276) from showing that Grouping is a feature of some "degraded form of language", he nevertheless concludes that "This principle can thus be seen as a 'fossil' feature of modern language". To make sense of the way in which Jackendoff uses the term "fossil" here, it has to be understood in the ad hoc sense of "a semantically based principle taking adjacency only into account". But this is not the meaning originally assigned by Jackendoff to the term "fossil", which gives rise to the question:

(5) What exactly is it that makes something a language "fossil"?

The answer to this question presupposes a theory that gives a restrictive characterization of language "fossils" on the basis of which features of modern language can be assigned or denied the status of "fossil" in a non-arbitrary way.

But Jackendoff needs more than a just a restrictive characterization of language "fossils". This is clear from some meta-questions which arise about his use (or non-use) of "fossil" evidence, questions such as the following three. One: Is it imperative – or merely desirable – that "fossil" evidence be furnished for claims about the existence or properties of stages in the evolution of language? Two: Are claims for which no "fossil" evidence has been offered unfounded, or improbable, or are they merely "not (yet) sufficiently well confirmed"? Three: Where claims seem to be at odds with "fossil" evidence, should they be considered "falsified" regardless of whether there are other (i.e., "non-fossil") kinds of evidence or considerations which appear to lend them some support? To be able to answer questions such as these in a reasoned way, Jackendoff needs an evidentiary theory: a theory that clarifies in an explicit way the status and power of "fossil" evidence in relation to other kinds of evidence that bear on accounts of language evolution. The third condition on using data about "degraded" forms of language as evidence for or against an account of the emergence of language, then, says that this has to be done in the framework of a theory of language "fossils" and an associated evidentiary theory.

15.7 CONCLUSION

So let us return to Jackendoff's claim that language "fossils" are "a new source of evidence on the issue" of how modern language emerged. To substantiate this claim – the preceding sections have shown – four theories are required:

(6) (a) a restrictive theory of what it is that makes a form of language "degraded";

(b) a bridge theory about how properties of "degraded" forms of language are interlinked with properties of stages of language evolution;

(c) a restrictive theory of what it is that makes something a language "fossil";

(d) a theory about the role(s) that "fossil" evidence could (not) play in the justification of accounts of language evolution and about the power that such evidence could (not) be accorded.

But, we have seen, Jackendoff has (so far) refrained from offering these theories. Which means that "fossil" evidence cannot (yet) be considered "a new source of evidence on the issue" of the emergence of language.

The poverty of restrictive theory which at present precludes the use of language "fossils" as a source of evidence about the way in which language emerged is, of course, but one specific instance of a fundamental weakness of many modern accounts of the evolution of language. More generally, poverty of restrictive theory is – as this book has sought to argue in some detail – the root cause of the difficulties involved in identifying what linguistic entities were affected by evolution, in discovering by what processes these entities evolved, and in ensuring that accounts of language evolution have the desired scientific substance. It all comes down to this: to arrive at a better understanding of what the evolution of language involved, we would need to make substantive progress in developing restrictive theories of the kinds touched on in this book.

NOTES

CHAPTER 1

1 For some discussion of these and other similarly speculative views of the origin of language, see Stam (1976, pp. 242-254). For a discussion of some of the speculative views expressed under die auspices of the Berlin Academy, see Trabant (2001).
2 Viewed from a modern perspective, such unconstrained speculations about the origin of language as those referred to above are foundationally flawed in other equally basic ways as well. For example, they are offered in the absence of adequate conceptions of what language is or of what it involves for something to come into existence or to develop out of something else.
3 For similar views, see Lewontin (1990b, p. 229).
4 For particulars, see Sections 6.4 and 13.4 below.
5 Stephen Jay Gould "evolved" from a scholar subscribing to a particular view of how language emerged (see Section 6.5 below for specifics) into one considering questions about the origins of language to be "intractable": " ... we know that many kinds of evolutionary events leave no empirical record – and that we therefore cannot formulate scientific questions about them. (For example, I doubt that we will be able to resolve the origins of human language, unless written expressions occurred far earlier than current belief and evidence now indicate.) (Gould 2002, p. 790)
6 A notion of "restrictive theory" played an important role in the development of linguistic theory. For this role, see Chomsky (1972b, pp. 128-129), Botha (1981, pp. 180-181, 339-340).

CHAPTER 2

1 For a charcterization of the Baldwin effect, see Section 7.4.1 below.
2 Chomsky (1981, pp. 34-35), while providing for "intermediate states" as well, has little to say about them.
3 For a characterization of the initial state of the language faculty, see also Chomsky (1980a, pp. 65, 187, 1987, pp. 34–35, 1986, pp. 25–26).
4 Chomsky (1981, pp. 34–35) has also called the initial state of the language faculty "universal grammar (UG)" or "the language acquisition device". For further discussion of this state, see Botha (1989, pp. 255ff.).

204 *Unravelling the Evolution of Language*

5   For Chomsky's general characterization of this state, see, for example, Chomsky (1986, pp. 24-26). For a discussion of important distinctions that need to be drawn in regard to this stable (or steady) state of the language faculty, see Botha (1989, pp. 25-27, 57ff.).
6   For a discussion of the nature of such "triggering" and "shaping", see Chomsky (1980a, pp. 33, 34, 45, 142) and Botha (1989, pp. 16-17).
7   Chomsky (1980a) has referred to this state variously as "knowledge of grammar", "grammatical competence", "mental grammar" and "internalized grammar". For this point of terminology, see Botha (1989, pp. 75-75).
8   For similar other remarks, see Chomsky (1986, p. 27, 1987, p.17).
9   See also Chomsky (1986, p. 22) for a distinction between "knowing a language" and "the known abstract entity".
10 The possibility that a language could also be an abstract Platonic entity has been rejected by Chomsky (1986, p. 33): "There is no initial plausibility to the idea that apart from the truths of grammar concerning the I-language and the truths of UG concerning S_0 there is an additional domain of fact about P[latonic]-language, independent of any psychological states of individuals". Platonic abstract objects incidentally, because they are entities that are non-biological, timeless, placeless and changeless, cannot be subject to evolution. For the characteristics of such entities, see Katz (1981, p. 181).
11 In essence, Chomsky's (1986, pp. 20-31, 1987, p. 33) criticisms of concepts of "E(xternal)language" concern the "artificial" character and their deviation from the common-sense concept of language.
12 Sober uses the expression "univocal object"; from the context, however, it is clear that "univocal" is intended to mean "unitary".
13 In what follows, I no longer put the expressions "characteristics", "features", "parts" and their loose synonyms in quotation marks. I do so purely for convenience; I do not mean to signal that these expressions are unproblematic in Pinker and Bloom's selectionist account of language evolution.
14 See Sections 8.4 and 8.5 below.
15 (18) and (19) refer to (A) and (B) respectively:
    (A) Stimulus-free and situationally independent assignment of structured signals to conceptual representations (asrbitrary sign formation);
    (B) Systematic, recursive combination of signs into structures supporting compositional interpretation (compositionality).
16 At the same colloquium, Wolfgang Klein (2001, p. 85) has contended that the first language or language system was created by the language faculty: " all the

human language faculty needed was a language. But no such linguistic system was available, so the language faculty had to create one."

CHAPTER 3

1   For an earlier, less developed version of this scenario, see Wilkins and Dumford (1990).
2   "Conceptual structure" (or CS) is the central concept of Jackendoff's (1983) theory of semantics: CS is a level of representation at which linguistic, sensory and motor information are integrated. For more particulars about the nature of conceptual structure, see note 6 to Chapter 11 below.
3   Additional assumptions are obviously required for fleshing out what "more" involves in this context.

CHAPTER 4

1   Edited by Hurford, Studdert-Kennedy and Knight, this volume was published in 1998 by Cambridge University Press under the title *Approaches to the Evolution of Language*.
2   The expression "language" is also used in a Chomskyan sense – that of "the language faculty" – by two other contributors to the Edinburgh discussion, namely Berwick (1998, pp. 320, 321, 322) and Newmeyer (1998, pp. 305, 308).
3   In terms of a variant of this question, the predecessor of language might have been an animal **cognitive** system rather than an animal **communication** system. This variant is defended in the Edinburgh discussion by Bickerton (1998) and Ulbaek (1998).
4   Such a "pan-selectionist stance" is attributed by Berwick (1998, p. 321) to Szathmáry (1996) and to Pinker and Bloom (1990).
5   For an earlier defence of this gradualist position, see Newmeyer (1990, 1991).
6   See Berwick (1998, p. 325) for this assumption.
7   For particulars of how these syntactic relations and constraints can be derived from Merge, see Berwick (1998, pp. 332–337).
8   These include the subsystems referred to as "Binding Theory", "Bounding Theory" and "Government Theory".
9   Theta analysis operates in terms of conceptual structure. Informally speaking, what it does is to assign roles to the participants in an event – "thematic roles" such as Agent, Theme and Goal.

CHAPTER 5

1   In a comprehensive linguistic ontology, various categories of entities would be provided for, including
    (a) linguistic objects such as language, languages, a language, etc.;
    (b) linguistic capacities such as the language faculty (with various steady states), the capacities underlying speech production and perception, etc.;
    (c) forms of linguistic behaviour such as speaking, hearing, signing, etc.;
    (d) (linguistic) processes such as those involved in language evolution (phylogeny), language acquisition (ontogeny), linguistic change (diachrony), language variation, etc.

CHAPTER 6

1   Gould's succinct account of the properties and evolution of this brooding chamber is based on work done by Lindberg and Dobbertsen (1981).
2   It is necessary to clarify the way in which the term "conception" is used as part of the expression "conception of language origin". A conception C of something S is taken here to differ from a theory T of S in two basic ways: (a) in regard to the specifics of what it asserts about S, C is less fully articulated than T; and (b) C is more highly speculative and less directly appraisable than T. In the sense intended, therefore, a conception of S is both in ontological and in epistemological terms a less fully developed construct than a theory of S. In the literature, the expressions "view" and "view-point" are often used as synonyms of "conception" in the sense just stipulated.
3   In the literature the terms "entity", "structure" and "system" are used loosely as synonyms in this context, as are the terms "feature", "trait", "property" and "character".
4   Griffiths (1992, p. 117) observes that Gould and Vrba offer two different characterizations of (an) exaptation, one of which represents a "fundamental confusion". The discussion below is not affected by this observation, if correct.
5   Some scholars have found the term "preadaptation" problematic because it could be taken, incorrectly, to imply foreordination. For some discussion of this misunderstanding, see Gould and Vrba (1982, p. 11), and Shelley (1999, pp. 65-66).
6   The use of the term "spandrel" in this context has been criticized on various counts. For an attempt at rebutting some of these criticisms see Gould (1997a, 1997b).

7   For this point, see Gould and Lewontin (1979, p. 153) and Gould and Vrba (1982, pp. 5–7) as well.
8   Gould (1991, p. 45) illustrates this "principle" with the aid of the following example: "We all understand this principle in the case of human artifacts: No one would claim that the US Mint made dimes thin so that all Americans could carry surrogate screw-drivers in their change purses".
9   To illustrate this point, Gould (1991, p. 55) observes that the penditive supports of a dome mounted on arches may cover more area than the dome itself.
10 In Gould's (1991, p. 55) view, San Marco offers a good example of this because mosaic decorations on the radially symmetrical central domes are designed in four-part symmetry, in clear harmony with the four penditives below. The design of the main structure is thus determined by both the form of the spandrels and their number.
11 A clad is a set of species descended from a common ancestral species (Ridley, 1993, p. 632). Cladistic analysis is analysis of the derived characters of organisms to infer the branching sequence in phylogeny based exclusively on derived characters (Mayr, 1997, p. 306). And a cladogram is the inferred branching pattern of a phylogenetic tree (Mayr, 1997, p. 306).
12 A homologous structure or character is one which (1) is shared by a set of species, and (2) is present in the common ancestor of these species (Ridley, 1993, p. 636, Mayr, 1997, p. 308). An analogous structure or character is one which (1) is shared by a set of species but (2) is not present in the common ancestor of these species (Ridley, 1993, p. 631).
13 In these speculations, Chomsky has used the term "language" as a synonym for "language faculty". See Section 2.3 for the (non-)distinction drawn by Chomsky between "language" and the "language faculty".
14 This point will be further pursued in Section 6.5.
15 An earlier formulation of this idea reads as follow: "This is a capacity that could not have been specifically selected, because it was never overt until human evolution reached essentially its present stage" (Chomsky, 1982a, p. 20).
16 In Chomsky's (1988, p. 168) view, it is not the case that people who could count or solve problems of arithmetic or number theory were able to survive to produce more offspring. Wynn and Bloom (1992, p. 410) maintain that "the capacity to count" evolved in animals as an adaptation through the process of natural selection.
17 There appears to be another inconsistency in Chomsky's thinking about the origin of the language faculty. In some formulations – for example, some of those

represented above – he portrays the process by which discrete infinity originated as a property of the language faculty as one that may be characterized in Gouldian terms as "spandrel cooption". In other formulations, however, he depicts this process as (possibly) one of function-shift: "In some cases it seems that organs develop to serve one purpose and, when they have reached a certain form in the evolutionary process, became available for different purposes, at which point the processes of natural selection may refine them further for these purposes. It has been suggested that the development of insect wings follow this pattern. Insects have the problem of heat exchange, and rudimentary wings can serve this function. When they reach a certain size, they become less useful for this purpose but begin to be useful for flight, at which point they evolve into wings. Possibly human mental capacities have in some cases evolved in similar way." (Chomsky, 1988, p. 167).

18 A problematic aspect of Gould's "translation" is that, whereas it attributes to Chomsky a certain view of the origin of "language", Chomsky's by-product conception of language origin is a conception of one fundamental feature of language, namely discrete infinity, only.

19 See also Gould (1993, p. 321) for the importance he assigns to these properties.

20 See also Pinker and Bloom (1990) for this point.

21 Piattelli-Palmarini (1989, 1990) subscribes to an exaptationist conception of language origin which in essential ways is similar to Gould's.

22 See, for example, Sober (1990, p. 764).

23 See Griffiths (1992, pp. 124–126) for a characterization of some of these phases. Botha (1997a, pp. 260–261) shows how the failure to draw a principled distinction between certain phases of language evolution is one of the factors making for a lack of focus in the discussion of Pinker and Bloom's (1990) selectionist theory.

24 For some clarification of the role accorded by Chomsky to the process of natural selection in language evolution, see Botha (1998b, p. 231–234). Chomsky (2000, p. 25) has recently drawn a distinction between three phases in the phylogenetic development of language referring to them as "pre-emergence", "emergence" and "evolution".

25 In Botha (1998b, p. 228–231) it is argued that Chomsky has not proposed what may be appropriately called a "theory of language evolution".

26 Recall that Gould (1997a, p. 10752) has argued that both types of features may in their modern form be "exquisitely well-crafted" for a current utility.

CHAPTER 7

1 Gould and Vrba (1982, p. 7) base this account on work by Ostrom (1974, 1979) and Bakker (1975).
2 For this distinction between adaptation and exaptation, see also Gould (1991, p. 46).
3 In the case of the Black Heron, Gould and Vrba (1982, pp. 7–8) observe, wings were coopted for a further use in fishing. In this connection, they cite McLachlan and Liversidge (1978, p. 39): "Its [i.e., the Black Heron's – R.P.B] fishing is performed standing in shallow water with wings outstretched and forward, forming an umbrella-like canopy which casts a shadow on the water. In this way its food can be seen".
4 See, for example, Mayr (1962, p. 593), Gould and Vrba (1982, p. 11) Shelley (1999) as well as Sections 7.2 and 7.3 below.
5 As observed by Lieberman (2000, p. i), this "model" was proposed for the first time nearly thirty years ago by him: "Almost thirty years have passed since I proposed that the neural mechanisms that confer human syntactic ability evolved from ones originally adapted for motor control". Lieberman has not modified the main claims of this "model" in essential ways over the years.
6 Lieberman (2001, p. 1) has recently admitted "in retrospect" that this claim was not original: Karl Lashley had come to a similar conclusion twenty years earlier "in a reference that I had missed".
7 For some criticisms of this theory of exaptation, see Griffiths (1992, pp. 115–123), Shelley (1999, p. 75) and Reeve and Sherman (1993, p. 3).
8 These include mechanisms involving in Bickerton's terminology such "vertical relationships" as the following: "command (the capacity of a syntactic constituent in a 'higher' position to influence one in a 'lower', but not vice versa); control (the capacity of a phonologically overt syntactic constituent to determine the referential content of a phonologically null constituent); and containment (factors creating limited domains which prevent co-reference between constituents within those domains and constituents outside them ..."
9 For the way in which Merge works, see Berwick (1998, p. 325) and Section 4.4 above. Merge, in essence, builds new hierarchical structure from old.
10 See Lieberman (2000, pp. 1,11,127–130, 164, 166; 2001, p. 21) for recent expressions of this aversion to Chomskyan views on Universal Grammar and syntax.
11 Maryanski (1995, p. 199) boils 1. and 2. down to the following: "Bipedalism, in association with selection for enhanced manual dexterity, triggered an expansion

of motor and parietal association cortex. Excess neural tissue then fashioned the parietal-occipital-temporal junction (POT) and Broca's area, which were later reappropriated for a 'conceptual structure' and language acquisition".

12 Wilkins and Wakefield do furnish what they consider evidence for the appearance of the reappropriated Broca's Area and the POT in *Homo habilis*. The nature of this evidence will be considered in Section 11.2 below.
13 This theory amends and extends earlier work done by Bickerton (1998) and Calvin (1993).
14 In earlier work, Bickerton (1990, p. 153) speculated that "[i]t was perhaps inevitable that a species with a rich PRS [i.e., a "primary representation system" – R.P.B.], an acute need for information, and control of an output channel would eventually stumble on protolanguage".
15 A social calculus should, in Calvin and Bickerton's (2000, p. 129) view, provide for two more basic abilities as well: an ability to distinguish individuals of the social group, and an ability to distinguish different types of actions.
16 Calvin and Bickerton (2000, p. 137) characterize an argument as the combination of a thematic role (AGENT, etc.) with whatever words represent a participant in an action, state or event.
17 Calvin and Bickerton (2000, p. 147) derive this characterization of organic selection from the work of Robert J. Richards, an authority on James Mark Baldwin. The Baldwin effect is a "form-follows-function principle" and should be distinguished from Lamarckism, which is the discredited belief that "what you do in your lifetime can somehow get into your genes". (Calvin and Bickerton, 2000, p. 146)
18 In Bickerton (1998) the terms "stage", "state", "step" and "level" are used loosely as synonyms. Nothing in Bickerton's reasoning, however, hinges on this variation in terminology.
19 The intermediate synchronic varieties mentioned by Bickerton (1998, p. 354) include pidgin languages, ape "language", and the language of children under two.
20 To the function and nature of licensing theories such as those mentioned in (b) and (c), we return in Chapter 11 below.
21 On the nature of *Just-so* stories, see Section 13.2 below.
22 First, nothing in the planning of ballistic movement gives an obvious precedent for the role of the subject NP in sentence structure. Second, the ballistic model is compatible with a kind of syntax in which there is no distinction between sentences and NPs.

23 Agrammatism involves speech that is syntactically disjointed, with grammatical words such as determiners, conjunctions, and auxiliaries left out. As for the quotation given above, it is not clear why Carstairs-McCarthy uses the term "neurological" rather than the term "neural" which he uses elsewhere.

CHAPTER 8

1 Modern authors describe the complexity of specifically the vertebrate eye in a much more detailed way. See in this connection, for example, Pinker and Bloom (1990, p. 709) for a representation of the standard modern description
2 Darwin initially "freely confessed" that to suppose that an organ of such "extreme perfection and complication" as the eye could have been formed by natural selection "seems ... absurd in the highest possible degree". For an account of Darwin's views on the evolution of the eye and of how those views have been misrepresented by antievolutionists, see Gould (1994, p. 10) and Dawkins (1996).
3 See in this connection, for example, Brandon and Hornstein (1986), Hurford (1989, 1991, 1992), Pinker and Bloom (1990), Newmeyer (1998), Donald (1991, 1993, 1999), Dunbar (1993), Aiello and Dunbar (1993), Maynard Smith and Szathmáry (1995, pp. 290–293). For selectionist accounts of various aspects of speech and of some of the mechanisms involved in the production or perception of speech, see for example, MacNeilage (1998a, 1998b), Studdert-Kennedy (1998, 2000) and Lindblom (1990, 1992, 1998).
4 As noted in Section 1.1.2 above, Pinker and Bloom's selectionist account was published and discussed as a target article in the interdisciplinary journal *Behavioral and Brain Sciences* (BBS), Vols. 13 (1990) and 17 (1994). This account is also outlined in part both in Pinker (1994, chapter 10; 1995) and in Bloom (1998, 1999).
5 These comments include the following: "In their remarkably well-written essay, based on a wealth of sources from many disciplines, Pinker and Bloom (P&B) offer a novel and sophisticated version of adaptationism" (Piattelli-Palmarini, 1990, p. 752). "Pinker and Bloom (P&B) have defended a selectionist account of language. The thoroughness with which they have done so is most welcome. I applaud P&B's account for its sophistication and persuasiveness" (Catania, 1990, p. 729). "The minor disagreements I have with Pinker and Bloom's (P&B's) admirable target article are trivial and beneath mention ..." (Ridley, 1990, p. 756). "That is why the target article is such a keen pleasure to read. P&B have found their way through a briar patch of rhetorical obfuscation to an impeccable understanding of modern Darwinism. P&B's central contention seems

inescapable" (Tooby and Cosmides, 1990, p. 761). "Pinker and Bloom (P&B) have done us a service in refuting the widespread belief among generativists that language could not have evolved by natural selection" (Broadwell, 1990, pp. 728–729). "Pinker and Bloom's (P&B's) target article is deeply satisfying and liberating" (Hurford, 1990, p. 736). "The authors are to be honored for a paper that goes a long way toward countering the intemperate anti-Darwinism that has become the mode in some cognitive science circles over the past decade" (Studdert-Kennedy, 1990, p. 758). "Because I find the general thrust of the Pinker and Bloom (P&B) target article to be compelling, this commentary will be devoted to further exploring the consequences of their hypothesis that the language faculty was shaped by natural selection" (Newmeyer, 1990 p. 745).

6   In *Behavioral and Brain Sciences*, Pinker and Bloom's target article is followed by commentary by some thirty-three "peers" which, in turn, is followed by a response from Pinker and Bloom. The debate has continued outside BBS, as witness, for example, Botha (1997a, 1997b, 1998a, 1998b), Gould (1997a, 1997b, 1997c), Grantham and Nichols (1999), Jenkins (2000), Knight, Studdert-Kennedy and Hurford (2000), and Lightfoot (2000).

7   Various aspects of Pinker and Bloom's characterization of the function of language have been criticized in the BBS debate. On the whole, however, their response to these criticisms has been adequate, as is shown in Botha (1997b, pp. 320–322).

8   Other examples of substantive universals furnished by Pinker and Bloom (1990, p. 713–714) include phrase structure rules, rules of linear order, case affixes, auxiliaries, and mechanisms of complementation and control.

9   Piattelli-Palmarini (1990, p. 753) offers the following "simple situation" to concretize his point: "John and Marcia are going to be married, and I want to assert now that one day, three months after their marriage (call it D day), John is going to discover that Marcia is pregnant on D day. Can I state this simple thought in a more compact, less cumbersome sentence ...? It seems not ...

(1) *John will discover that Marcia is pregnant,*

won't do, because (1) is also true if John will discover on D day that Marcia is pregnant now, at this very moment.

(2) *John will discover that Marcia will be pregnant*

won't do either, because (2) is true also if, on D day, John will discover that Marcia will be pregnant at some time *after* D day. It is easy to see that other attempts are equally unsuccessful, even allowing ourselves to [sic] plainly ungrammatical constructions:

(3) *John will have discovered that Marcia (is) (was) (will be) (*will have been)(has been) pregnant."*
(Piattelli-Palmarini, 1990, p. 753)

10 "Spandrel" – as we have seen in Section 6.2 – is a term taken over by Gould and Lewontin (1979) from architecture for denoting biological structures or traits that have uses, roles or utilities for which they were not originally designed.

11 Structure-dependency is a universal constraint on the class of possible grammatical rules. Structure-dependent rules refer to structural properties of constituents of sentences. Structure-independent rules, by contrast, refer only to the linear position of such constituents. What (the universal of) structure-dependency states is that language uses structure-dependent grammatical rules only. For an informal illustration of the nature of structure-dependent grammatical rules, see Chomsky (1988, pp. 41–46).

12 The Case Filter embodies the requirement that all overt NPs must be assigned abstract case. For an illustration of the Case Filter, see Haegeman (1991, p. 141, 156).

13 Allen and Bekoff (1995, p. 617) illustrate these points with reference to the behaviour of a hare confronted by a fox. The hare's behaviour, it has been hypothesized, is to indicate to the fox that it has been detected. This hypothesis, in Allen and Bekoff's view, "is justified if it is reasonable to believe that bipedal standing by ancestral hares had this effect on ancestral foxes, and this effect was (partially) responsible for the transmission of this trait from ancestral hares to descendants". On their analysis, "A corresponding design claim about bipedal standing would ... require showing that this trait is a direct modification of some ancestral trait that was less efficient with respect to its effect on foxes".

14 This characterization of complexity is consonant with those offered by Williams and by Dawkins. On Dawkins's (1988) characterization, a complex thing —
  (a) is something that has a heterogeneous structure (p. 6);
  (b) is something whose constituent parts are arranged in a way that is unlikely to have arisen by chance alone (p. 7);
  (c) is something that is good for or at something (in virtue of having a particular internal structure) (p. 9).

15 Pinker and Bloom (1990, p. 718) base their ideas about the principle (or requirement) of parity on work by Liberman and Mattingly (1989). The principle states that any communication system requires a coding protocol that can be arbitrary as long as it is shared.

16 Reeve and Sherman (1993, p. 7) illustrate the former kind of traits with reference to the camouflaging of certain moths. In particular, they refer to the case of a white moth that is camouflaged from avian predators when it rests on the trunk of light-coloured trees. They ask their readers to imagine that a black morph appears as a result of mutation at a single locus. Such black moths, they observe, would be safe on dark-coloured tree trunks; this would then enable them to migrate deeper into the forest, and there they would be able to establish themselves and to reproduce effectively. And yet, under certain teleonomic criteria for adaptation, black coloration of this sort might fail to be considered an adaptation – because it happens not to require any complex biological machinery or extreme fine-tuning.

17 Fodor (1998, pp. 208–209) has argued that the notion of adaptive complexity is problematic in an even more fundamental way. In his view, what matters to the question of whether the mind is an adaptation is not how complex our behaviour is, but how much change you would have to make in an ape's brain to produce the cognitive structure of a human mind. And he argues that "exactly nothing" is known about this. We will be returning to this argument in Section 12.4 below.

CHAPTER 9

1 For some of the others, see, for example, Griffiths (1992) and Shelley (1999).
2 Reeve and Sherman use the expressions "original role" and "current function" where Gould and Vrba (1982) would probably have used the expressions "(original) function" and "current role/utility/use", respectively.

CHAPTER 10

1 In the literature on language evolution, no explicit distinction is drawn among "testability", "falsifiability" and "refutability". The non-systematic use of the expressions "account", "theory", "scenario", "model" and "explanation" represents another case of terminological variation that is found in this literature.
2 For this conventional way of drawing the distinction between testability-in-principle and testability-in-practice, see Hempel (1966, p. 30ff.) and Botha (1981, pp. 378-379).
3 For some discussion of these factors, see, for example, Botha (1981, pp. 379-381).
4 For some discussion of the nature of protective devices, see Botha (1978, 1981, pp. 381–382, 413–417).

5   Below I will follow the terminological practice of the BBS discussants of informally using the expressions "claim" and "account" instead of "hypothesis" and "theory", respectively.
6   The grounds for not conflating claims of the first three categories will become clear as we proceed.
7   For criticisms of Pinker and Bloom's selection of linguistic universals, see, for example, Pesetsky and Block (1990, pp. 751–752).
8   The example used by Pinker and Bloom is that of the [NP-to-VP] filter. This used to be invoked to explain the ungrammaticality of strings such as *John to have won is surprising*; today, however, it is seen as a consequence of the Case Filter. According to the authors, one might legitimately have wondered what good the older filter was doing in a grammar, but "one could hardly dispense with something like the Case Filter".
9   Commenting critically on a more general claim of Pinker and Bloom's, Lewontin (1990a, p. 741), in similar vein, draws attention to their "confusion of might with must": "Of course, the language faculty might have increased the survivorship and reproduction of its possessors relative to others, so it might have been selected. But was it?" The problem of "speculative" modals is not restricted to selectionist accounts of the evolution of language. Consider in this regard the following comments by Orr (1996, p. 471) on Dennett's (1995a) selectionist account of the evolution of morality: "Dennett's treatment of evolutionary ethics is symptomatic of the problem plaguing his entire book: he is forever suggesting that the universal acid of natural selection *may* be involved here or there. Natural selection of alternative universes may explain why we live in a world having just these physical constants (I spared you this one). Selection may explain why 'strong' artificial intelligence is destined to work (nature got semantics out of syntax, so digital computers can too). Selection may explain the spread of ethical codes among humans. But at each milepost the sceptical reader grumbles, 'But maybe not'. After all, the evidence for each claim is non-existent (alternative universes, origin of morality) to negative (Darwinian evolution of memes)."
10 Hornstein (1990, p. 736) is not willing to do this: "In fact, despite Pinker and Bloom's sensitivity to providing 'just-so' stories in Section 3.1, that indeed is all they provide".
11 These include dismissing data that conflicted with this thesis and using rhetorical ploys or sleights of hand. For some discussion of these, see Feyerabend (1979, p. 88), Botha (1982, p. 35) and the references given there.

CHAPTER 11

1   Holloway (1983, p. 219) draws a distinction between various kinds of information available from endocasts, including information about (i) absolute size, (ii) relative size, when postcranial remains exist, (iii) convolutional patterns, sometimes present, but rarely so, (iv) lobar division, depending on the presence of convolutional patterns, (v) morphometric properties, such as indices, radial and linear distance, asymmetries, etc., and (vi) meningeal (and other blood supply) patterns. A seventh kind of information that may be included, according to Holloway, is about cranial foramina, and cranial nerves. All of these kinds of information depend, in Holloway's (1983, p. 219) view, on the completeness of the endocast, the degree of cranial deformation during and after death, and the intactness of the internal table of bone.

2   Wilkins and Wakefield cite the following specifics: "With respect to posterior organization, the degree of development of the inferior parietal lobule of *H. habilis* appears to exceed that of the australopithecine; sulcal evidence of the presence of well-developed supramarginal and angular gyri is apparent in this specimen. (Similar evidence for parietal expansion is also demonstrated on three habiline endocasts from Olduvai Gorge, Tanzania ... . With the emergence of a substantial inferior parietal lobule (and the decided lack, subsequently, of an observable lunate sulcus), *H. habilis* appears to have been the first species in which researchers might agree that there is human posterior neural organization. The habiline may therefore be considered the first potential possessor of uniquely human modality-free sensory representation." (Wilkins and Wakefield, 1995, p. 171)

3   To these observations, Wilkins and Wakefield add the following: " ... the sulci that have been identified as the horizontal and ascending branches of the Sylvian sulcus on the Koobi Fora habiline endocast represent, in extant humans, the anterior and posterior boundaries of the pars triangularis (part of the inferior frontal gyrus ...) An impression of the pars opercularis (the remaining portion of the inferior frontal gyrus) is preserved on an *H. habilis* specimen from Olduvai Gorge ...; on two additional habiline specimens from this site, humanlike frontal lobe morphology has been verified ... ." (Wilkins and Wakefield, 1995, p. 172)

4   Holloway (1995, p. 192) draws attention to "some additional ugly facts": "Similarly, concerning the Olduvai Gorge hominids referred to as *Homo habilis*, there is a substantial lack of such evidence. Unfortunately, there is no good evidence that 'the presence of well-developed supramarginal and angular gyri is apparent in this specimen', or that 'similar evidence for parietal expansion is also

demonstrated on three habiline endocasts from Olduvai Gorge.' The parietal, temporal, and occipital lobes have no certain convolutional detail, and in the case of OH 7, which was crushed flat into several pieces, there is no occipital portion at all." The target of these critical remarks by Holloway includes Wilkins and Wakefield's claims quoted in note 2 above.

5 On an account by Dick et al. (2001, p. 759) "[l]ocalizationists argue in favor of the idea that language (or specific subcomponents of language) is represented and processed in one or more bounded regions of the brain". This belief is according to them (2001, p. 760) usually accompanied by two corollaries: "(a) there is a transparent mapping between specific functions (i.e., specific behaviors, experiences, and domains of knowledge, or all of these) and the neural regions that mediate those functions, and (b) these neural regions are dedicated exclusively to the functional domains they serve (e.g., an area that mediates motor behavior)." Wilkins and Wakefield (1995, p. 206) do not accept (b), maintaining that the neuroanatomical structures exapted for language "show evidence of their original function"

6 Wilkins and Wakefield (1995, p. 175) suggest that structured, modality-neutral representation is the essence of conceptual structure, and that conceptual structure is not part of the linguistic system per se but is related to it through a set of correspondence rules. Following Jackendoff (1983, p. 17), Wilkins and Wakefield (1995, p. 175) take conceptual structure to be a single level of mental representation at which linguistic, sensory and motor information are compatible. It is made up of basic ontological categories and constituents put together by specific rules of combination. These rules construct higher-level constituents, such as STATES and EVENTS, out of basic categories, such as THINGS and PATHS. Wilkins and Wakefield (1995, p. 175) illustrate this with reference to the sentence *Ben threw the ball to the dog*, which "would include a representation of an EVENT in which a THING (a ball) goes along a PATH from THING [sic] (Ben) to a different THING (the dog). Because this is a causal event, one THING (Ben) CAUSEs the ACT in which the THING (ball) is acted on".

7 For the view that Wilkins and Wakefield's localizationist neuro-linguistic theory is simply "wrong", see Lieberman (2000, pp. 4, 145–146, 159) Lieberman (2000, p. 4) adopts a non-localizationist position on brain activity in terms of which a particular aspect of behaviour usually involves activity of various neuroanatomical structures distributed through the brain. In accordance with this position, he (2000, p. 1) maintains that there exists a functional language system that is distributed over many parts of the human brain, including the neocortex

and subcortical basal ganglia. In a recent article, Dick et al. (2001, p. 760) provide evidence in favour of a "distributive approach" to grammar too. This evidence contradicts the claim that deficits in the processing of grammar necessarily derive from damage to a localized, bounded, and self-contained module or organ dedicated exclusively to this aspect of language. They "show" two general things: (a) deficits in grammatical processing (both receptive and expressive are not restricted to any single type of aphasia, and hence are not associated with damage to specific regions; and (b) the specific profile of deficits referred to as "receptive agrammatism" can be reproduced by testing college students under adverse processing conditions (e.g., temporal or spectral degradation of the acoustic signal, or both), suggesting that these grammatical deficits may have causes that lie outside of the linguistic domain.

8   See Section 10.2 above for a distinction among the various categories of claims expressed by this account.
9   For this tripartite distinction, see Chomsky (1980a, pp. 51–52, 1986a, pp. 9–10) and Botha (1989, pp. 47–48, 91–92).
10 This requirement obviously applies to Calvin and Bickerton's exaptationist theory (see (12)(b) and (c) in Section 7.4.2 above) and Carstairs-McCarthy's co-optationist scenario (see Sections 7.5.3 and 7.5.4 above) as well.
11 The basis for assigning or denying data or facts the status of "evidence" is actually more complex: as has been shown in earlier sections, that basis consists in the nature of the connection between what the data or facts are about and what the claims making up the account are about.

CHAPTER 12

1   For some general discussion of this point, see Weitzenfeld (1984, p. 139ff.) and Waters (1986, p. 502). See Waters (1986) also for a discussion of some of the problems with giving a logical reconstruction of arguments from analogy.
2   For a more technical approach to estimating the probability that a biological structure is an adaptation, see Tooby (1999, pp. 4–5).
3   For a statement of this criticism in terms of the notion of "eminently workable design", see Gould (1997c, p. 57).
4   For further clarification of the sense in which Chomsky uses the expressions "incoherent" and "irrational" in this context, see Botha (1998b, p. 233) and Jenkins (2000, pp. 180–180).
5   To illustrate the contribution of the physical channel, Chomsky refers to, amongst other things, the Fibonacci series. This series – which he claims to be "showing

up all over the place" – is a series of numbers each of which is the sum of the two numbers before it. For some discussion of the Fibonacci series as a "design principle", see Jenkins (2000, pp. 147–151).

6   Gould (1997a, p. 34) elaborates on the characterization by saying that "... the ultra-Darwinists share a conviction that natural selection regulates everything of any importance in evolution, and that adaptation emerges as a universal result and ultimate test of selection's ubiquity". For an account of how "ultra-Darwinism" originated in the work of George Williams (1966) and of how it was extended in the work of Richard Dawkins (1976), see Eldredge (1995, pp. 35–40).

7   Here is a list of some of the factors in question: (a) chance (Gould, 1997b, p. 147), (b) physical constraints on biological form (as a special case of physical law) (Maynard Smith et al., 1985, p. 267, Jenkins, 2000, pp. 188–192), (c) allometry (Lewontin, 1987, p. 167, Gould and Lewontin, 1979, p. 590), (d) random genetic drift (Gould and Lewontin, 1979, pp. 590–591), (e) pleiotropy (Lewontin, 1978, p. 168), (f) ontogenetic developmental constraints (Maynard Smith et al., 1985, p. 272), (g) organic selection or the Baldwin effect (Baldwin, 1902, pp. 135–159, Richards, 1987, pp. 398-404, 457-503), (h) exaptation (Gould and Vrba, 1982, Section 6.2 above), (i) random fixation of mutation (Lewontin, 1978, p. 168) or of selectively neutral or nearly neutral mutants (Kimura, 1983) and (j) self-organization (Kauffman, 1995).

8   This problematic aspect of Pinker and Bloom's selectionist account has been identified by BBS commentators as well, as noted in Section 8.4 above. For details of Gould's criticisms of evolutionary psychology, see Gould (1997a, 1997b, 1997c, 2000). For criticisms of specifically Pinker's views, see Gould (1997c).

9   His argument is directed at this view as it is formulated by Plotkin (1997, pp. 53–54), Pinker (1997b, p. 155), Cosmides and Tooby (1992, p. 53), and Dawkins (1996, p. 202). According to Fodor (2000), this view is expressed so frequently in the literature that "a chap could come down with déjà lu".

10 Fodor (2000, p. 5) is "on the balance not inclined to celebrate how much we have so far learned about how minds work. The bottom line [of his book *The Mind Doesn't Work That Way* – R.P.B] will be that the current situation in cognitive science is light years from being satisfactory. Perhaps somebody will fix this eventually; but not, I should think, in the foreseeable future, and not with tools that we currently have in hand."

11 Chomsky's (early) view of the (exaptive) emergence of a component of the human language faculty is examined in Section 6.4 above.

12 For criticisms of other rhetorical "ploys" used by Pinker and Bloom – and also of their "patronizing tone" – see Piattelli-Palmarini (1990, p. 753).
13 The debate about the "ultra-Darwinian" research paradigm of evolutionary psychology is rich in rhetoric used for purposes such as persuasion, derision and so on. For some examples, see Maynard Smith (1995), Dennett (1997), Pinker (1997a), Gould (1997a, 1997b, 1997c, 2000), Tooby and Cosmides (1997), Steen (1997), Tooby (1999), Kurzban (2002)

CHAPTER 13

1 These papers are published in a volume edited by Carruthers and Chamberlin (2000).
2 Selectionist accounts of the evolution of various features of the mind offered by Pinker (1997b) have been criticized for essentially the same reasons by Jones (1997).
3 Chomsky's distinction between what he calls a "Just So Story" and a "fable" seems to be entirely terminological.
4 Chomsky (1996a, pp. 29–30) has phrased these questions in various, essentially equivalent ways, including the following one: "Suppose we have some account of general properties P of the systems [of the mind/brain – R.P.B.] with which language interacts at the interface. We can now ask a question that is not precise, but is not vacuous either: How good a solution is language to the conditions P? How perfectly does language satisfy the general conditions imposed at the interface? If a divine architect were faced with the problem of designing something to satisfy these conditions, would actual human language be one of the candidates, or close to it?" For other similar formulations, see Chomsky (1995a, p. 221, 1995b, p. 32).
5 For this answer, see also Chomsky (1995b, p. 32, 1996a, p. 30, 1998, p. 15).
6 For some discussion of this point, see Freidin (1997).
7 Chomsky (1998, p. 17) expands as follows on this supposition: "The creature shared our modes of perceptual organization, our beliefs and desires, our hopes and fears, insofar as these are not formed and mediated by language. Perhaps it had a 'language of thought' in the sense of Jerry Fodor and others, but no way to form linguistic expressions associated with the thoughts that this LINGUA MENTIS makes available".
8 This problem is often phrased in the form of a question: "How is it (logically) possible for children, on the basis of insufficient evidence about or severely

limited experience of their language, to acquire the complex and rich system that represents their knowledge of the language?"

9 In the context of language acquisition, Chomsky (1980b, p. 42) draws a distinction between the poverty of the evidence (or stimulus) and the degeneracy of the evidence (or stimulus). He considers the stimulus degenerate in that the data-base of language acquisition contains expressions that are not well formed, including, for example, slips of the tongue, incomplete utterances, utterances characterized by pauses, false starts, endings that do not match their beginnings, etc. The stimulus is impoverished, however, in the sense that it contains no evidence at all for certain properties and principles of (the grammars of) the languages acquired by children.

10 Chomsky (1981, pp. 34–35) has also referred to the initial state of the language faculty as "universal grammar" or "UG". See also Section 2.3 in this connection.

11 For some discussion of the nature of such "triggering" and "shaping", see Chomsky (1980a, pp. 33, 34, 45, 142).

12 The distinction between the logical problem of language acquisition and the psychological problem of language acquisition is elucidated in various contributions to the volume in which Chomsky (1981) was published.

13 Ray Jackendoff (1997, p. 20) is rather doubtful about whether language is characterized by nonredundant perfection. "... I would expect the design of language to involve a lot of Good Tricks (to use Dennett's term) that make language more or less good enough, and that get along well enough with each other and the preexisting systems. But nonredundant perfection? I doubt it." In his view, language has "overlapping systems" as well as systems that serve multiple purposes.

14 Chomsky (1982a, p.23, 1996b, p.42, 1997), of course, has provided himself in a speculative mode for a role for natural selection in the evolution of language. For a discussion of this point, see Botha (1998b, pp. 231-234).

CHAPTER 14

1 In this connection, see for example Gould (2002, pp. 790, 839-840) and Tooby (1999).

CHAPTER 15

1 Jackendoff uses both the notion of a "step" and that of a "stage" in his discussion without clarifying the way in which they are interrelated. Presumably, more than one "step" may be needed to get to one and the same "stage". Likewise, he

refrains from drawing explicitly a distinction between "(modern) language" and "the language capacity".
2   For Bickerton's notion of "protolanguage", see Section 7.4.1 above.
3   To what Grouping involves, we will return in Section 15.6 below.
4   There is a considerable body of work on what is portrayed as simplified forms of language occurring in such domains as language contact/genesis, acquisition, attrition, loss, pathology, register variation and so on.

BIBLIOGRAPHY

Aiello, L.C., Dunbar, R.I.M., 1993. Neocortex size, group size and the evolution of language. Current Anthropology 34, 184–193.

Aitchison, J., 1994. The Seeds of Speech. Language Origin and Language Evolution. Cambridge University Press. Cambridge.

Aitchison, J., 1998. On discontinuing the continuity–discontinuity debate. In: Hurford, J.R., Studdert-Kennedy, M., Knight, C. (Eds.), Approaches to the Evolution of Language, Cambridge, Cambridge University Press, pp. 17–28.

Allen, C., Bekoff, M., 1995. Biological function, adaptation, and natural design. Philosophy of Science 62, 609–622.

Bakker, R.T., 1975. Dinosaur renaissance. Scientific American 232(4), 58–78.

Baldwin, J.M., 1902. Development and Evolution. The Macmillan Company, London.

Batali, J., 1998. Computational simulations of the emergence of grammar. In: Hurford, J.R., Studdert-Kennedy, M., Knight, C. (Eds.), Approaches to the Evolution of Language, Cambridge, Cambridge University Press, pp. 405–426.

Berwick, R.C., 1998. Language evolution and the Minimalist Program: The origins of syntax. In: Hurford, J.R., Studdert-Kennedy, M., Knight, C. (Eds.), Approaches to the Evolution of Language, Cambridge, Cambridge University Press, pp. 320–340.

Berwick, R.C., Weinberg, A.S., 1984. The Grammatical Basis of Linguistic Performance. MIT Press, Cambridge, MA.

Bever, T.G., Carrithers, C., Cowart, W., Townsend, D.J., 1989. Language processing and familial handedness. In: Galaburda, A. (Ed.), From Reading to Neurons, MIT Press, Cambridge, MA., pp. 331–357.

Bickerton, D., 1986. More than nature needs? A reply to Premack. Cognition 23, 73–79.

Bickerton, D., 1990. Language and Species. University of Chicago Press, Chicago.

Bickerton, D., 1995. Language and Human Behavior. University of Washington Press, Seattle.

Bickerton, D., 1998. Catastrophic evolution: the case for a single step from protolanguage to full human language. In: Hurford, J.R., Studdert-Kennedy, M., Knight, C. (Eds.), Approaches to the Evolution of Language, Cambridge, Cambridge University Press, pp. 341–358.

Bierwisch, M., 2001. The apparent paradox of language evolution: can Universal Grammar be explained by adaptive selection? In: Trabant, J., Ward, S. (eds.), New Essays on the Origin of Language. Mouton de Gruyter, Berlin, pp. 55–79.

Bloom, P. 1998. Some issues in the evolution of language and thought. In: Cummins, M.C., Allen, C. (Eds.), The Evolution of Mind, Oxford University Press, pp. 204–223.

Bloom, P., 1999. The evolution of certain novel human capacities. In: Corballis, M.C., Lea, S.E.G. (Eds.), The Descent of Mind. Psychological Perspectives on Hominid Evolution, University of Oxford, Oxford, pp. 295–310.

Boorse, C., 1973. Wright on functions. Philosophical Review 82, 139–168.

Botha, R.P., 1978. Protecting general-linguistic hypotheses from refutation. Stellenbosch Papers in Linguistics 1, 1–38.

Botha, R.P., 1981. The Conduct of Linguistic Inquiry. A Systematic Introduction to the Methodology of Generative Grammar. Mouton Publishers, The Hague etc.

Botha, R.P., 1982. On "the Galilean style" of linguistic inquiry. Lingua 58, 1–50.

Botha, R.P., 1989. Challenging Chomsky. The Generative Garden Game. Basil Blackwell, Oxford.

Botha, R.P., 1997a. Neo-Darwinian accounts of the evolution of language: 1. Questions about their explanatory focus. Language & Communication 17, 249–267.

Botha, R.P., 1997b. Neo-Darwinian accounts of the evolution of language: 2. Questions about complex design. Language & Communication 17, 319–340.

Botha, R.P., 1998a. Neo-Darwinian accounts of the evolution of language: 3. Questions about their evidential bases, logic and rhetoric. Language & Communication 18, 227–249.

Botha, R.P., 1998b. Neo-Darwinian accounts of the evolution of language: 4. Questions about their comparative merit. Language & Communication 18, 227–249.

Botha, R.P., 1999. On Chomsky's 'fable' of instantaneous language evolution. Language and Communication 19, 243–257.

Botha, R.P., 2000. Discussing the evolution of the assorted beasts called *language*. Language & Communication 20, 149–160.

Botha, R.P., 2001a. On the role of bridge theories in accounts of the evolution of language. Language & Communication 21, 61–71.

Botha, R.P., 2001b. How much of language, if any, came about in the same sort of way as the brooding chamber of snails? Language & Communication 21, 225–243.

Botha, R.P., 2002a. Are there features of language that arose like birds' feathers? Language & Communication 22, 17–35.
Botha, R.P., 2002b. Did language evolve like the vertebrate eye? Language & Communication 22, 131–158.
Brandon, R.N., Hornstein, N., 1986. From icons to symbols: some speculations on the origin of language. Biology and Philosophy 1, 169–189.
Broadwell, G.A., 1990. Linguistic function and linguistic evolution. Behavioral and Brain Sciences 13, 728–729.
Byrne, R., 1995. The Thinking Ape: Evolutionary Origins of Intelligence. Oxford University Press, Oxford.
Calvin, W.H., 1993. The unitary hypothesis: a common neural circuitry for novel manipulations, language, plan-ahead, and throwing. In: Gibson, K.R., Ingold, T. (Eds.), Tools, Language and Cognition in Human Evolution, Cambridge University Press, Cambridge, 1993, pp. 230–250.
Calvin, W.H., Bickerton, D., 2000. Lingua ex Machina. Reconciling Darwin and Chomsky with the Human Brain. MIT Press, Cambridge, MA.
Carpenter, R.H.S., 1990. Neurophysiology. 2nd ed. Edward Arnold, London.
Carruthers, P., Chamberlin, A. (Eds.), 2000. Evolution and the Human Mind: Modularity, Language and Meta-Cognition. Cambridge University Press, Cambridge.
Carstairs-McCarthy, A., 1999. The Origins of Complex Language. Oxford, Oxford University Press.
Catania, A.C., 1990. What good is five percent of a language competence? Behavioral and Brain Sciences 13, 729–731.
Catania, A.C., 1995. Single words, multiple words, and the functions of language. Behavioral and Brain Sciences 18, 184–185.
Chomsky, N., 1972a. Language and Mind. Enlarged Edition. Harcourt, Brace Javanovich, New York.
Chomsky, N., 1972b. Some empirical issues in the theory of transformational grammar. In: Chomsky, N., Studies on Semantics in Generative Grammar. Mouton, The Hague, pp. 120–202.
Chomsky, N., 1980a. Rules and Representations. Columbia University Press, New York.
Chomsky, N., 1980b. Rules and Representations. Behavioral and Brain Sciences 3, 1–15, 42–61.

Chomsky, N., 1981. Principles and parameters in syntactic theory. In: Hornstein, L..N., Lightfoot, D. (Eds.), Explanation in Linguistics. The Logical Problem of Language Acquisition. Longman, London, pp. 32–75.

Chomsky, N., 1982a. The Generative Enterprise. A Discussion with Riny Huybregts and Henk van Riemsdijk. Foris Publications, Dordrecht.

Chomsky, N., 1982b. Discussion of Putnam's comments. In: Piattelli-Palmarini, M. (Ed.), Language and Learning. The Debates between Jean Piaget and Noam Chomsky. Routledge and Kegan Paul, London, pp. 310–324.

Chomsky, N., 1986. Knowledge of Language: Its Nature, Origin and Use. Praeger, New York.

Chomsky, N., 1987. Language in a Psychological Setting. Sophia Linguistica 22. The Graduate School of Languages and Linguistics, Tokyo.

Chomsky, N., 1988. Language and Problems of Knowledge. The Managua Lectures. MIT Press, Cambridge, MA.

Chomsky, N., 1989. Mental constructions and social reality. Paper delivered at Conference on Knowledge and Language, May 1989, Groningen.

Chomsky, N., 1991a. A personal view. In: Kasher, A. (Ed.), The Chomskyan Turn, Basil Blackwell, Oxford, pp. 3–25.

Chomsky, N., 1991b. Linguistics and cognitive science: problems and mysteries. In: Kasher, A. (Ed.), The Chomskyan Turn. Basil Blackwell, Oxford, pp. 26–53.

Chomsky, N., 1995a. The Minimalist Program. MIT Press, Cambridge, MA.

Chomsky, N., 1995b. Language is the perfect solution! Interview with L. Cheng and R. Sybesma. Glot International 1, 31–34.

Chomsky, N., 1996a. Powers and Prospects. Reflections on Human Nature and Social Order. South End Press, Boston.

Chomsky, N., 1996b. Language and evolution. Letter to the New York Review of Books, 1 February 1996, p. 41.

Chomsky, N., 1997. The state of the minimalist art. Lecture presented at the University of Cape Town, 29 May 1997.

Chomsky, N., 1998. Language and mind: current thoughts on ancient problems. Part I and Part II. Lectures presented at Universidade de Brasilia. Published under the title "Linguagem e mente. Pensamentos atuais sobre antigos problemas" in Pesquisa Linguistica 3.4. Page references are to the English manuscript.

Chomsky, N., 2000. An interview on minimalism (with Adriana Beletti and Luigi Rizzi). University of Siena, Nov. 8–9, 1999.

Chomsky, N., Halle, M., 1968. The Sound Pattern of English. Harper and Row, New York.

Cosmides, L., Tooby, J., 1992. Cognitive adaptations for social exchange. In: Barkow, J., Cosmides, L., Tooby, J. (Eds.), The Adapted Mind: Evolutionary Psychology and the Generation of Culture. Oxford University Press, Oxford, pp. 163–227.

Cummins, R., 1984. Functional analysis. In: Sober, E. (Ed.), Conceptual Issues in Evolutionary Biology, MIT Press, Cambridge, MA, pp. 386–407.

Darwin, C., 1859. On the Origin of Species. John Murray, London.

Darwin, C., 1871. The Descent of Man, and Selection in Relation to Sex. John Murray, London.

Darwin, C., 1872. On the Origin of Species. Second Edition. John Murray, London.

Dawkins, R., 1976. The Selfish Gene. Oxford University Press, Oxford.

Dawkins, R., 1983. Universal Darwinism. In: Bendall, D.S. (Ed.), Evolution from Molecules to Man, Cambridge University Press, Cambridge, pp. 403–425.

Dawkins, R., 1986. The Blind Watchmaker. Longman, Harlow.

Dawkins, R., 1988. The Blind Watchmaker. Penguin Books, London.

Dawkins, R., 1996. Climbing Mount Improbable. W.W. Norton & Company, New York.

Dennett, D., 1995a. Darwin's Dangerous Idea. Evolution and the Meaning of Life. Simon and Schuster, New York.

Dennett, D., 1995b. Interview. Omni 17(8), 119–124.

Dennett, D.C., 1997. "Darwinian fundamentalism": an exchange. Letter to the Editors of New York Review of Books, 14 August 1997, pp. 64–65.

Dick, F., Bates, E., Wulfeck, B., Utman, J.A., Dronkers, N., 2001. Language deficits, localization, and grammar: evidence for a distributive model of language breakdown in aphasic patients and neurologically intact individuals. Psychological Review 108, 759–788.

Dingwall, W.O., 1995. Complex behaviors: Evolution and the brain. Behavioral and Brain Sciences 18, 186–188.

Donald, M., 1991. Origins of the Modern Mind: Three Stages in the Evolution of Culture and Cognition. MIT Press, Cambridge.

Donald, M., 1993. Précis of Origins of the Modern Mind: Three Stages in the Evolution of Culture and Cognition. Behavioral and Brain Sciences 16, 737–748, 775–791.

Donald, M., 1995. Neurolinguistic models and fossil reconstructions. Behavioral and Brain Sciences 18, 188–189.

Donald, M., 1998. Mimesis and the executive suite: missing links in language evolution. In: Hurford, J.R., Studdert-Kennedy, M., Knight, C. (Eds.), Approaches to the Evolution of Language, Cambridge, Cambridge University Press, pp. 44–67.

Donald, M. 1999. Preconditions for the evolution of protolanguages. In: Corballis, M.C., Lea, S.E.G. (Eds.), The Descent of Mind. Psychological Perspectives on Hominid Evolution. Oxford University Press, Oxford.

du Boulay, G.H., 1965. Principles of X-ray Diagnosis of the Skull. Butterworth, London.

Dunbar, R., 1993. Coevolution of neocortical size, group size and language in humans. Behavioral and Brain Sciences 16, 681–694, 721–735.

Dunbar, R., 1998. Theory of mind and the evolution of language. In: Hurford, J.R., Studdert-Kennedy, M., Knight, C. (Eds.), Approaches to the Evolution of Language, Cambridge, Cambridge University Press, pp. 92–110.

Eldredge, N., 1995. Reinventing Darwin: The great evolutionary debate. Weidenfeld and Nicolson, London.

Feyerabend, P.K., 1979. Against method. Outline of an anarchist theory of knowledge. Verso, London.

Fitch, R.H., Tallal, P., 1995. A case for auditory temporal processing as an evolutionary precursor to speech processing and language function. Behavioral and Brain Sciences 18, 189.

Fodor, J., 1998. In Critical Condition. Polemical Essays on Cognitive Science and the Philosophy of Mind. MIT Press, Cambridge, MA.

Fodor, J., 2000. The Mind Doesn't Work that Way. The Scope and Limits of Computational Psychology. MIT Press, Cambridge, MA.

Fodor, J., 2001. Review of Carruthers, P., Chamberlin, A. (Eds.), Evolution and the Human Mind: Modularity, Language and Meta-Cognition. Cambridge University Press, Cambridge, 2000. The British Journal for the Philosophy of Science 52, 623–628.

Frazier, L., 1990. Seeing language evolution in the eye. Adaptive complexity or visual illusion. Behavioral and Brain Sciences 13, 731–732.

Freidin, R., 1997. Review of Chomsky, N., The Minimalist Program, MIT Press, Cambridge, MA. Language 73, 571–582.

Freyd, J., 1990. Natural selection or shareability? Behavioral and Brain Sciences 13, pp. 732–734.

Gould, S.J., 1980. The Panda's Thumb. Penguin. London.

Gould, S.J., 1991. Exaptation: a crucial tool for evolutionary psychology. Journal of Social Issues 47, 43–65.

Gould, S.J., 1993. Eight Little Piggies. Reflections on Natural History. Penguin Books, London.
Gould, S.J. 1994. Common pathways of illumination. Natural History 12, 10–20.
Gould, S.J. 1997a. The exaptive excellence of spandrels as a term and prototype. Proc. Natl. Acad. Sci. USA 94, 10750–10755
Gould, S.J., 1997b. Darwinian fundamentalism. The New York Review of Books, 12 June 1997, 34–37.
Gould, S.J., 1997c. Evolution: the pleasures of pluralism. The New York Review of Books, 26 June 1997, 47–52.
Gould, S.J., 1997d. Evolutionary psychology: an exchange. Letter to the New York Review of Books, 9 October 1997, 56–58.
Gould, S.J., 1998. On transmitting Boyle's Law to Darwin's revolution. In: Fabian, A.C. (Ed.), Evolution: Society, Science and the Universe. Cambridge University Press, Cambridge, pp. 4–27.
Gould, S.J., 2000. More things in heaven and earth. In: Rose, H., Rose, S. (Eds.), Alas Poor Darwin: Arguments Against Evolutionary Psychology, Harmony Books, New York, pp. 101–126.
Gould, S.J., 2002. The Structure of Evolutionary Theory. The Belknap Press of Harvard University Press, Cambridge, MA and London.
Gould, S.J., Lewontin, R.C., 1979. The spandrels of San Marco and the Panglossian paradigm: a critique of the adaptationist programme. Proceedings of the Royal Society of London 205, 581–598.
Gould, S.J., Vrba, E.S., 1982. Exaptation – a missing term in the science of form. Paleobiology 8, 4–15.
Grantham, T., Nichols, S., 1999. Evolutionary psychology: Ultimate explanations and Panglossian predictions. In: Hardcastle, V.G. (Ed.), Where Biology Meets Psychology. Philosophical Essays, The MIT Press, Cambridge, MA, pp. 47–66.
Greenfield, P.M., 1991. Language, tools and brain: The ontogency and philogeny of hierarchically organized sequential behavior. Behavioral and Brain Sciences 14, pp. 531–551.
Griffiths, P., 1992. Adaptive explanation and the concept of a vestige. In: Griffiths, P. (Ed.), Trees of Life. Essays in Philosophy of Biology. Kluwer Academic Publishers, Dordrecht, pp. 111–131.
Haegeman, L., 1991. Introduction to Government and Binding Theory. Basil Blackwell, Oxford.
Hauser, M.D., Wolfe, N.D., 1995. Human Language: Are nonhuman precursors lacking? Behavioral and Brain Sciences 18, 190–191.

Hempel, C.G., 1966. Philosophy of Natural Science. Prentice-Hall, Englewood Cliffs, N.J.
Holloway, R.L., 1976. Paleoneurological evidence for language origins. Annals of the New York Academy of Sciences 280, 330–348.
Holloway, R.L., 1983. Human paleontological evidence relevant to language behaviour. Human Neurobiology 2, 105–114.
Holloway, R.L., 1995. Evidence for POT expansion in early *Homo*: a pretty theory with ugly (or no) paleoneurological facts. Behavioral and Brain Sciences 18, 191–193.
Hornstein, N., 1990. Selecting grammars. Behavioral and Brain Sciences 13, 735–736.
Hurford, J.R., 1989. Biological evolution of the Saussurean sign as a component of the language acquisition device. Lingua 79, pp. 187–222.
Hurford, J.R., 1990. Beyond the roadblock of linguistic evolution studies. Behavioral and Brain Sciences 13, 736–737.
Hurford, J.R., 1991. The evolution of the critical period for language acquisition. Cognition 40, 159–201.
Hurford, J.R., 1992. An approach to the phylogeny of the language faculty. In: Hawkins, J.A., Gell-Mann, M. (Eds.), The Evolution of Human Languages, Adison-Wesley Publishing Company, Redwood City, California, pp. 273–303.
Hurford, J.R., 1998. Introduction: the emergence of syntax. In: Hurford, J.R., Studdert-Kennedy, M., Knight, C. (Eds.), Approaches to the Evolution of Language, Cambridge, Cambridge University Press, pp. 299–304.
Jackendoff, R., 1983. Semantics and cognition. MIT Press, Cambridge, MA.
Jackendoff, R., 1997. The Architecture of the Language Faculty. MIT Press, Cambridge, MA.
Jackendoff, R., 1999. Possible stages in the evolution of the language capacity. *Trends in Cognitive Science* 3(7), 272–279.
Jackendoff, R., 2002. Foundations of Language: Brain, Meaning, Grammar, Evolution. Oxford University Press, Oxford.
Jacobs, B., Horner, J.M., 1995. Language as a multimodal sensory enhancement system. Behavioral and Brain Sciences 18, 194–195.
Jenkins, L., 2000. Biolinguistics. Exploring the Biology of Language. Cambridge University Press, Cambridge.
Jerison, H.J., 1995. Issues in neo- and paleoneurology of language. Behavioral and Brain Sciences 18, 195–196.

Jones, S., 1997. The set within the skull. The New York Review of Books, 6 November, 1997, pp. 13–16.
Katz, J.J., 1981. Language and other Abstract Objects. Basil Blackwell. Oxford.
Kauffman, S., 1995. At Home in the Universe. The Search for Laws of Self-organization and Complexity. Oxford University Press, New York.
Kendon, A., 1991. Some considerations for a theory of language origins. *Man* (N.S.) 26, pp. 199–220.
Kimura, M., 1979. The neutral theory of molecular evolution. Scientific American 241 (November), 98–126.
Kimura, M., 1983. The Neutral Theory of Molecular Evolution. Cambridge University Press, Cambridge.
Kirby, S., 1998. Fitness and the selective adaptation of language. In: Hurford, J.R., Studdert-Kennedy, M., Knight, C. (Eds.), Approaches to the Evolution of Language, Cambridge, Cambridge University Press, pp. 359–383.
Kirby, S., 2000. Syntax without natural selection: How compositionality emerges from vocabulary in a population of learners. In: Knight, C., Studdert-Kennedy, M., Hurford, J.R. (Eds.), The Evolutionary Emergence of Language. Social Functions and the Origins of Linguistic Form, Cambridge University Press. Cambridge, pp. 302–323.
Klein, W., 2001. Elementary forms of linguistic organization. In: Trabant, J., Ward, S. (Eds.), New Essays on the Origin of Language, Mouton de Gruyter, Berlin, pp. 81–102.
Klein, W., Perdue, C., 1996. The Basic Variety, or: Couldn't natural languages be much simpler? Second Language Research 13, 301–347.
Knight, C., Studdert-Kennedy, M., Hurford, J.R., 2000. Language: A Darwinian adaptation. In: Knight, C., Studdert-Kennedy, M., Hurford, J.R. (Eds.), The Evolutionary Emergence of Language. Social Functions and the Origins of Linguistic Form, Cambridge University Press, Cambridge, pp. 1–15.
Kurzban, R., 2002. Alas poor evolutionary psychology: Unfairly accused, unjustly condemned. Human Nature Review 2, 99–109.
http://human-nature.com/nibbs/02/apd.html
Lakatos, I., 1971. History of science and its rational reconstructions. In: Buck, P.C., Cohen, R.S. (Eds.), PSA 1970. In Memory of Rudolf Carnap. Boston Studies in the Philosophy of Science. Vol. VIII, D. Reidel Publishing Company, Dordrecht and Boston, pp. 91–136.
Laudan, L., 1996. Beyond Positivism and Relativism. Theory, Method and Evidence. Westview Press, Boulder, Colorado.

Lewontin, R.C., 1978. Adaptation. Scientific American 239, 157–170.
Lewontin, R.C., 1990a. How much did the brain have to change for speech? Behavioral and Brain Sciences 13, 740–741.
Lewontin, R.C., 1990b. The evolution of cognition. In: Osherson, D.N., Smith, E.E. (Eds.). Thinking, An Invitation to Cognitive Science. MIT Press, Cambridge, MA., pp. 229–240.
Lieberman, P., 1975. On the Origins of Language. An Introduction to the Evolution of Human Speech. MacMillan Publishing Co., New York.
Lieberman, P., 1984. The Biology and Evolution of Language. Harvard University Press, Cambridge, MA.
Lieberman, P., 1985. On the evolution of human syntactic ability. Its preadaptive bases – motor control and speech. Journal of Human Evolution 14, 657–666.
Lieberman, P., 1989. Some biological constraints on universal grammar and learnability. In: Rice, M., Schiefelbusch, R.L. (Eds.), The Teachability of Language, Paul H. Brookes, Baltimore, MD., pp. 199–225.Lieberman, P., 1990. "Not invented here". Behavioral and Brain Sciences 13, 741–742.
Lieberman, P., 1991a. Uniquely Human. The Evolution of Speech, Thought, and Selfless Behavior. Harvard University Press, Cambridge, MA.
Lieberman, P., 1991b. Speech and brain evolution. Behavioral and Brain Sciences 14, 566–568.
Lieberman, P., 1995. Manual versus speech motor control and the evolution of language. Behavioral and Brain Sciences 18, 197–198.
Lieberman, P., 2000. Human Language and our Reptilian Brain. The Subcortical Bases of Speech, Syntax and Thought. Harvard University Press, Cambridge, MA.
Lieberman, P., 2001. On the subcortical bases of the evolution of language. In: Trabant, J., Ward, S. (Eds.), New Essays on the Origin of Language, Mouton de Gruyter, Berlin, pp. 21–40.
Lightfoot, D., 2000. The spandrels of the linguistic genotype. In: Knight, C., Studdert-Kennedy, M., Hurford, J.R. (Eds.), The Evolutionary Emergence of Language. Social Functions and the Origins of Linguistic Form. Cambridge University Press, Cambridge, pp. 242–264.
Lindberg, D.R., Dobbertsen, R.A., 1981. Umbilical brood protection and sexual dimorphism in the boreal trochid gastropod *Margarites vorticiterus* Dall. Journal of Invertebrate Reproduction 3, 347-355.
Lindblom, B., 1990. Adaptive complexity in sound patterns. Behavioral and Brain Sciences 13, 743–744.

Lindblom, B., 1992. Phonological units as adaptive emergents of lexical development. In: Ferguson, C.A., Menn, L., Stoel-Gammon, C. (Eds.), Phonological Development: Models, Research, Implications. York Press, Timonium, MD, pp. 131–163.

Liska, J., 1995. Semiogenesis as a continuous, not a discrete, phenomenon. Behavioral and Brain Sciences 18, 198–199.

MacNeilage, P.F., 1998a. Evolution of the mechanism of language output: comparative neurobiology of vocal and manual communication. In: Hurford, J.R., Studdert-Kennedy, M., Knight, C. (Eds.), Approaches to the Evolution of Language, Cambridge, Cambridge University Press, pp. 222–241.

MacNeilage, P.F. 1998b. The frame/content theory of evolution of speech production. Behavioral and Brain Sciences 21, 499–511, 532–546.

Maryanski, A., 1995. Hominid tool-language connection: Some missing evolutionary links? Behavioral and Brain Sciences 18, 199–200.

Maynard Smith, J., 1995. Genes, memes and minds: Review of Dennett, D.C., Darwin's Dangerous Idea. New York Review of Books, 30 November 1995, pp. 46–48.

Maynard Smith, J., Burian, R., Kauffman, S., Alberch, P., Campbell, J., Goodwin, B., Lande, R., Raup, D., Wolpert, L., 1985. Developmental constraints and evolution. The Quarterly Review of Biology 60, 265–287.

Maynard Smith, J., Szathmáry, E., 1995. The Major Transitions in Evolution. W.H. Freeman/Spektrum, Oxford.

Mayr, E., 1962. Animal Species and Evolution. Belknap Press of Harvard University Press, Cambridge, MA.

Mayr, E., 1997. This is Biology. The Science of the Living World. The Belknap Press of Harvard University Press, Cambridge, MA.

McLachlan, G.R., Liversidge, R., 1987. Robert's Birds of South Africa. 4th Edition. John Voelcker Bird Book Fund, Cape Town.

Newmeyer, F.J., 1990. Natural selection and the autonomy of syntax. Behavioral and Brain Sciences 13, 745–746.

Newmeyer, F.J., 1991. Functional explanation in linguistics and the origins of language. Language & Communication 11, 3–28.

Newmeyer, F.J., 1998. On the supposed 'counterfactuality' of Universal Grammar: some evolutionary implications. In: Hurford, J.R., Studdert-Kennedy, M., Knight, C. (Eds.), Approaches to the Evolution of Language, Cambridge, Cambridge University Press, pp. 305–319.

Newmeyer, F., 2000. Three book-length studies of language evolution. Journal of Linguistics 36, 383–395.

Ninio, A., 1990. The genome might as well store the entire language in the environment. Behavioral and Brain Sciences 13, 746–747.

Orr, H.A., 1996. Dennett's dangerous idea. Evolution 50, 467–472.

Ostrom, J., 1974. *Archaeopteryx* and the origin of flight. Quarterly Review of Biology 49, 27–47.

Ostrom, J., 1979. Bird flight: How did it begin? American Scientist 67, 46–56.

Otero, C.P., 1990. The emergence of *homo loquens* and the laws of physics. Behavioral and Brain Sciences 13, 747–750.

Page, R., Mitchell, S., 1990. Self-organization and adaptation in insect societies. In: Fine, A. et al. (Eds.), PSA 1990, Vol. 2, Philosophy of Science Association, East Lansing, MI, pp. 289–298.

Pesetsky, D., Block, N., 1990. Complexity and adaptation. Behavioral and Brain Sciences 13, 750–752.

Piattelli-Palmarini, M., 1989. Evolution, selection and cognition: From "learning" to parameter setting in biology and the study of language. Cognition 31, 1–44.

Piattelli-Palmarini, M., 1990. An ideological battle over modals and quantifiers. Behavioral and Brain Sciences 13, 752–754.

Pinker, S., 1994. The Language Instinct. How the Mind Creates Language. William Morrow and Company, Inc., New York.

Pinker, S., 1995. Language is a human instinct. In: Brockman, J., (Ed.), The Third Culture: Beyond the Scientific Revolution, Simon and Schuster, New York, pp. 223–236.

Pinker, S., 1997a. Evolutionary psychology: an exchange. Letter to the New York Review of Books, 9 September 1997, pp. 55–56.

Pinker, S., 1997b. How the Mind Works. Norton, New York.

Pinker, S., 1997c. Evolutionary perspectives. In: Gazzaniga, M.S. (Ed.), Conversations with the Cognitive Neurosciences, MIT Press, Cambridge, MA, pp. 111–129.

Pinker, S., 1998. The evolution of the human language faculty. In: Jablonski, N.G., Aiello, L.C. (Eds.), The Origin and Diversification of Language, Memoirs of the California Academy of Sciences 24, San Fransisco, pp. 117–126.

Pinker, S., Bloom, P., 1990. Natural language and natural selection. Behavioral and Brain Sciences 13, 707–727, 765–784.

Pinker, S., Bloom, P., 1994. Continued commentary on Steven Pinker and Paul Bloom (1990), Natural language and natural selection, BBS 13: 707–784. Behavioral and Brain Sciences 17, 180–185.

Plotkin, H., 1997. Evolution in Mind. Alan Lane, London.

Premack, D., 1986. Pangloss to Cyrano de Bergerac: "Nonsense, it's perfect!" Cognition 23, pp. 81–88.

Reeve, H.K., Sherman, P.W., 1993. Adaptation and the goals of evolutionary theory. Quarterly Review of Biology 68, 1–32.

Richards, R.J., 1987. Darwin and the Emergence of Evolutionary Theories of Mind and Behavior. University of Chicago Press, Chicago.

Ridley, M., 1990. Arbitrariness is no argument against adaptation. Behavioral and Brain Sciences 13, 756.

Ridley, M., 1993. Evolution. Blackwell Scientific Publications, Boston.

Shelley, C., 1999. Preadaptation and the explanation of human evolution. Biology and Philosophy 14, 65–82.

Sober, E., 1990. Anatomizing the rhinoceros. Behavioral and Brain Sciences 13, 764–765.

Sperber, D., 1990. The evolution of the language faculty: a paradox and its solution. Behavioral and Brain Sciences 13, 756–758.

Stam, J.H., 1976. Inquiries into the Origin of Language. The Fate of a Question. Harper and Row Publishers, New York etc.

Steels, L., 1998. Synthesizing the origins of language and meaning using coevolution, self-organization and level formation. In: Hurford, J.R., Studdert-Kennedy, M., Knight, C. (Eds.), Approaches to the Evolution of Language, Cambridge, Cambridge University Press, pp. 384–404.

Steen, F.F., 1997. Gould on adaptationism and evolutionary psychology. http://cogweb.ucla.edu/Debate/On_Gould.html

Studdert-Kennedy, M., 1990. This view of language. Behavioral and Brain Sciences 13, 756–758.

Studdert-Kennedy, M., Knight, C., Hurford, J.R., 1998. Introduction: new approaches to language evolution. In: Hurford, J.R., Studdert-Kennedy, M., Knight, C. (Eds.), Approaches to the Evolution of Language, Cambridge University Press, Cambridge, pp. 1–5.

Studdert-Kennedy, M., 2000. Evolutionary implications of the particulate principle: Imitation and the dissociation of phonetic form from semantic function. In: Knight, C., Studdert-Kennedy, M., Hurford, J.R. (Eds.), The Evolutionary

Emergence of Language. Social Function and the Origins of Linguistic Form, Cambridge University Press, Cambridge, pp. 161–176.

Szathmáry, E., 1996. From RNA to language. Current Biology 6, 764.

Szathmáry, E., 2001. Origin of the human language faculty: the language amoeba hypothesis. In: Trabant, J., Ward, S. (Eds.), New Essays on the Origin of Language, Mouton de Gruyter, Berlin, pp. 41–51.

Tooby, J., 1999. The most testable concept in biology, Part I. HBES Newsletter, View from the President's Window – Fall 1999.
http://www.psych.ucsb.edu/research/cep/viewfall99.html

Tooby, J., Cosmides, L., 1990. Toward an adaptationist psycholinguistics. Behavioral and Brain Sciences 13, 760–762.

Tooby, J., Cosmides, L., 1997. Letter to the Editor of The New York Review of Books on Stephen Jay Gould's "Darwinian fundamentalism" (12 June 1997) and "Evolution: The pleasures of pluralism" (June 26, 1997).
http://cogweb.english.ucsb.edu/Debate/CEP_Gould.html

Trabant, J., 1996. Thunder, girls, and sheep, and other origins of language. In: Trabant, J. (Ed.), Origins of Language, Collegium Budapest Workshop Series No. 2, pp. 39–69.

Trabant, J., 2001. Introduction: New perspectives on an old academic question. In: Trabant, J., Ward, S. (Eds.), New Essays on the Origin of Language, Mouton de Gruyter, Berlin, pp. 1–17.

Ulbaek, I., 1998. The origins of language and cognition. In: Hurford, J.R., Studdert-Kennedy, M., Knight, C. (Eds.), Approaches to the Evolution of Language, Cambridge, Cambridge University Press, pp. 30–43.

Uriagereka, J., 2001. Review of Carstairs-McCarthy, A., The Origins of Complex Language. An Inquiry into the Evolutionary Beginnings of Sentences, Syllables, and Truth, Oxford University Press, Oxford, 1999. Language 77, 368–373.

Walker, S.F., 1995. Bartering old stone tools: When did communicative ability and conceptual structure began to interact? Behavioral and Brain Sciences 18, 203–204.

Waters, C.K., 1986. Taking analogical inference seriously: Darwin's argument from artificial selection. In Fine, A., Machamer, P. (Eds.), PSA 1986, The Philosophy of Science Foundation, East Lansing, Mich., pp. 502–513.

Weitzenfeld, J.S., 1984. Valid reasoning by analogy. Philosophy of Science 51, 137–149.

Whitcombe, E., 1995. Paleoneurology of language: Grounds for skepticism. Behavioral and Brain Sciences 18, 204–305.

Whitney, W., 1873. Oriental and Linguistic Studies, Vol. 1. Charles Scribner's Sons, New York.
Wilkins, W.K., Dumford, J., 1990. In defense of exaptation. Behavioral and Brain Sciences 13, 763–764.
Wilkins, W.K., Wakefield, J., 1995. Brain evolution and neurolinguistic preconditions. Behavioral and Brain Sciences 18, 161–182, 205–226.
Wilkins, W.K., Wakefield, J., 1996. Further issues in neurolinguistic preconditions. Behavioral and Brain Sciences 19, 793–798.
Williams, G.C., 1966. Adaptation and Natural Selection. Princeton University Press, Princeton, N.Y.
Worden, R., 1998. The evolution of language from social intelligence. In: Hurford, J.R., Studdert-Kennedy, M., Knight, C. (Eds.), Approaches to the Evolution of Language, Cambridge, Cambridge University Press, pp. 148–166.
Wynn, K., Bloom, P., 1992. The origins of psychological axioms of arithmetic and geometry. Mind and Language 7, 409–416.

INDEX

abstracted language, 19
abstraction, 57, 58, 59, 173, 180, 181, 182, 183, 185, 186, 187, 188, 189, 190
accounts of language evolution, adaptationist; *see* selectionist
  by-product, 50
  co-optationist, 50
  exaptationist, 78
  preadaptive, 68, 116
  reappropriationist, 73
  selectionist, 10, 94, 104, 113, 123, 126, 134, 136, 157, 158, 177, 206
adaptation, (as a process), 7, 16, 51, 52, 53, 54, 67, 69, 70, 71, 72, 75, 94, 95, 108, 111, 112, 115, 116, 125, 131, 133, 158, 165, 175, 209, 211, 216, 220, 221, 225, 233, 236, 237; *see also* natural selection
adaptationism, strong vs extreme, 121
adaptations, (as products), 51, 52, 53, 60, 63, 64, 65, 67, 73, 106, 110, 112, 113, 116, 125, 176, 229
adaptive complexity, 14, 93, 95, 106, 107, 108, 110, 111, 135, 163, 216; *see also* complex design
adaptive properties of language, 108, 111
agrammatism, 90, 220
ambient language, 17
analogous structure, 209
analogy, 20, 53, 61, 100, 157, 158, 159, 162, 165, 167, 168, 170, 171, 172, 177, 178, 180, 182, 183, 184, 187, 189, 192, 220, 238
  arguments from, 119, 131
arguments, non-empirical, *see* analogy, arguments from; ignorance arguments from; necessity, arguments from; probability arguments from
argument clusters, 170
argument structure (in language evolution), 77, 78

Baldwin effect, 17, 205, 212, 221; *see also* organic selection
Basic Variety, The, 197; *see also* BV
Binding Theory, 207, 231
bridge theory/theories, 146, 147, 148, 149, 150, 156, 192, 199, 200, 202
Broca's aphasia, 90, 91
Broca's area, 27, 28, 68, 71, 73, 87, 90, 91, 107, 142, 143, 144, 149, 150, 212
built-in arbitrariness, 129
BV, 197, 198, 199; *see also* Basic Variety, The
by-product conceptions of language origin, 50

case filter, 100
communication, 2, 14, 17, 24, 29, 30, 33, 36, 37, 69, 71, 94, 95, 96, 100, 101, 106, 116, 125, 126, 129, 130, 133, 159, 207, 215, 235
communicative function, 96, 124, 125, 131, 132, 158

complex design, 14, 15, 93, 94, 95, 96, 112, 121, 131, 135, 160, 162, 163, 164, 165, 167, 175, 226; *see also* adaptive complexity

complex properties of language, 100, 108

complexity, adaptive vs. arbitrary, 93; *see also* adaptive complexity

conceptual structure, 28, 30, 143, 196, 207, 212, 219, 238

continuity vs. discontinuity of language evolution, 36, 37, 38

co-optation, 6, 47, 51, 73, 84, 85, 87, 89, 90, 91, 115

correlates of language, 33

data, 4, 5, 8, 18, 29, 71, 75, 78, 81, 90, 91, 109, 111, 119, 122, 123, 134, 141, 142, 143, 144, 145, 146, 148, 150, 151, 152, 154, 155, 156, 157, 183, 184, 185, 186, 187, 189, 192, 193, 198, 199, 200, 201, 217, 220, 223; *see also* evidence; facts

degraded (forms of) language, 198-201

demarcation criterion, 138, 170; *see also* scientific (value)

design of language, 123, 132, 179, 180, 187, 190, 223; *see also* perfection of language

discrete infinity, 49, 55, 56, 57, 58, 61, 64, 65, 210

displacement (in syntax), evolution of, 86

embedding/recursion, evolution of, 86

emergence/evolution of syntax, 39-41, 69-73, 77-78, 81-84

endocast(s), 143, 144, 145, 146, 147, 148, 150, 218, 219

evidence, 2, 3, 4, 5, 6, 8, 14, 16, 22, 29, 30, 38, 47, 50, 52, 54, 55, 57, 61, 63, 75, 76, 78, 79, 80, 81, 84, 85, 86, 87, 89, 91, 100, 116, 119, 122, 123, 125, 128, 130, 133, 134, 135, 136, 138, 141, 142, 143, 144, 145, 148, 149, 150, 154, 155, 156, 157, 159, 168, 173, 176, 178, 183, 185, 186, 187, 188, 189, 190, 192, 193, 195, 197, 198, 199, 200, 201, 202, 205, 212, 217, 218, 219, 220, 222, 223, 229, 232; *see also* data; facts

evidence/data about language evolution,
"fossil", 192, 201, 202
direct vs indirect, 119, 141-142
historical vs nonhistorical, 141, 150
paleoneurological, 142, 143, 144, 148

evidential paucity, 119, 157

evolution of language, 1, 2, 3, 4, 5, 6, 7, 8, 19, 23, 34, 36, 37, 38, 40, 46, 48, 50, 74, 87, 94, 96, 98, 102, 108, 116, 122, 124, 130, 134, 136, 142, 151, 163, 164, 168, 173, 177, 179, 188, 189, 190, 191, 192, 193, 195, 199, 200, 201, 202, 217, 223, 225, 226, 230, 234, 239; *see also* language evolution

evolutionary by-products, 52

evolutionary stories, (plausible), 173, 174, 190, 193

exaptation, (as a process), 7, 51, 52, 53, 59, 60, 61, 62, 67, 68, 70, 73, 78, 81, 91, 115, 116, 208, 211, 221, 239

exaptationist theory of language evolution, 78

exaptations, (as products), 51, 52, 60, 61, 67, 116

fable, evolutionary, 178, 182, 188, 190, 191, 193, 222, 226
facts, 4, 5, 8, 14, 19, 24, 58, 94, 108, 111, 122, 136, 144, 156, 157, 175, 176, 179, 218, 220, 232; *see also* data; evidence
falsificationist methodology, 137
Fibonacci series, 220
"fossil" evidence, 200, 201, 202
formal grammatical system, 27, 28, 29, 30
form-function fit,
    arbitrariness, 103-104
    dysfunctionality, 97-99
    functionlessness, 101-103
    non-uniqueness, 99-101
function of language, 96, 97
    evolutionarily significant, 33, 95, 96
function-shift, 7, 51, 210; *see also* function-shift; preadaptation

generalization, evolutionary process of, 71, 72
genesis of language, 2, 6, 119
gradualness vs. non-gradualness of language evolution, 39

handedness, 33, 141, 144, 152, 154, 155, 225
Homo habilis, 27, 73, 76, 141, 142, 143, 144, 145, 149, 212, 218
homologous structure, 209

ignorance, arguments from, 119, 157, 165, 167, 168, 172, 192
I-language, 19, 206

inferential jumps, 146, 147, 150
instantaneous language acquisition, 180, 182, 183, 185, 186, 187, 188, 189, 190
instantaneous language evolution, 173, 178, 180, 181, 182, 183, 184, 186, 187, 188, 189, 190, 226

Just-so stories, 5, 173, 174, 175, 176, 178, 212; *see also* evolutionary stories, (plausible); fable, evolutionary

knowledge of language, 18, 19, 44, 183

Lamarckism, 212
language, (human), 8-9, 11-12, 13-21, 23-25, 27-32, 33-41, 42-46
    abstracted language, 19
    ambient language, 17
    "degraded" (forms of) language, 198-201
    I-language, 19
    "language itself", 16-35
    "language themselves", 35
    pidgin languages, 76, 197, 198, 199
    protolanguage, 41, 46, 77, 78, 79, 80, 196, 198, 200, 212, 224, 225
    "shared language", 20, 21
    "true" language, 78, 79, 80
language "fossils", 195, 197, 200, 201, 202
language acquisition device, 14, 205, 232
language behaviour, 44, 109, 232
language capacity, 24, 33, 36, 143, 144, 145, 146, 148, 149, 150, 196, 197, 224, 232

language evolution, 1, 3, 4, 5, 6, 7, 8, 1, 10, 18, 21, 23, 24, 28, 31, 32, 33, 34, 36, 38, 39, 40, 41, 43, 44, 45, 46, 47, 48, 68, 72, 77, 78, 81, 82, 94, 113, 119, 121, 123, 135, 136, 138, 141, 142, 150, 155, 156, 157, 158, 167, 168, 169, 170, 171, 172, 173, 178, 180, 181, 182, 183, 184, 186, 187, 189, 190, 191, 192, 193, 195, 197, 200, 201, 202, 208, 210, 216, 226, 229, 230, 236, 237; see also accounts of language evolution; evidence/data about language evolution; evolution of language; instantaneous language evolution; processes of language evolution

language faculty, (the human), 4, 13-22, 44; see also universal grammar; UG

lateralization, 144

linguistic competence, 4, 107, 109, 154, 197

linguistic entities, 8, 35, 44, 45, 68, 90, 115, 116, 119, 141, 145, 202; see also linguistic ontology, (a)

linguistic judgements, 109

linguistic ontology, (a), 18, 19, 20, 21, 24, 39, 40, 44, 45, 46, 154, 208; see also linguistic entities

linguistic phylogeny, 2

linguistic universals, 97, 124, 135, 217; see also substantive linguistic universals

localizationist neurolinguistic theory/theories, 89, 149

manual motor control, 68, 69

Merge, 40, 41, 72, 207, 211

method of comparative anatomy, 54, 55, 61

Minimalist Program, 40, 41, 179, 225, 228, 230; see also syntax, minimalist

mosaic evolution, 34, 37, 38

natural selection, 3, 7, 13, 14, 15, 16, 19, 20, 21, 22, 23, 34, 47, 51, 56, 58, 65, 67, 69, 70, 72, 73, 74, 75, 76, 86, 93, 94, 95, 99, 100, 101, 104, 111, 112, 113, 121, 124, 125, 151, 157, 158, 159, 160, 161, 162, 163, 164, 165, 167, 168, 169, 171, 173, 174, 175, 176, 177, 178, 209, 210, 213, 214, 217, 221, 223, 233, 236, 237

necessity, 91, 97, 119, 150
arguments from, 119, 157, 159, 160, 161, 162, 164, 165, 168, 170, 171, 172, 177, 178, 192

neural preconditions for language, 27, 28, 29, 74, 142

neuroanatomical substrate of language, 28, 31

number faculty, (evolution of), 55, 57, 58, 59

ontological arbitrariness, 11, 44

ontological domains, 145, 154, 192

ontological opacity, 11, 44

organic selection, 78, 80, 212, 221; see also Baldwin effect

origin of language, 2, 3, 4, 60, 64, 169, 205, 227

paleoneurological data/evidence, 143, 144, 145, 146, 148, 150

parity, see requirement of parity

paucity of factual evidence, 141, 191, 195

perfection of language, 179, 181, 182
pidgin languages, 198, 199, 212
POT, 27, 28, 68, 73, 74, 142, 143, 144, 148, 149, 150, 212, 232
poverty of restrictive theory, 7, 202
preadaptation, 7, 27, 47, 51, 70, 71, 72, 73, 75, 115, 116, 208; *see also* function-shift; reappropriation
preadaptive model of language evolution, 68, 116
probability, arguments from, 119, 157, 159, 160, 161, 164, 165, 168, 169, 170, 171, 172, 177, 178, 186, 192, 220
processes of language evolution, *see* adaptation; Baldwin effect; co-optation; function-shift; generalization; natural selection; organic selection; preadaptation; reappropriation
protolanguage, 41, 76, 77, 78, 79, 80, 196, 198, 200, 212, 224, 225

reappropriation, 27, 73, 74, 75, 76; *see also* function-shift; preadaptation 142, 143
reappropriationist scenario of language evolution, 73-76
reciprocal altruism, 77
recursion/embedding, evolution of, 86
relevance (of data), 6, 91, 141, 145, 150, 156, 157, 200
requirement of parity, 130, 131
restrictive theory, 7, 8, 9, 44, 46, 65, 68, 76, 120, 158, 191, 201, 202, 205
rhetoric, 157, 168, 169, 222, 226
rhetorical devices, 157, 168, 169, 170

science, substance of, 120; *see also* theory of science
scientific (value), 2, 3, 8, 119, 121, 137, 138, 169; *see also* theory of science; demarcation criterion
selectionist account of language evolution, 10, 94, 104, 113, 123, 126, 134, 136, 157, 158, 177, 206
"shared language", 20, 21
social calculus, (in language evolution), 68, 77, 212
spandrel(s), 47, 51, 52, 53, 54, 55, 58, 60, 61, 62, 63, 65, 98, 102, 115, 208, 209, 210, 231, 234
speech, 3, 7, 30, 31, 44, 45, 68, 69, 70, 71, 72, 87, 88, 91, 116, 183, 208, 213, 230, 234, 235
speech production, 68, 71, 116
"stages"/"steps" in language evolution, 195-196
structure-dependence/dependency, 100, 102, 125, 215
Subjacency, 126, 127, 128, 129
substantive linguistic universals, 97, 124, 135; *see also* linguistic universals
syllable structure, (in language evolution), 68, 82, 83, 84, 85, 86, 87
syntax,
 ballistic model of, 88
 emergence/evolution of, 39-41, 69-73, 77-78, 81-84
 Government Binding model of, 40-41
 minimalist, 40, 41; *see also* Minimalist Program
 syllable-based, 83-84

testability, 119, 121, 122, 123, 125, 126, 127, 128, 129, 130, 132, 134, 136, 137, 138, 142, 151, 155, 169, 170, 177, 191, 193, 216
testability-in-practice, 122, 123, 128, 216
testability-in-principle, 122, 123, 130, 216
thematic roles, (in language evolution), 77, 207
theory of science, 191, 192, 193; *see also* scientific value; science, substance of
theta analysis, 41
trade-off's in evolution, 178

UG, 28, 30, 39, 63, 99, 106, 168, 185, 205, 206, 223; *see also* universal grammar
ultra-Darwinism, 162, 163, 221
universal grammar, 14, 38, 97, 101, 151, 152, 205, 223, 234; *see also* UG

vertebrate eye, evolution of, 93-94
Wernicke/Geschwind theory, 149
Wernicke's aphasia, 89, 91
Wernicke's area, 27, 73, 90, 107, 149

X-bar theory, 100, 110